Shiva's Trident

Shiva's Trident
The Consciousness of Freedom and the Means to Liberation

Swami Khecaranatha

Copyright © 2013 by Swami Khecaranatha

The Kabir poem on page 161 is republished with permission of Beacon Press, from *The Kabir Book: Forty-four of the Ecstatic Poems of Kabir*, by Robert Bly, 1977; permission conveyed through Copyright Clearance Center, Inc.

The quote from Abhinavagupta's Tantrasāra on page 186 is used by permission of Christopher Wallis, from his book *Tantra Illuminated*, Anusara Press, 2012.

The original illustrations of Śiva, Parā, and Trident Man are printed with permission of the artist, Ekabhūmi Charles Ellik.

The photos of the Parādevī *pūjā* on pages 176 and 177 are courtesy of Scott Eaton.

ISBN-13: 978-1492902515
ISBN-10: 1492902519

All rights reserved. Printed in the United States of America. No part of this book may be reproduced in any manner whatsoever without written permission, except in the case of brief quotations embedded in articles and reviews. For permissions, contact *Nathaji@trikashala.com*.

Swami Khecaranatha's books are published under his own imprint, Prasad Press.

*This book is dedicated to you, dear reader.
My sincere and humble wish is that reading it will
help you to understand that you are Lord Śiva,
ever shining and manifesting as all things.*

Also by Swami Khecaranatha

*Depth Over Time: Kundalini MahaYoga:
A Path of Transformation and Liberation*
(Author House, 2010)

Merging With the Divine: One Day at a Time
(Prasad Press, 2012)

*The Heart of Recognition: The Wisdom & Practices of the
Pratyabhijna Hrdayam*
(Prasad Press, 2013)

All books and audio/video recordings, including several guided meditations, are available online and may be ordered from *SwamiKhecaranatha.com*.

Acknowledgments

This book is the result of the work of a team of people whose many talents have brought it to published form. I am grateful for their assistance and wish to extend my thanks to all of them.

I want to express my gratitude to my editor, Christine Sheridan, for guiding the book to completion with one-pointed dedication, care, and sensitivity.

I owe thanks to Ellen Jefferds for her meticulous work in creating the layout of the interior of the book, and to Keith Jefferds for his extraordinary cover design. I am grateful to Nikolay Beliov, Gayatri Brughera, Ellen Jefferds, and Sassi LaMuth, who read early drafts of the manuscript and provided invaluable feedback that helped bring clarity and flow to the content, and also to Kurt Keutzer for his help with the Sanskrit transliterations.

Next, I want to acknowledge the artist Ekabhūmi Charles Ellik, who created the exquisite renderings of Śiva, Parā, and the image I call Trident Man.

I am indebted to the many scholars and practitioners upon whose work I have drawn and whose guidance has been indispensable. Among these I want to acknowledge Alexis Sanderson for bringing to life both the *paddhati* for the Parādevī *pūjā* and the image of Trident Man that is integral to that *pūjā*.

Special thanks are also due to Mark Dyczkowski for providing me with the quote by Abhinavagupta that is the focal point of this book, and for his mentorship in my study of Shaivite scripture. I must also thank Christopher Wallis for his insight into the practices of the Parādevī *pūjā*.

Above all, I wish to express my gratitude to my gurus, Bhagavan Nityananda and Swami Rudrananda, at whose feet I serve, and finally to Lord Śiva, the Supreme Guru and Self of all, whose Grace sets us free.

Table of Contents

From the Author, About His Lineage — i

Introduction: The Journey as God — xv

SECTION ONE: The Consciousness of Freedom

1. The Nature and Powers of Consciousness — 5
2. Śiva's Trident: Will, Knowledge, and Action — 19
3. God's Powers Are Our Powers — 57

SECTION TWO: The Descent of Consciousness

4. The *Tattvas*, Part One: The Divine Reality — 73
5. The *Tattvas*, Part Two: *Māyā* — 89
6. The *Tattvas*, Part Three: The Human Experience — 109

SECTION THREE: The Ascent of Consciousness

7. Trident Man: *Kuṇḍalinī* Rising — 127
8. The *Upāyas*: The Means to Liberation — 183
9. The Four Gates: Inner Practice, Grace, Devotion, Selfless Service — 201
10. Surrender Is the Key — 245

Conclusion: Śiva's Grace: The Heart of it All — 273

Appendix: Guided Meditations — 284

Glossary and Pronunciation Guide — 290

From the Author, About His Lineage

A lineage is an unbroken transmission of living spiritual force, passed from heart to heart. It flows from one generation to the next—from a teacher to the student he or she wishes to initiate as a lineage carrier. Whether that initiation is an elaborate ceremony, or simply the words of the teacher spoken to the heart of the student, it is the power of initiation that installs the seed of the living spiritual force in the recipient. Although this force manifests within a teacher, this living energy is greater than that which is carried within any particular person. A lineage carrier is the servant of that force.

KUṆḌALINĪ MAHĀYOGA: THE PRACTICE OF THIS LINEAGE

While the term "Kuṇḍalinī MahāYoga" emerged around the seventeenth century, the practice of awakening *kuṇḍalinī* has been a fundamental part of nondual Tantric traditions for many centuries before that. The practice of Kuṇḍalinī Yoga, which some scholars have dated back to 2000 B.C., has always been an inner practice carefully passed from teacher to student through oral and energetic transmission. While the emphasis on inner practice remained constant, a philosophical written tradition began to emerge in the seventh and eighth centuries.

These inspired writings and commentaries arose from the direct inner experiences of committed practitioners, and are based on their ardent study of early spiritual practices and traditions, which blossomed from the hearts of early masters called *mahāsiddhas*. The term comes from the Sanskrit words *mahā*, which means "great," and *siddha*, which denotes a person who has attained perfection of inner awareness and energy. These *mahāsiddhas* were the preceptors of the earliest spiritual practices.

Throughout history there has been an underlying current of spiritual wisdom and energy that has manifested in various ways in many different times and places. Such a current preserves an unbroken connection with the Divine Source of living spiritual energy. Down through the ages, great realized masters, or *mahāsiddhas*, have served as the preceptors of that Divine energy in various yogic and Tantric traditions. A profound expression of that spiritual energy has most recently emerged in the form of two twentieth-century realized saints: Bhagavan Nityananda and Swami Rudrananda (Rudi). They were modern-day *mahāsiddhas* and the wellspring of my immediate lineage, extending the profound tradition of Kuṇḍalinī MahāYoga into the present.

In the preface to my book *Depth Over Time*, my friend and scriptural mentor Mark Dyczkowski expressed the profound connection between the lineage that I carry and the teachings and practices of nondual Kashmir Shaivism. The following excerpts from that preface eloquently elucidate my own teachings within the context Tantric Shaivism, Kuṇḍalinī Yoga, and *śaktipāta*, a significant aspect of those traditions:

This beautiful phrase [below] written by Abhinavagupta concisely describes the power of śaktipāta, and its vital role in the awakening of kuṇḍalinī within the individual:

The moon-like teacher whose (spiritual) darkness has been dispersed by the lunar rays of divine insight (pratibhā) removes the darkness (of their ignorance) and the heat (of their suffering).

To see how this works according to the nondual Śaiva and Śakti Tantras of the Trika, we need to examine briefly what they have to say about śaktipāta, initiation, and practice. Śaktipāta removes the darkness of the restrictions that contract consciousness from its pervasive unlimited expanse down to a speck of light that is the essential consciousness in the core of our Being. Dualist Shaivites believe that these restrictions are an independent material substance that covers the consciousness of the individual soul. Accordingly, they maintain that it can be removed by the appropriate action, as is chaff from rice by beating it, or a cataract from an eye by surgery. Initiation, they say, is the action that removes the impurities. By the power of the appropriate mantras the teacher . . . leads his disciple's soul through the worlds of the cosmic order and their corresponding metaphysical principles up into Śiva, the highest principle. There . . . the teacher conjoins the disciple's soul with Śiva.

Nondual Kashmiri Shaivites accept that this procedure works but believe that it is slow and inefficient because it is not fueled directly by Śiva's Śakti. They stated emphatically that the best and most efficient way is to awaken kuṇḍalinī, which from the non-dualist point of view, is equally both Śiva's Śakti and that of the individual soul. Consciousness is the one reality, which we experience as Deity—who nourishes us and all Its creation with the power of Its empowering grace. Through this force all things are created, sustained in their Being, and withdrawn back into Deity, who is Universal Consciousness.

Inherent in the freedom of consciousness is the power to act and perceive. Consciousness makes of us perceivers and agents. It is the source of the awareness we have of ourselves and of the world that consciousness manifests from within Itself. Consciousness passively illumines its manifestation within an unconfined expanse of power. Its own nature as the perceiver is derived from its own reflective awareness. As such, it operates as the power of knowledge. Operating as the power of action, consciousness is an agent, just as when it operates as the power of knowledge, it is a perceiver. Thus consciousness is Deity worshiped as Śiva and His power, kuṇḍalinī śakti, through which He generates all things—both individual perceivers and their objects. All this is manifested and known within Himself, like images in a mirror.

This is the dynamic energy of kuṇḍalinī (śakti), which generates, sustains, and withdraws the world of manifestation reflected in the pure mirror of Śiva's Divine Light. We can experience this flow—or at least catch a glimpse of it—by paying attention, as Khecaranatha teaches, to the pulsing core of the consciousness of our innermost Being. Here, in the Center, free of all notions of difference, time, and space, we experience the supreme, perpetual flow of kuṇḍalinī. Further out, as it were, in the physical and subtle body, the same flow manifests as that of the breath. Here we experience the flow of the kuṇḍalinī of the Breath—prāṇa kuṇḍalinī. The vital breath is the first transformation of consciousness. Withdrawing into itself, consciousness leaves behind an Emptiness into which it pours out as the vital breath. Travelling down the channel it opens up for itself, it generates and vitalizes the physical and subtle bodies.

From this channel, called suṣumṇa, develop other channels from which others branch off until, like the veins of a leaf, they cover every part of the body. Clearly, the central suṣumṇa is the most important. The vital force travels out from and back to its original source of pure Divine Consciousness. This flow stimulates the activity of the inner subtle body and the outer physical body. Thus the inner breathing of the descending and ascending flow of kuṇḍalinī generates the outer breathing—that is, inhalation and exhalation. We are not normally aware of this link. We do not normally experience the flow of kuṇḍalinī without making an effort to do so, although it does sometimes happen spontaneously.

Eloquently, and in great detail, Khecaranatha expounds the practice that arouses kuṇḍalinī. From the point of view of practice at the corporeal level, we must wake up the sleeping, potential reflective awareness of this flow and accompany it with our attention, first up and then back down. The ascending flow passes through a series of doors, levels, or configurations of energies—cakras—and pierces through the knots that block its ascent. At each stage the kuṇḍalinī of the Breath vitalizes aspects of the physical, mental, emotive, and vital subtle bodies. First exercising attention on the breath, then on the flow of the inner vital force of kuṇḍalinī, we awaken our dormant awareness of this flow. In this way we "purify" it and it purifies us. As kuṇḍalinī moves through these dimensions of the individual, lower, more contracted states are integrated into higher, more expanded ones.

The Tantric traditions that focus on the worship of Goddesses such as Tripurā, Kālī, and Kubjikā, as well as Anuttara Trika, the one Kashmiris considered to be the most secret and elevated, teach this higher form of initiation. It is śaktipāta, called "Initiation by Piercing."

Awakening the reflective awareness of this process by an intense descent of empowering grace—śaktipāta—the initiate experiences the Goddess Kuṇḍalinī rising through the cakras, piercing through them as She goes. In this way She burns up the impurities and ignorance that sully and condition consciousness.

This takes place just by the gracious look of the teacher, or by a touch, or just a thought. The Anuttara Trika practices taught by Abhinavagupta accommodate both the slower method of ritual initiation and the more direct method of śaktipāta. The initiation by which the initiate ascends progressively through the metaphysical principles is done in its Trika form. This involves the visualization of Śiva's Trident projected along the axis of the body. The prongs of the trident extend out of the top of the head. On them are the three Goddesses of the Trika—Parā, Parāparā, and Aparā. They are the three aspects of the one Goddess who embodies the triadic energy of kuṇḍalinī. While this is an important and powerful initiation, the direct awakening of kuṇḍalinī in the Initiation by Piercing—śaktipāta— is the higher initiation and is considered to be the most excellent by the Kashmiris.

This form of higher initiation is the essence of the practice taught by Swami Khecaranatha. He has attained, through the transmission of his teachers and a lifetime of teaching, practice and personal experience, a deep understanding of Kashmiri Shaivism and Anuttara Trika. Thus, he summates, in his realization and teachings, what was considered by the Kashmiri Shaivites to be the most elevated teachings of all the Tantric schools.

When I first began practicing with my teacher, Swami Rudrananda (Rudi), it was indeed that direct transmission—śaktipāta—that unleashed the power of kuṇḍalinī within me. Rudi did not study scripture and, in fact, the exposition of nondual Shaivism was virtually unknown in the West until after his passing. However, as I began to study the scripture and traditions for myself, I was amazed at the profound connections to these traditions expressed in Rudi's teaching.

The more deeply I penetrated into the Shaivite traditions, the more I understood the knowledge of Rudi's teachings—knowledge he extracted from within himself through his own disciplined inner practice. Over the past thirty years, and particularly throughout the past decade, I have ardently studied the teachings of Shaivism and now offer my teachings within the sophisticated framework graciously handed down to us by the early Tantric masters.

I have a deep awareness that the sacred knowledge of those early Shaivite saints was in fact transmitted to and received by Rudi. While traveling in India and Nepal about a year before his passing, Rudi was told by an astrologer that he would meet a great saint who would be eight hundred to a thousand years of age. For Rudi, such an extraordinary encounter was not only entirely within the realm of possibility but very likely, as those sorts of profound spiritual experiences occurred regularly as part of his inner growth and development.

As he traveled around India, he worked deeply in himself to try to open to that connection, and, in searching for the elusive saint, he actually tapped many elderly looking *sādhus* on the shoulder. Toward the end of his trip, he and a few students were in his hotel room, and an ancient master did appear to Rudi in spirit form, completely visible to everyone in the room. This figure simply materialized and walked right into Rudi, who experienced a profound energy and wealth of knowledge being "downloaded" into him. That wisdom and energy began to transform Rudi from that moment until he took *mahāsamadhi*, not long after.

The last time I was in Varanasi, Mark Dyczkowski and I were discussing the Tantrāloka and the lineage of masters that came before and after Abhinavagupta. All of a sudden, like a bolt of lightning, it was crystal clear to me that the saint who had appeared to Rudi was, in fact, an ancient master of that same nondual Shaivite tradition. I could feel the timeless thread of knowledge and energy extending back to the preceptors of this tradition, and I knew without a doubt that through Rudi's transmission I had received that same connection, which was now flowering.

Although I continue to feel a deeper and deeper connection to and understanding of the practices of Tantric Shaivism, I want to be clear to my readers that this book is not intended to be an academic study of the writings and teachings of the great Tantric masters, and certainly not of Abhinavagupta's profound teachings in the Tantrāloka or other writings of the Trika. What I can say for certain is that his writings, insofar as they have been available to me, have deeply inspired me and have resonated with my own inner experience. The interpretations of the Trika tradition and the Śiva's Trident *maṇḍala* in this book are my own, based on my own experience and practice.

As a lineage carrier in this tradition, I feel a deep gratitude to every teacher who has gone before me. They have passed down an enormous wealth of knowledge and have provided the practical means to enable generations of spiritual seekers to gain their liberation. My own meeting with my teacher, Swami Rudrananda, in 1971 demonstrates that it is possible, in one moment of life, for our consciousness and experience to be totally transformed.

The unconditional love and the powerful, transformative spiritual energy that radiated from Rudi penetrated deeply into me, cutting through what felt like lifetimes of confusion and pain. My heart exploded open—the first of many incredible gifts of Grace that I received from my teacher. Every moment since has been an expression of gratitude and devotion focused on an unwavering commitment to growth. This clarity of focus is the best way I know to honor Rudi.

SWAMI RUDRANANDA: HIS PRACTICE AND TEACHINGS

Rudi called his practice "the work." He developed a powerful set of techniques, including a unique "open-eyes class," for giving *śaktipāta*, which literally means "descent of Grace." This transmission of higher spiritual energy from teacher to student is an integral part of his practice of Kuṇḍalinī MahāYoga. Although he did not study scripture, Rudi's practice and teachings were a perfect expression of the most sacred of the Tantric Shaivite traditions (often referred to as Kashmir Shaivism), which we will explore in this book.

Rudi was a complex man, but he lived in profound inner simplicity. He was extraordinarily powerful, yet gentle and full of love and Grace. Rudi was unconditionally focused on the dissolution of any limitation within himself as the means to allow God to emerge and reveal Himself. Rudi had been aware of his spiritual potential as a very young boy and spoke of continual inspirational visions and experiences that guided him on his path.

His earliest teachers were Tibetan Buddhists, and in his early twenties he studied the teachings of Gurdjieff and Pak Subud. However, Rudi's most powerful relationships were with the Indian masters Sri Shankaracharya of Puri, Bhagavan Nityananda, and Swami Muktananda. It was the latter who recognized Rudi as a swami in 1966, and gave him the name Rudrananda.

If I had to describe Rudi's spiritual teaching, I would say there are three elements that are central to his practice:

- cultivating a deep inner wish to grow
- working internally to establish a flow of energy through the psychic system
- living in a state of surrender

None of these elements function without the others. They fit into one dynamic. Rudi taught us that these qualities must be brought into our practice and into our everyday lives. The discipline he required of himself and his students was the foundation of his teachings. Rudi made it very clear that attaining liberation in this lifetime was our right, and that freedom was available to anyone who wanted it. He emphasized that cultivating the wish to grow would transform our experience and consciousness if we worked with depth over time. That depth is accomplished through opening our hearts, feeling the flow of spiritual energy within and with all of life, and surrendering to God.

In February 1973, Rudi departed from this world in a small plane crash in the Catskill Mountains. Remarkably, the other three passengers walked away with only minor injuries. Rudi's last words, dictated on the plane moments before it crashed, perfectly express the essence of his life and his teaching:

> *The last year of my life has prepared me for the deeper understanding that Divine Consciousness can come only through unconditional surrender. That state is reached by surrendering ourselves and the tensions that bind and restrict us, keeping us from expressing the power of creation that is our true essence. It is God flowing through us and showing us that we are nothing but Him. I want to live as an expression of that higher creative will, and from a deeper sense of surrender.*

While Rudi had several teachers, it was his relationship with the great saint Bhagavan Nityananda that catapulted his growth into its most profound dimensions. Rudi said, "My first meeting with the renowned Indian guru Bhagavan Nityananda was of such depth that it changed the course of my life." There are conflicting accounts as to how many times Rudi met Nityananda in person. Whether it was once or a few times, it was the relationship that developed after the saint's passing that was the most important expression of their connection. Rudi described this profound relationship as existing on a spiritual level that was not limited by the absence of Nityananda's physical form.

BHAGAVAN NITYANANDA

Nityananda, whose name means "Bliss of the eternal," lived in southwestern India from around the turn of the twentieth century until 1961. Details of his early life are difficult to verify, but from the 1920s until his passing, he was surrounded by an ever-increasing number of disciples and devotees. By the late 1930s, he was established in Ganeshpuri, a small village in the countryside near Mumbai, and an active ashram developed around him. In India today, he continues to be revered as a great saint.

Nityananda lived as the Divine expression of stillness, purity, and joy, and his teaching was profoundly simple. Like the ancient sages of many traditions, the essence of his teaching was that liberation occurs within every person when they merge their own individual consciousness into the Divine, and he clearly emphasized the awakening of the *kuṇḍalinī* as the path to liberation. To realize the universal nature of one's own awareness, to be absorbed into the heart of God, is the goal of spiritual practice. Over the past forty years of my own practice and the study of nondual Kashmir Shaivism, it has become evident that Nityananda's teachings clearly reflect the essence of that tradition.

The *Nityananda Sutras* outline the elements that are the essence of his experience, and therefore of his teaching:

- developing the subtle discrimination to see the One in the many
- cultivating detachment
- expressing devotion
- establishing an inner practice
- living in profound simplicity
- discovering unconditional joy
- living in Grace and communion with the Divine

Nityananda often sat in a room in the ashram that was lit only by a few bare light bulbs, resting there quietly, with his eyes open. People came from considerable distances to see him because in India, the mere viewing, or *darśana*, of a spiritual teacher is considered to be a profound blessing. The powerful forces of *śaktipāta* that continuously emitted from Nityananda permeated the environment around him. His presence attracted thousands of people who wanted to receive his *darśana*. Each person who came in contact with this saint experienced the miracle of Pure Consciousness in human form. Bhagavan Nityananda was a holy person who was considered to be an *avadhūta*. Timeless and eternal, the *avadhūta* is a direct link to the Absolute, encompassing all the teachers who preceded him and all who follow.

Introduction: The Journey as God

Introduction

The Journey as God

The purpose of life is freedom. The purpose of our individual lives is to experience and celebrate that freedom. While the consciousness of freedom is very different from any other consciousness you will ever function from, Tantric practices emphatically assert that it is each individual's Divine right to experience and live in that state of liberation. While there are many authentic spiritual practices that allow for the attainment of that highest goal, this book seeks to explore and make accessible the practice of Anuttara Trika, a thousand-year-old school within the nondual Kashmir Shaivite Tantric tradition. This tradition focuses on the merging of individual consciousness with God's Consciousness and is the practice I've taught for more than forty years. Throughout the book I will use the terms Kashmir Shaivism, Tantric Shaivism, Trika, or simply Tantric practices interchangeably, all referring to the same nondual tradition.

Nondual Tantric Shaivism uses the terms Consciousness (Śiva) and energy (Śakti) to describe the fundamental structure of the universe. Śiva, or Consciousness Itself, are the terms we use in our practice to denote God. Readers unfamiliar with Shaivite practices can feel free to substitute their own language for the terms "Śiva" or "God." Śiva is the very foundation of existence, while the dynamic energy of Śakti creates the manifest world. Tantric Shaivism posits that these two inseparable principles, Consciousness and energy, represent the underlying unity of all of life: one magnificent expression of God's absolute, autonomous freedom, or *svātantrya*. Further, Tantric tradition maintains that if we could only recognize ourselves as we truly are, we would discover that we are Śiva incarnate, and that His *svātantrya* is none other than our own.

KASHMIR SHAIVISM

The nondual Tantric tradition known as Kashmir Shaivism is a thousand-year-old philosophical system characterized by its assertion that universal Divine Consciousness, or Śiva, is the fundamental substance of the entire universe. There is nothing other than, or occurring outside of, this Supreme Consciousness, and therefore there is no duality. The goal of this system of yoga is for practitioners to realize their identity as Śiva by merging their individual consciousness into Divine Consciousness.

Although many Shaivite texts were written earlier, Tantric Shaivism reached its high point in the eleventh century as the great Kashmiri master Abhinavagupta synthesized the teachings of the various Tantric traditions (including Kaula, Krama Trika, and Pratyabhijñā) in his opus Tantrāloka (Light on the Tantras). It's important to note that many other traditions before and around this time taught that infinite awareness is outside of the individual, and that the phenomenal world is an illusion, or *māyā*. Entire philosophical systems were built on that dualistic understanding.

Tantric practices diverged from that point of view in their understanding of the manifest world as not only real but *līlā*, the play of Divine Consciousness. In other words, everything exists because of—and has its being rooted in—Supreme Consciousness. Shaivism is not a philosophy of opinions but the direct experience of practitioners who discovered within themselves the experience of union with Śiva. Out of their practice and the internalization of their awareness arose the whole philosophical Shaivite exposition, written down several centuries after they discovered and refined it.

Abhinavagupta aligned and synthesized the various systems within Shaivism, for which he is understood as perhaps the greatest saint within the Tantric tradition. One of India's most prolific philosophers, mystics, and aestheticians, he was a master in seven traditions. Through that mastery, he was able to formulate one system, called Anuttara Trika, to express that synthesis. Through his own self-discovery, and that of the saints who walked before him, he was able elucidate a clear, concise, and incredibly sophisticated path to God.

Abhinavagupta's eloquent expression of Tantric Shaivism is truly amazing. In that period, many traditions asserted that God is outside of and separate from the individual. Accordingly, one can love and worship God, build temples and sing to God, but there's a limit to one's own experience. Departing radically from that, Tantric practices emphatically declared that there is no separation between God and the individual, and that such a notion is a misunderstanding. There is only God and His manifest expressions. Further, the purpose of individuated life, the purpose for which you were created, is to discover the highest truth in yourself: You are Śiva. You are God, and you have the Divine right to know and experience that. Your individuated experience has been Divinely offered to you so that you can discover that experience in yourself. This was a fairly significant point of difference.

The Śiva's Trident *maṇḍala*, the image around which the teachings and practices in this book are focused, is a profoundly simple and sophisticated description and methodology of recognizing just that. Tantric practices commonly use sacred, diagrammatic images called *maṇḍalas* to convey the ultimate reality and imprint its experience on practitioners through contemplation and ritual. This *maṇḍala*, formally called *triśūlābjamaṇḍala*, is taken from Abhinavagupta's Tantrāloka. Often referred to as Śiva's Trident, this image is also known as Paramaśiva *maṇḍala*, or *Anuttara maṇḍala*, because *"anuttara"* means "none higher." "Paramaśiva" means "beyond Śiva."

This specific *maṇḍala* is used within Trika Shaivism, the nondualistic school of Shaivite practices elaborated by Abhinavagupta, through his careful extraction and synthesis of the various Tantric practices and scriptures. Trika is one of the major schools of nondual Shaivism, and the one that Abhinavagupta is most associated with. The term "Trika" refers to the triad of Śiva's will, knowledge, and action, as well as Consciousness, energy, and the individual—three expressions of an undifferentiated Unity.

One of the most extraordinary things about the trident *maṇḍala* is that it is a self-portrait. It is God's self-portrait, and therefore our self-portrait. In its representation of Consciousness and Its powers, or Śiva and His powers—which are not separate or different from our own—the *maṇḍala* depicts the essence of all Trika Shaivism. The key to understanding it is recognizing that if it expresses God's power, it also expresses our power. If it is God's experience, it should be our experience; if it isn't, it should be the experience we seek. The understanding imparted through this image, along with the practices embedded within it, is that we *are* God. We *are* Śiva.

The *maṇḍala* is an amazing image depicting the entire expression of Consciousness and Its manifestation, how the simplicity of Consciousness expresses Itself through the sophistication of Its own capacity and awareness. It's a profoundly simple and beautiful explanation of how, through Śiva's power, His Śakti, and therefore our power, we can recognize ourselves as the source and holder of the powers of the universe. This *maṇḍala* is thus an eloquent visualization of supreme, universal awareness, as well as the individual's capacity to perceive and experience that awareness—a visual symbol of spiritual liberation according to the practice of Anuttara Trika. For me, this image depicts the essence of Kuṇḍalinī MahāYoga because the trident represents the pathway of Consciousness as it rises through the psychic body back to Its source.

Within the Trika tradition, this *maṇḍala* depicts how Infinite Consciousness—using the powers inherent within Itself—unfolds all of manifestation, and, specifically relevant to us, gives life to us. According to Trika Shaivism, the universe was created by the five powers of Divine Consciousness: Consciousness Itself, bliss, will, knowledge, and action. The entire *maṇḍala* represents the field of God's Consciousness. Emerging from that field is a large central lotus, which represents bliss. This *maṇḍala* is also sometimes described as the Parādevī *maṇḍala* because emerging from the trident, out of Śiva Himself, are the three goddesses of the Trika representing His Divine powers of will, knowledge, and action: Parā, Parāparā, and Aparā. The three prongs of the trident represent those three Divine energies through which the emission of the universe takes place.

How fascinating to recognize that the powers that create life—will, knowledge, and action—are shown emerging directly from the power of bliss, not the other way around, contrary to what we believe about our experience of life. Think of the profound shift that would occur in our experience if we understood that joy is something we infuse into the dynamics of our life, instead of perpetually seeking it outside ourselves, through doing, having, and knowing things.

In the image, the trident itself symbolizes the *suṣumṇa*, the central and most important energetic channel of the individual psychic body, which is where we personally experience the five Divine powers of Consciousness, bliss, will, knowledge, and action. The prominence and centrality given to the individual within this sacred *maṇḍala* is significant because our individuated lives, Divinely offered to us, are our means to discovering the highest truth in God.

The dot in the center of the diagram is a *bindu*, the single, miniscule point of Infinite Consciousness, God's Presence. Everything unfolds from that, and that unfolding is God's expression of Consciousness and freedom. Our meditation and spiritual practices are how we return to that point, how we get back home, which is really what any authentic spiritual practice is about. As we return to that point, we penetrate through and understand each dimension of Consciousness and energy.

THE TATTVAS

Embedded within the trident *maṇḍala* is the understanding of the *tattvas*, which we will explore in detail in Section Two. *Tattva* literally means "that-ness," and refers to the thirty-six levels of existence or Consciousness that Śiva stratifies Himself into in the creation of the world. Through His own joy and will to express His freedom, He creates the entire manifest universe, which is simply one continuum of Divine Consciousness and energy vibrating at different frequencies. As It unfolds and descends, It goes through a process of contraction, from pure Infinite Consciousness all the way down to slower and denser frequencies like inert matter. Within this spectrum of contraction and densification, the human being shows up.

My friend Mark Dyczkowski, an authentic practitioner as well as a respected scholar of Kashmir Shaivism, describes the Tantric model of the *tattvas* as a series of thirty-six "metaphysical principles" that make up a seemingly linear—although actually always pulsating in and out—model of reality and how things (i.e., the world as we know it, including us) come into being.

As the manifest universe gets created, with it arises the appearance of duality. In Shaivism, form is understood as the *appearance* of duality, not the reality of duality. As human beings, our experience in life is in the world of form; we don't see the *source* of form. While Tantric practices never deny the experience of duality, it is understood as a limited experience. In reality, there is no duality; there's only the experience of it.

The *tattva*s therefore are a way of mapping out apparent duality within a singular state of Oneness, which exists both in creation and in us. Within this model, individuated human consciousness is depicted as none other than God's supreme and unbounded Consciousness, albeit in a contracted and limited form. The model describes how Infinite Consciousness descends into manifestation and gives rise to duality. At the same time, it also describes how individuated consciousness can ascend back through those same levels of awareness to its infinite Source. This is the purpose of spiritual practice: to ascend back through the *tattvas*, all the levels of "suchness," through multiplicity, God's own emission, and achieve union with our Divine Source. The purification of the *tattvas*, which is the purification of our understanding of Consciousness Itself, is in my experience the practice of Kuṇḍalinī MahāYoga, the raising of the dormant vital energy and Consciousness within us back to their Source.

THE FOUR GATES

At its highest, Tantric Shaivism says that we are already free, and there is nothing we need to do other than to realize that. Yet for most of us, that recognition unfolds gradually through a combination of God's Grace, our personal wish to grow, and some form of disciplined *sādhana*, or spiritual practice. As Rudi always said, "the equation for spirituality is depth over time." In keeping with this, we see that the trident *maṇḍala* has four gates, which I have described as Grace, inner practice, selfless service, and devotion. We enter the spiritual dimension through these gates. While ultimately there is no inside or outside to the field of Consciousness from which we arose, the problem is that we perceive ourselves to be outside it, and that perception limits our capacity to function from inside that centeredness and openness. These gates represent the four entryways into the heart of Consciousness.

In my practice of Kuṇḍalinī MahāYoga and AnuttaraTrika, there are many ways we approach the involution process, and we will discuss them at length. These include selfless service, the practice of surrender, interaction with a teacher, and meditation. We will also explore an inner practice that attunes us to the internal breath, which is the breath that arises and subsides within the *suṣumṇa*, without external breath. In addition, it's through the receiving of Grace and the awakening of the *kuṇḍalinī* that we begin to dissolve the veils of duality—I am separate, I am different, I am the doer—that are part of our misunderstanding. We pierce those veils by awakening the *kuṇḍalinī* energy within us and allowing it to rise up through the *suṣumṇa*, open the *cakras*, pierce the *granthi* (the dense knots and blockages within the psychic body), and reveal Unity. In my practice the primary method for receiving Grace is through *śaktipāta* from an authentic teacher.

The most important aspect to recognize about the *maṇḍala* is that the field of consciousness it represents—*svātantrya*, absolute, autonomous freedom—is always ever present. The consciousness of freedom is the consciousness of choosing to enter that space, through one or all of those gates simultaneously.

THE UPĀYAS

In Tantric tradition, the means to liberation, the means of ascent back through the *tattvas*, are called *upāyas*. In brief, there are four *upāyas* that function within us simultaneously. While they are not strictly linear, and none is more important than the others, one or more may be more predominant in our practice and experience at any given point. The four *upāyas* are:

- *Āṇavopāya*: the path of individual effort
- *Śāktopāya*: the path of energy
- *Śāmbhavopāya*: the path of awareness
- *Anupāya*: no path, the path of Grace

Within each *upāya* there are many different dynamics, aspects, and practices, and they all lead to each other. If we look at the *maṇḍala*, we'll understand that service, for example, functions within all of the *upāyas*. The only exception to that would be *anupāya*, the path of Grace, because Grace comes from only two sources: God and guru, which, in reality, is really one source, as God and guru are never separate. *Anupāya* is simply being melted by God's Grace. *Śaktipāta* is the descent and transmission of that Grace.

Spiritual *sādhana* is a conscious choice and a conscious process. Inherent within the discussion of the consciousness of freedom and becoming one with Śiva is the recognition that we get to choose. At every level it's a conscious choice and effort. The efforts we make as we move from *āṇavopāya* to *anupāya* may have a different *rasa*, or flavor, but they are all simply ways of focusing and directing our awareness back into that field of Consciousness. What does this tell us about the purpose of our spiritual life? We can become one with God. It isn't to be prettier or richer, to have more relationships or less hang-ups. It is for one thing only: to become one with God.

The true essence of spiritual practice is to penetrate through the experience of duality, of which we are an effect. Transcending the appearance of duality is part of Śiva's plan, part of His Consciousness and will. Divine will at some point decides to play hide-and-seek. Why did Śiva decide to play this game? When you were six years old why did *you* play hide-and-seek? It was fun. What does that say about our experience and all the things we do as part of our life and our spiritual *sādhana*? It should be fun; its purpose is the discovery and expression of joy.

Śiva's Trident: A Road Map to Freedom

One of the things I love most about this *maṇḍala* is the prominence of the large lotus in the center, which in my view represents both joy and the heart. This is a clear statement that the purpose of life is to experience the joy of living, that life is the expression of the unconditional joy of our own existence. That bliss is the state of unconditionality, the state of surrender. We must discover bliss, and any condition that seems to be a barrier to that bliss represents our misperception that it's a barrier. In fact, it's probably the doorway. The powers that emerge out of Śiva's Consciousness are the same powers we use to discover that joy. In discovering autonomous bliss, we can discover God.

What this suggests is that if we're not happy, we're not going to find joy. We must truly love our life and find the simple gratitude for the opportunity to discover the highest truth in ourselves. The things we're attached to, reach for, hold on to, and reject are not what we need to live in joy. We need nothing to live in joy. When you find yourself reaching for something because part of you feels incomplete, stop reaching. Open your heart. Find that fullness inside. Then everything that's part of your life is part of that same fullness.

You may be reading this thinking, "It cannot be possible that I could simply live in joy." But it is that very thought that limits the capacity to experience it. Spiritual *sādhana* is about transforming our perception of what is possible. Rudi once described God showing up and telling him: "You must work and teach every day of your life until the day you die. And never forget, you're not here to serve the world; you're here to serve Me." What an amazing message, from God Himself, that if we mistake the world for the source of the world, if we get lost in the world in the search for the source of the world, we will never discover it. We must penetrate through and consume it. Rudi translated that understanding into one of the most Tantric statements ever made: "Life must be consumed whole, with all its pain, joy, and sorrow." Without negating any of it, he understood that God's emission is the celebration of freedom and, at the same time, the obscuration of that freedom.

In the Bhagavad Gītā, Lord Kṛṣṇa says to Arjuna: "Among thousands of men, only a few strive to attain perfection, and of those who strive, only a few know Me in truth." It's such a beautiful statement, and it makes very clear the importance and power of our wish to grow. What distinguishes one person from the other thousands? What distinguishes the person who knows God in truth? The wish to grow. Rudi built his entire freedom on that: discovering that wish inside him, holding on to the wish when something tried to get in the way of it, and surrendering himself to that wish no matter the cost. The choice is yours: Are you among the thousands who strive? Are you among the few who truly discover the truth in yourself?

Every day I am astonished at the choice each of us has to live in a deeper dimension within ourselves, from which we can truly surrender in the face of whatever adversity we may be facing, so that we recognize how precious and extraordinary life is because it allows us the opportunity to know God. My goal in writing this book is to inspire readers to make the conscious choice to use the understandings and methods embedded within the iconography of Śiva's Trident in their own search for that ultimate reality.

Right now, at this very moment, we have everything we need in our life to experience God's Consciousness. All of our practice, rigor, sacrifice, and surrender simply bring us to the recognition that we always had it all along. And that is the point of the *maṇḍala*: God's emission creates incredible multiplicity that can catch and confuse us. But just as we misunderstand multiplicity and duality, and we suffer because of that misunderstanding, we can reach inside and find joy, in the very same conditions that two-billionths of a second before we were suffering from. Rather than rejecting multiplicity or saying it's unreal, we discover its source. Ultimately, we must engage and penetrate through duality to be free of duality. This is the fundamental canon of Tantric Shaivism, which separates it from all other practices. There isn't God and the illusion of the world. There is only God.

The word "Trika" means three, and the classical, philosophical texts of Kashmir Shaivism are replete with triadic symbolism. One example would be the three goddesses who sit atop the three prongs of Śiva's Trident: Parā, Parāparā, and Aparā, who are the goddesses of Śiva's powers of will, knowledge, and action. Shaivite scripture also discusses the trinity of the known, the knower, and the means of knowing. In the context of this exposition of the Śiva's Trident *maṇḍala*, another triad relates to the three ways we will approach the exploration of the iconography of the *maṇḍala* itself, which are reflected in the three sections into which the book is divided.

The first section is concerned with the nature of Divine Consciousness Itself, particularly Śiva's five Divine pure energies (which are also the five highest *tattvas*), and how they can point us to freedom. In the second section, which pertains to the complete model of the thirty-six *tattvas*, we will explore the descent of that Supreme Consciousness into manifestation. It is this Self-willed descent or contraction of Consciousness, meticulously laid out in the *tattvas*, that leads to the appearance of duality, as well as to our human experiences of limitation, misunderstanding, and suffering. The third section will focus on the *upāyas* and our *sādhana*—our path out of suffering and our means to spiritual liberation.

There is beautiful language in many different traditions describing the process of spiritual *sādhana* and freedom. One says it's the journey *to* God. Another expresses it as the journey *in* God. The Shaivite Tantrics say it's the journey *as* God. Of course, there's no real distinction between them. We have this sense of wishing to know God. We reach for God. We offer ourselves to God. As some degree of our separation begins to fade, we realize we are just moving in God. This journey, so articulately described within the *maṇḍala*, is the descent of

Consciousness and Its return. If we don't get caught up in the details of that, we come to understand and experience that there is—and always ever was—only God in the journey.

SECTION ONE
The Consciousness of Freedom

The Nature and Powers of Consciousness

The Nature and Powers of Consciousness

In the words of the renowned, eleventh-century Kashmiri master Abhinavagupta:

> *The highest insight of Anuttara Trika is union with Śakti, the triad of energies of will, knowledge, and action. This is Śiva's Trident, the three aspects of His absolute nature and freedom, which He possesses by virtue of His union with His own emission. In the practice of Anuttara Trika, the sādhaka penetrates the energy of emission, becoming one with Śiva, the source and holder of the powers of the universe. . . . This is done through the practice of Kuṇḍalinī Yoga. There is no other Divine fire able to consume the whole of duality than kuṇḍalinī.*

What's amazing to me is that not only is Abhinavagupta describing the ultimate goal of spiritual practice—our return home by penetrating through dualistic experience and understanding into Unity—he's stating that the energy underlying the entire universe is *conscious* energy. He's describing how Divine Consciousness creates the entire universe within Itself, and how It comes to recognize Its own experience of Itself. Because of that recognition, Consciousness expresses Its creative force from Its own joy and urge to celebrate Itself. In this chapter we will explore how that creation occurs through Śiva's energies of will, knowledge, and action within His own awareness, and how we use those exact same powers every day in the creation of our own lives. For instance, as our individual will generates an impulse, our mind uses limited knowledge and formulates an idea, and then we act.

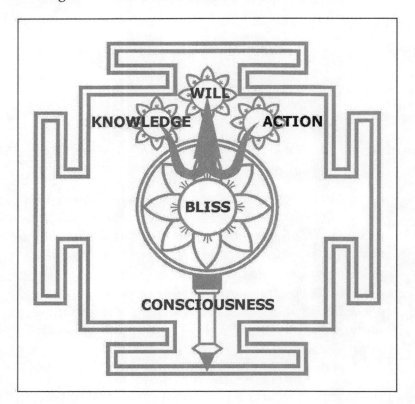

Śiva's Trident *maṇḍala* is a sophisticated depiction of the understanding expressed in Abhinavagupta's statement, a graphic symbol of the energies that emerge from the highest Consciousness. The *maṇḍala*, in other words, depicts the five powers of Consciousness, which are the energies of life itself.

In Tantric scripture, these powers are discussed as the five aspects of Śakti within and expressed by Śiva. They are:

1. Consciousness, or *cit śakti*, the energy of Consciousness Itself, the capacity for self-awareness

2. Bliss, or *ānanda śakti*, the energy of bliss, the essential joy of experiencing one's own existence

3. Will, or *icchā śakti*, the energy of desire or will, the capacity to express infinite freedom

4. Knowledge, or *jñāna śakti*, the energy of knowledge, the capacity for perfect knowing

5. Action, or *kriyā śakti*, the energy of action, the capacity to act

These five different expressions enable Śiva to manifest Himself as the universe by means of His intrinsic Divine power of *svātantrya* (His free and independent will), using His own Consciousness and energy as the material, and Himself as the screen on which He manifests. Thus, the manifest universe in all its infinite variety of objects is only One Thing — the Supreme's Self-manifestation. This is the Self-expansion of His own Śakti. As we will explore in the next section, these five energies are in fact the first five *tattvas*. One of the most important things to understand is that our existence is the *effect* of these five energies, yet it is not different or separate from them. Our life is the expression of God's freedom and joy. This immediately begins the debate: If that's true, then why do I suffer? That's a good question, and the answer is because we misunderstand, misinterpret, and ultimately misuse these powers. Yet also inherent within the trident *maṇḍala* is our pathway out of suffering, if we know how to look for it.

In the above quotation, Abhinavagupta says that we have been given the power to free ourselves. If we wish to achieve infinite, endless union with God—which is our Divine right—we must discover the source of Consciousness. We do so by penetrating back through that which was emitted within Divine Consciousness by Its powers of bliss, will, knowledge, and action, i.e., the manifest universe that arises from those powers. If we get caught in external life, we miss the source of life, and this poignantly describes our typical experience. We search endlessly to find the meaning of life in external life because we misunderstand it as something separate from ourselves. We think of life as the beautiful trees, the pretty girls, the cute guys, which, of course, it is. The trick is that the very things we must penetrate through in order to understand that they are not the ultimate experience in life, are usually the same things that catch and confuse us, binding us in our misunderstanding.

This is why we must deeply engage life to be free of the binding and suffering of life, and we must go through duality to be free of duality. Liberation, which is the discovery of bliss and the experience of autonomous freedom, is the understanding that there can be One and many at the same time. This is the point of *sādhana*, and if we're serious about our practice, we surrender everything that gets in the way of that experience. This is why Nityananda said, "Surrender everything that keeps you from Śiva." He didn't qualify that statement. Ultimately, there is only one thing that gets in the way of that experience, and that is our limited understanding. It's not our wives, our husbands, our jobs, our kids, or our lack of money. It is none of those conditions. It is our limited understanding.

Śiva and Śakti, Consciousness and the energy of bliss, are the Divine forces underlying all manifest life, and they are never separate. Śiva and Śakti are God and His creative power, the light of life and the self-awareness of that light. At the same time, the description of Divine Consciousness embedded within the trident *maṇḍala* expresses the subtle understanding of how, from Consciousness Itself, a sophisticated matrix of energies arises that are the capacities of Consciousness.

Śakti isn't just energy. It is multidimensional and has a multiplicity of dynamic aspects. It is conscious and therefore has the ability to be aware of itself, to create and decipher the different frequencies of energy within itself. As we will explore below, each of those energies has a specific resonance and purpose; and it is how these cosmic forces interact, create one another, and express themselves in their own perfection that create all life, including *our* life. In order to distinguish among and penetrate through these energies, we must bring to our *sādhana* the most profound, subtle, and discriminating awareness. Ultimately, this is what determines our level of mastery of our own experience.

Svātantrya

These five powers of Divine Consciousness could be called the DNA of Śiva's *svātantrya*, His absolute, autonomous freedom. In Kashmir Shaivism, *svātantrya* is understood to be the sole cause of the creation of the universe. It is the primordial force that manifests the world within the Supreme Consciousness of Śiva. Willed into existence by this sovereign force, the world has no external cause outside of Śiva's *svātantrya*. It is the very seed of the universe, and the ultimate creative force.

Svātantrya is the underlying field of autonomous freedom from which the five powers of Divine Consciousness are expressed. It is the awareness of the entire consciousness of freedom, as yet undifferentiated into the various powers. *Svātantrya* is the heart and the Grace of God, the essence of Consciousness, the fundamental quality of the Supreme Subject. All of the manifestation and multiplicity that arise from the creative expression of these five powers are simply the expression of the absolute power of *svātantrya*. As such, it is the one and only force that unifies all of the energies of creation.

The reason this is important to us is because this is the experience we seek. Kashmir Shaivism maintains that spiritual liberation necessitates the assimilation of the energies inherent in freedom. As the root cause of all the energies of emission, *svātantrya* automatically represents both the purpose and the culmination of our *sādhana*. All of the spiritual means and practices of the *upāyas* are subsumed under the umbrella of *svātantrya*, as it is the sole mediator of Divine Grace. *Svātantrya* is the same force that allows Śiva to become a limited individual, i.e., to become us—which never changes His eternal nature. It is simultaneously the Grace that allows the limited individual to recognize his or her Divine Self, to become God.

Simply put, *svātantrya* is the purpose of life: discovering and experiencing that freedom, and allowing our lives to express themselves from that freedom. How different would our lives be if we allowed that to happen? Think of the implications in your own life of being absolutely free of all limited awareness. This is the goal of spiritual practice, and in the words of my teacher Rudi, "Anything less is a sad reward for all your hard work." The consciousness of freedom is the consciousness of choice, so let's not focus on just getting past our pain, suffering, and struggles. Rather, let's focus on achieving absolute, unconditional freedom, the source of the joy of life.

Spanda

From the time of Abhinavagupta, Kashmir Shaivism was associated with four main schools or traditions, one of which was the Spanda Śāstra (*śāstra* means teaching or body of knowledge). This particular school of thought is often described as focused on the "vibration," or movement, of Consciousness.

Spanda is also described as the energy of joy just beginning to manifest out of the Consciousness from which it arises.

The most important text in this tradition, the Spandakārikā, states that the universe is nothing but vibrating energy. Its central tenet is that everything is *spanda*, both objective, exterior reality and the subjective world. Nothing exists without movement, yet the ultimate movement happens not in space or time but within Supreme Consciousness Itself.

Abhinavagupta uses the expression "some sort of movement" to imply a distinction from physical movement. It is a vibration within the Divine, a throb or pulsation, the essence of which is ecstatic, Self-recurrent Consciousness. The entire universe pulsates with this vibrating energy, both on the macrocosmic level and within us as individuals. It is the quivering forth of this vibrating energy that gives life to the galaxies as well as to the arising of every thought we have, every breath we take, and every beat of our hearts. The masters of this tradition sought to locate that vibrating energy within every moment of life.

Spanda is also another way of describing the unity of stillness, Consciousness, and energy that is shown in the *maṇḍala*, as well as the source of the *maṇḍala*. The dot in the center of the diagram is the *bindu*, that single point of vibrating Consciousness that is at once infinitesimally small and the entire universe. This is God's Presence, and everything that unfolds from that is His expression of Consciousness and freedom.

In one sense, spiritual practice is the discovery of that point. In order to discover it we must penetrate through manifest emission to reach the stillpoint within the pulsation of creation. Another way to think of it is that there's one single point from which all multiplicity is expressed; in other words, Spanda tradition states that all multiplicity arises from One

Thing. Yet so beautifully articulated within the Tantric system is that they are never separate. It's not that there's One Thing that created everything else. Out of Itself, and out of the bliss of Its own existence, Consciousness, this thing called God, created multiplicity. As a result, we have the opportunity—and the requirement—to penetrate back through it. The entirety of this incredible, extraordinary universe arises from that single pulsation of Consciousness, the heartbeat of Śiva.

Let's proceed with an overview of the five energies of Śiva, which also happen to be the five highest and the most subtle of all the *tattvas*.

CIT ŚAKTI: THE POWER OF CONSCIOUSNESS ITSELF

These Divine energies—Consciousness, bliss, will, knowledge, and action—all start with the power of Consciousness Itself, or *cit śakti*. This is Śiva—infinite, omnipresent Consciousness. *Cit śakti* is the source of all energies, and, ultimately, all of manifestation. It is Pure Presence, both still and dynamic at the same time. The essential quality that *cit śakti* possesses is Self-awareness, the power to know Itself. Consciousness is not just an inert presence; inherent within It is the power to be aware. The reason It's called *cit śakti* is because *śakti* means energy, and *cit śakti* is the very energy of Consciousness Itself.

Cit śakti is pure, Infinite Consciousness—transcendental, unmanifest, and formless. It's completely present yet has no form. The *bindu* point in the middle of the *maṇḍala* is God's Presence: full, pregnant Consciousness. Held within that Consciousness and Its power is a radiance and effulgence that just can't contain itself, from which Its dynamic aspect begins to become manifest, which is the act of looking back and recognizing Itself. As this all happens within Pure Consciousness, the word "manifest" here doesn't imply form. It is manifest only as awareness.

Ananda Śakti: The Power of Bliss

The most prominent visual aspect of the *maṇḍala* is the large lotus in the center, which represents the second energy of Consciousness, the energy of bliss, which is called *ānanda śakti*. The reason this lotus is so prominent in the image is because the very first thing that arises out of the power and awareness of Consciousness is the bliss of Its own Self-awareness. How amazing to understand that as energy explodes out of Consciousness, the very first thing that emerges is joy, which is also the cause of that explosion. The effulgence of Consciousness is so powerful that the first thing It expresses is the pure, unbounded, unconditional joy of Its own fullness.

The lotus in the *maṇḍala* is a graphic symbol of God's experience of joy. This is not a depiction of bliss dissolving into Pure Consciousness, but rather, it is the *expression* of Pure Consciousness. What is that joy experiencing? Itself: Consciousness. It is aware of Itself, and It is fulfilled in that. Nothing else needs to happen. And yet, as we will see, that very fulfillment is the source from which the urge to create arises. Śiva's impulse to express and share His experience emerges not from a lack of fulfillment but from the richness and effulgence of His own joy.

This *maṇḍala* helps us to understand how the initial experience of Consciousness begins with joy, with bliss, with the recognition: "There is nothing that I am not. There is nothing outside of me." The joy of that recognition is the emergent quality of Consciousness. Just think of that for a moment: Joy is an energy! And if it's an energy, we can tune in to it. Imagine how different our lives would be if we functioned from fulfillment instead of seeking it, if we recognized fulfillment within ourselves and understood that we don't need anything else to experience that joy. Simply because we exist, that infinite, unbounded joy is accessible to us every moment of our lives. Therefore, living in and functioning from that joy is a conscious choice. Similarly, not living in and functioning from joy is also a choice.

This book is a discussion of the consciousness of freedom. In our lives, this plays out as the choice to live from the joy of freedom, as opposed to living from a place of suffering from which we are trying to be free—an infinitesimal shift yet an infinite difference in experience. That bliss is energy. That joy is unconditionality. Think of all the moments of joy in your life, whether it's simply having a cup of tea or holding a child's hand. What happens when you truly rest within the stillness and fullness of joy? Nothing else needs to happen. There's nothing you need to add to or subtract from it; it's just perfect effulgence.

Śiva and Śakti, Prakāśa and Vimarśa

Another way of understanding Śiva and Śakti, Consciousness and energy, and specifically the energy of bliss, is as *prakāśa* and *vimarśa*. Tantric exposition asserts that the world is based on those two interactive principles. *Prakāśa* is understood as the pure light of Consciousness that illuminates all of life, while *vimarśa* is the ability to be self-aware, the self-reflective capacity of Consciousness to see the light and recognize Itself as that light. The illuminating power of *prakāśa* is present within every level of creation. *Vimarśa* is the mirror of Consciousness that reflects all that light, the self-referential capacity of Infinite Consciousness to know and experience Itself, to not just *be* a light bulb but to *know* it, and to experience everything It shines on as Itself—because It creates out of Itself everything It shines on. *Prakāśa* and *vimarśa* are of the nature of absolute Divine sovereignty. Eternal and infinite, from within the light of Its own Self, Divine Consciousness creates the universe. Being the Divine, It also decides that not only is It going to *be* the light of life, It's going to *know* and *experience* Its own sovereignty.

The important thing to understand is that we are not separate from that. We *are* that. Those same Divine capacities to illuminate life and to be aware of ourselves is how we come to know the source of those capacities: infinite, absolute Consciousness. This is the highest teaching: We *are* that light. It emerges from us and it creates us, all at the same time. By the power of *vimarśa*, not only do we have within us the capacity to be aware of our own state or level of consciousness, we also have the power to change our level of consciousness.

Will, Knowledge, and Action

The next three powers of Consciousness—will, knowledge, and action—arise from the bliss of Consciousness. Before proceeding with that discussion, the critical question we need to ask is this: If we are not separate from Supreme Consciousness, if we are Śiva, and Śiva is overjoyed with the experience of His own existence, why aren't we? Śiva created us in His own image, with all the same powers. Unfortunately, we misunderstand and therefore use those powers in a limited way, and from the same limited place in ourselves. We do this over and over again, and every time we do, we tie a little more tension around Śiva's light.

At the end of the day, we choose and create our own reality, just as Śiva does. If the unbounded joy of existence expressed by that lotus is not our experience, it means that somewhere along the way we forgot or misinterpreted that fact. We forgot who we really are and we've used our limted will, knowledge, and action to perpetuate our state. The fundamental purpose of our spiritual practice is to dissolve our misunderstanding and lead us back to that experience, to know our true Self.

As we move forward I hope it becomes clear what this discussion means to your individual experience, and to achieving your freedom. It is fundamentally relevant because it is the *source* of your experience. The consciousness of freedom is the determination of which level of understanding you function from within those powers. In the following chapter, we'll explore the three powers of will, knowledge, and action at length, particularly in the context of surrender, the foundation of our spiritual practice.

Shiva's Trident: Will, Knowledge, and Action

Shiva's Trident: Will, Knowledge, and Action

Arising directly out of the dynamic interplay between Consciousness and bliss—*prakāśa* and *vimarśa*—is the third power of Consciousness, *icchā śakti*, the will to create. As it emerges, it translates itself into knowledge (*jñāna śakti*), action (*kriyā śakti*), and, ultimately, all of manifestation. Embedded within the *maṇḍala* is the sophisticated articulation of that emission, which is called *visarga*. Depicted in the *maṇḍala* are the field of Consciousness and the huge lotus radiating the bliss of Its own experience. Arising out of the infinite light of Consciousness and the bliss of Its experience of knowing Itself, *visarga* is simply the cup runneth over. It is the dynamic stillness of *prakāśa* and *vimarśa*, Consciousness and joy, saying, "Let's express Myself." From this state of *svātantrya*, which is absolute, autonomous freedom, and without any form as yet, the triadic powers of will, knowledge, and action, the three prongs of Śiva's Trident, begin to emerge.

Will, knowledge, and action are always interrelated, both for Śiva and for us. In our own experience, we can recognize that first we have the urge to do something, then we figure out how to do it, and then we do it. From the generation of a single thought to the most momentous events in our lives, all of our experience follows this pathway and occurs via these three powers. At the Divine level, these are the same powers Śiva uses to create the universe and to give life to us. We've been endowed with these same capacities, and we use them at every moment to create our own lives. The difference between Śiva and us is that we understand and use these capacities in a limited way.

The emission Abhinavagupta refers to in the keynote quote is the emission of God's powers of will, knowledge, and action. What he's saying is that we must penetrate back through even those powers by becoming one with them, recognizing that they are God's expression of the joy and infinite freedom He dwells with as Himself. What an amazingly powerful statement to understand, that the highest of all Tantric practices is to penetrate through those three powers in order to experience them as our power.

We experience our own lives as limited expressions of those powers in the sense that we experience ourselves as having an individual will and a certain amount of knowledge. Mostly we experience our life as action, that we're doing something. What we're attempting in our *sādhana*, which is every breath we take, is to free ourselves of that limited perspective and experience. As we surrender our limited perspective and experience long enough, deeply enough, we begin to allow those energies to rise back to their source, and to experience them in a higher awareness.

In truly seeking to find that state of freedom, we must at some point surrender our limited will—and thus our limited knowledge and actions—to God's will. We must use our will to align with God's will. That is the highest service, and the highest state of freedom. Surrendering our will, our limited knowledge—that is, what we think we know—and even surrendering our need to act, is how we penetrate those powers. As we do so, we begin to understand that the reason we walk on this earth is because of God's will. Our entire *sādhana* is to surrender until we come to that recognition and experience.

This is why surrender is the foundation of spiritual *sādhana*. Developing the capacity to surrender in our engagement with the world is how we begin to let go of our individual will, our knowledge of who and what we think we are, and our actions taken from that perspective. If we're still fighting with our partner about what side of the bed we get to sleep on or worrying about our financial security, we aren't within a million miles of the dissolution of the emission of God's powers.

Śiva's Trident is a direct invitation to the highest practice, which is to penetrate through those three powers, because in penetrating through those, Śiva's just there. The essence of *sādhana* is the discovery that those energies and the Consciousness from which they arose are never separate from each other. It is living from and through those energies that penetrates the veils of duality. So let's discuss each of these three powers, in both their Divine and limited capacities, and explore how in each of those dimensions surrender is the pivotal point in attaining spiritual freedom and beginning to live our lives as joyous expressions of Śiva's *svātantrya*.

ICCHĀ ŚAKTI: THE POWER OF WILL

From the *svātantrya* of Divine Consciousness and from the blissful energy of *ānanda śakti*, the next energy that arises is *icchā śakti*, pure, infinite will. How incredible it is that out of unconditionality and effulgent joy, the next energy that arises is the power whereby God experiences Himself as an unlimited, independent force, ready and able to perform any action He wishes.

Divine will is the primordial impulse toward creation. It is Śiva thinking, "I exist, established in My own bliss and Consciousness. Because I experience the joy of that and want to express it, I'm going to create the effect of that bliss." The power of *icchā śakti*—Śiva's will to express joy—arises directly from His experience of joy, yet this power expresses itself entirely within Śiva's own awareness. Through His will, He expresses a perfect reflection of Himself, yet there's no form to it and there doesn't need to be any form. *Visarga*—the creation and emission of the universe as the expression of Divine sovereignty—occurs prior to any manifestation.

In the Tantrāloka, Abhinavagupta describes *icchā śakti* as Sadāśiva, which translates as "eternally Śiva," meaning that as the universe begins to come into existence, even only as a concept, the Absolute loses none of Its Divinity. In Śiva's will to express perfection and freedom, He conceives the entire universe without any sense of it being different or separate from Himself. What we come to recognize is that everything expressed out of joy is part of that joy, and thus, how perfect all of manifest life must be, because Śiva designed it. And He did a pretty good job. It manifest pretty amazingly, even just on this planet.

Perfection, however, didn't mean that every detail was worked out. Because the only thing happening was the will to express freedom, getting it right didn't mean that every thread of the warp and weave of the fabric had to be worked out. Śiva thought, "I'll work it out as it happens. I'm allowing this expression to emerge from My will to express freedom, so I don't need to control it. I know it's coming from my pure joy, so I don't need to know in advance." Do you think there's any implication for this in our lives?

God's Will Is Freedom

Pure, infinite, Divine will is God's power and intention to express freedom, not manifestation. Even though manifestation ultimately emerges out of that expression, God's intention is simply to expand freedom. In doing so, creation is the choice. He thought, "I will create freedom, and it will look like the universe," thus expressing and containing all possibilities and limitless variation.

How does this apply to our experience? Just like Śiva, we too have this power of will, and therefore the responsibility, the choice, and the gift of creating our own life. Just as Śiva creates this freedom in His own awareness, we also have the power to close our eyes and say, "I am free." Why wouldn't we create our life as an expression of our freedom? How could anything ever bind us if we did so? Exercising our will to create our life is our Divine right. If what we create is the expression of our freedom, then we no longer need to search for freedom in our life. When we search for freedom in external life, we start placing conditions and defining what a free life should look like based on our limited understanding of freedom: "This is a free life; this is not. This binds me; this does not."

Part of our unconsciousness is that we are not aware of that choice and therefore we don't make it, and we continue to function from a place in ourselves that's unaware of that choice. This is the mystery. We don't know we have a choice and therefore we keep functioning from a place that doesn't know it has a choice. At some point, we must get quiet enough to recognize that at every moment of life, we choose what depth of consciousness we function from. We come to realize that we have that opportunity.

The Śiva's Trident *maṇḍala* represents one unified field of Consciousness and energy expressing Its own freedom, which is Śiva's will. Since we have been given the same free will to create our life, if we aren't creating a life of freedom, perhaps it's because we've chosen to use our will to create something else. Our problems arise when there is a millimeter of difference between whether we are crystal clear that we are living in God's will, or if there is the tendency to express our own limited will. In His benevolence, God gave us free will to align ourselves with His will, which might be considered a design flaw because so often we don't choose it! Our individual will gives us the power to deny even the Grace of God, and, unfortunately, most often we do.

When we exert our own will, God's desire to express His own freedom becomes limited and expressed by us as the desire for something outside ourselves. We experience the power of will as desire—the desire to make something happen or stop something from happening—instead of understanding our will as simply the perpetuation of freedom. Śiva's will is the expression of freedom, end of discussion. There is no detail involved in that. If we truly surrender and begin to understand that, then our will is not separate from that, and our idea that God's will has something to do with our plan for our life evaporates. Only when we are bound by condition, thinking that if we surrender our will and live in God's will, then we'll be rich, or we'll be this or that, are we misunderstanding.

God's will is the expansion of freedom. There is no form or condition in freedom. Through *vimarśa*, our self-reflective capacity, we can know this in ourselves. Whenever we chase, cling, or reject, whenever we try to change something with the idea that changing it will change our experience, that's our will. That's being willful and functioning from a place of incompleteness. If we're complete, life is perfect as it is. This is why so many practices and scriptures emphasize the development of the capacity to be aware of our own state, as it is the prerequisite for changing our experience from one of limitation to one of expansion.

We can have our individual will and still be an expression of God's will. Both can function at the same time once we understand the power of Divine will as it lives in us, as our will. Because Divine will is the emission of the joy of Consciousness Itself, when we use our will to surrender to Divine will, our experience is one of unconditional joy. It is only by surrendering our will long enough, over and over again, that we begin to see that we are simply allowing God's will to flow through us.

THE DESIGNER AND THE WEAVER

Remember that will, *icchā śakti*, is energy. The energy of will arises from the energy of bliss, *ānanda śakti*, because it is the energy of *expressing* that bliss. The purpose of will is to express joy and freedom, not create binding out of it. The absolute, autonomous will of Śiva that creates all of manifestation is the same autonomous will we have to create our own lives. And we do, every moment of every day. The problem and the challenge for us is that we misunderstand the purpose of having that will, and so instead of creating joy and freedom, we use it to reinforce our current level of consciousness. This is how Divine will becomes individual willfulness.

In his book *Behind the Cosmic Curtain*, Rudi beautifully encapsulates this entire discussion of God's will versus our will, writing:

> *Those who pick apart the threads weaken the fabric of creation by applying their mind to the design, because to them God's will is not acceptable as their own. We must first surrender to the miracle of creation; then the pattern will emerge. Life is composed of an endless variety of threads of many colors. The need to reduce them to a certain type of design constricts the creative output. All the tension put into the weaving is man's limitation of God's purpose.*

As Rudi so eloquently explains, we are not the designers of our lives; we are simply the weavers, and we are being weaved. How beautiful. The highest choice and use of our own will is to surrender it. In doing so, we recognize that we are simply not doing what we think we're doing, and we begin to truly free ourselves from the misunderstanding that we are doing anything at all except living as the spontaneous, free expression of God. We begin to penetrate back through the veil that we are the doer and experience that only Śiva is doing. The willingness and the choice to allow the design of our life to express itself is the essence of surrender. It is only through surrendering our own will that God's will can show us the perfection of our life.

We think we can design our life a little bit better than God can. We think perfection will show up if we design it. Our life is already perfect because it is trying to free us. Every moment of life is Divinely offered to us in order to point us toward understanding our freedom and living in joy. What could be more perfect? But we will never have that experience until we ask for it and live it and are truly willing to let go of our design. We must let go of the idea that we are the designer, or that we need to redesign anything. Instead of trying to redesign our life, we can allow our consciousness to be transformed.

The central lotus in the *maṇḍala* represents the unfolding experience of bliss, surrender, and freedom from condition. This is a clue that we must love our life no matter what the condition, because the conditions have been designed and woven into our life in order to free us. Instead of being still and quiet enough to hear the resonance of that weave being created in our life, we have a constant dialogue with God about the conditions that we think shouldn't be there, and this is what allows us to disconnect and reject the Grace of God in our lives. In our heart, in a place of stillness, it is absolutely obvious when it's our will versus God's will.

Surrendering Our Will Into God's Will

What we have in our life at this very moment is God's will. We can huff and puff and blow the house down, but if God doesn't will it for us, it won't happen. God wills one thing: the perpetual expansion of freedom, and He wishes it for us. We, on the other hand, reject that freedom because it doesn't fit our design. If we could for one moment truly let go of everything we think we need and perpetually reach for, we would be free. Our will is how we let go.

It is very easy to allow God to be the doer of everybody else's life. Sometimes we even think we're messengers of God's will concerning how He wants everybody else's life to be. Then we have these interesting dialogues with people in our lives in which we make comments like, "I'll really be committed to you when you've grown and changed, when you look, feel, act, and treat me the way I want you to treat me." Such statements are expressions of our will and our conditions, and this is how relationships become incredible expressions of demand instead of beautiful expressions of love and support. This is a simple example of how those powers play out in our lives. I suggest we start from the top and give our will away. It has no relevance whether the person we're engaged with needs to change or not. The issue is whether we're willing to change.

Yet we get something wonderful out of it: freedom. We get to function, experience, and express from the unconditional joy of needing nothing in order to have the highest inner experience. While it may appear as if we're giving up or giving in to another person, all we're really doing is offering ourselves in service to a higher will. All of the conditions for offering our life in service to God evaporate as soon as we understand that the details involved in doing so are not that important.

God does not script our lives at the mundane level. His will is the perpetual expansion of freedom. We can do anything we want, as long as it's not contracting that state of freedom. At a certain point we understand that surrender is not about letting go of any particular thing. It is a state of awareness, of allowing God to be the doer. Anything we do from that state expands and allows God's will to express itself. People always ask what the purpose of life is. The purpose of life is to live God's will. Everything and anything else we might do within that context is irrelevant to God.

So do anything you want, but always hold that in the context of what you really want, which is freedom. And when you find yourself in that moment where you know you need to make that offering of your will, and you begin to be afraid, reach inside and ask for help: "May my will be Your will. May I live in unconditional bliss." This is the power of your will, your wish to grow. That wish turns into commitment to growing, and ultimately the surrender of growing no matter what the condition is, whatever we get or don't get. This is how Divine will becomes manifest within us.

Will is the expression of choice, and there is no distinction between Consciousness, choice, and will. *Svātantrya*—absolute, autonomous freedom and the bliss that arises from it—is the state of surrender, and gratitude is the emergent quality of that state. How can we be anything but grateful when we recognize that we are or can be free?

"Pain Is God Loving You"

Surrender is simple; we complicate it because we aren't willing to understand that when we say, "May my will be Your will," we are actually saying, "May I live in freedom." We translate it into: "May I live in freedom and have everything I want exactly the way I want it." As soon as we don't have what we want, we believe we're not living in freedom. Perhaps not getting what we want is the very test that will free us from condition.

We create the very dynamics in the world to test our willingness to not be attached to the dynamics of the world. Our life is a mirage of ourselves, painted on the canvas of our own consciousness. When Rudi talked about being tested that's exactly what he meant, because the very vibration of our wish to grow attracts to us some form or circumstance that tests whether or not we're serious.

When you are in pain and can't surrender, that's the moment to let go. That's the moment to recognize that God is trying to make you bigger. Rudi said it very directly: "Pain is God loving you." Why is this so? Because He wants us to grow and be free. The pain is simply our resistance to that freedom, our resistance to opening and allowing our own perception to be blown apart. If we let go in those moments what we find is the power of bliss, the power of unconditional surrender. They're not separate. Bliss is the joy of experiencing our own existence as it is in this moment.

Whenever you find yourself struggling, ask yourself, "Is this worth sacrificing my own unconditional joy?" Our capacity for self-reflection, to know our own state, is the gift of Consciousness that allows us at any and every moment to stop, take a breath, and say, "This is not my beautiful life. This suffering, this tediousness, this mundaneness is not what I choose." Even though you may find yourself drowning in it, you are your own life preserver, and the cord of that life preserver is anchored in your will: "I wish to not live this mundane, superficial, petty existence. I wish to live in God." Every moment of your life is that choice. This is why the consciousness of freedom is the consciousness of choice.

Divine will as it manifests in us is the continuation of God's infinite will to express freedom and joy. Everything that we do that pushes against that and causes us to be unhappy is our will. All of it. Not some of it. Not some of the time. Not only in certain circumstances. When we ultimately surrender the veil of duality of thinking we are the doer, God just expresses Himself through us, with no particular plan except the expression of freedom. Surrendering totally into the will of God doesn't mean that we're just going to sit like a lump for the rest of our life. Out of that will comes knowing exactly what to do and the capacity to do it, the state of illuminated clarity. We no longer question whether it's God's will or our will because it's perfectly clear.

Here's a clue. If we're struggling about whether something is or isn't God's will, guess what? It's ours. The reason we don't understand this is because we want to attach a result even to our surrender. The only result of surrender is surrender. It doesn't have to manifest in any form. It is a state of awareness and freedom. *Svātantrya*, the pure, absolute freedom from which Śiva created us, is the same pure, absolute freedom from which we offer ourselves back to Him. The highest expression of our own will is to surrender it, because when we offer our individual will back into Divine will, we free ourselves from individuality.

JÑĀNA ŚAKTI: THE POWER OF KNOWLEDGE

If Divine will is perfect in its understanding and in its own bliss, then everything that emerges and manifests from it must also be perfect. Śiva knows exactly what He wants to create in order to share His freedom and joy, and He knows how to do so. That power of knowing, *jñāna śakti*, is the same as *vimarśa*, the attribute of Consciousness to know Itself. Knowing yourself is the highest knowledge, even if you're Śiva!

Jñāna śakti is God's power of pure, infinite knowledge whereby He is able to know all things. As He conceives in His mind the universe to be created, He holds within Himself all the patterns and structures that will form the universe. In this sense, the world is created, but only in an internal sense, within the Supreme Subject, as there is no difference yet between the Creator and the created. Since the world exists only in His awareness, He even knows what the universe is going to look like and He hasn't manifested it yet. This is omniscience. In the Upaniṣads, the Lord says, "I am Brahmā. All this is Me."

Divine Will means that Śiva is ready, willing, and able to perform, but before He does so, He must have knowledge. "I've looked back at myself and I know what I look like. Now I can act." From that crystal clarity emerges the will to go forward. Within Śiva's own Consciousness He begins to conceive of the world and all the patterns and structures that will form creation. Does that mean He said, "There will be Uranus and Pluto and quark 212"? He didn't need to, because inherent in that level of awareness is perfect knowledge of all things.

Since Śiva is free, He doesn't need to know the details. Because He knows that manifestation will unfold out of its own perfection, He doesn't have to worry, "Will what arises out of Me be perfect?" This is not a question Śiva asks Himself. In His perfection, Śiva creates this incredible, beautiful manifestation, knowing it will look like Him, because it *is* Him.

What's important to understand about *jñāna śakti* is its inherent awareness of how energy manifests into form. Knowledge means knowing how to express will, and that power arises directly out of will, whether it's Śiva's will or our own. It is having an intention, knowing what to do with it, and then doing it. As a tennis player, when that ball comes at me and I've got my forehand lined up, I know exactly what I'm going to do with it. I know how to apply my own will. It's that simple. Because I'm functioning from that clarity, there isn't this Ping-Pong game going on in my mind: "Do I hit it? Do I not hit it? Is it this? Is it that?"

This is Śiva's supreme knowledge. He knows that creation, arising from His own Consciousness and freedom, will express that same freedom and perfection. He doesn't need a plan. At Śiva's level, this is the knowledge of perfection, and the knowledge that perfection is perfectly free.

The Highest Knowledge

Vimarśa, the self-referential capacity to know our own state, is how we know whether we're free or bound, and what allows us to change that state. The capacity to be self-aware enables us to recognize the dimension of ourselves we're functioning in and to choose a deeper one. This is our right and our choice. It says in the Tantrāloka, "I bow to the one goddess in the form of Self-consciousness. That Self-consciousness is not the psychosomatic state, which masquerades as the self." The real issue is what we do with that knowledge. Most people are vaguely aware that they're bound, but they don't know why and don't have a clue what to do about it. This is, unfortunately, the bane of human existence.

All action arises from knowledge, which means we better know what we're doing before we do something. We better know how our words are going affect the people in our lives and our relationships with them. *Vimarśa* is the ability to recognize what level of consciousness our words and actions emerge from. *Jñāna śakti* is the next energy that arises after will, and it is critical because will and knowledge ultimately express themselves as action. We must be honest with ourselves in order to know if our will is coming from a place in us that feels incomplete and needs something. We must be still in order to discern this because, unfortunately, most of our urges come from a place of need, of not feeling whole in ourselves.

In the creation of the universe, Śiva got it right before He acted, something we ought to think about. Before you speak, get it right, and do not act until you know. If you're not sure if you know, think very carefully about where it's coming from in you. What part of your will are you expressing? Are you allowing God's will to show itself through you, or have you begun to define things through your own will? If you're unsure, surrender, and don't act. You might think, "But if I don't act, then this won't happen. And if *that* doesn't happen, then this can't happen, and I'll never get what I want." Maybe the best thing that could ever happen to you is that you never get what you want.

It is the self-reflective awareness of *vimarśa* that makes Consciousness conscious. What good is being conscious if we're not aware of it? The wish to grow is Śiva's *vimarśa*, His own wish to know Himself. We think we're sitting here saying, "I wish to grow," when really it's Śiva saying, "I wish to know Myself again." And He wishes to know Himself through us.

Knowledge in the highest sense is the capacity to know oneself and understand that all of life happens from within. Śiva knows Himself, and He creates all of manifestation Himself before there's ever form. He got it right from the very start, knowing, "All of this is perfect. I know how it will look, and therefore acting is simple. I just do it." In us, this unlimited knowledge contracts into limited knowledge, and as we will see, the mind only has a capacity for limited knowledge.

Recognizing Limited Knowledge

Abhinavagupta says, "The state of *khecara* is the state of liberation that comes from the liberation of the mind. When our awareness is not trapped in the smallness of the mind, it can connect to the grandness of Divine Consciousness." We completely misunderstand who we are, and we project our lives based on that misunderstanding. Because we're attached to our perspective, we insist on defending it, and we often attack the people who have a different view and dare to suggest that ours is not really what we think it is. What we think we know limits us, which is why true *sādhakas* must seek to have everything they think they know disproved.

This is why it is often said that freedom is the thought-free state. It is being so deeply immersed in Consciousness that thought does not even arise. We all know how easily thoughts create elaborate fantasies in our minds. We get caught in something, somebody, some situation. One thought leads to two thoughts, which multiply into many. We create this incredible reality and forget that it's not reality!

The Spandakārikā, one of the foundational texts of Tantric Shaivism, describes how all of life arises and subsides from one single point, and that everything that manifests from that stillpoint is part of the whole. The early practitioners of the Spanda tradition explored how that foundational principle applies to everything in life, including the thought-constructs of the mind. A line in that text states, "The rise in the bound soul of all sorts of thought-constructs marks the disappearance of supreme immortality, and therefore he loses his freedom."

We have all had this experience. A thought arises, and instead of allowing it to subside, we maintain it. We express it, extrapolate it, and allow one thought to lead to another. A powerful practice in the Spandakārikā is the surrendering of thought-construct. As it arises, instead of allowing it to form and draw content to itself, which then has to be explained and proved, we recognize the thought as energy. Rather than engaging it and giving it life, we simply allow it to subside.

In the words of Nityananda, "If you have mind, you want everything; if you have no mind, you want nothing." It is our subtle discrimination that gives us the capacity to recognize openness, stillness, and Presence within us, as well as when thoughts start to arise that limit those attributes. The practice is catching ourselves before thought starts to perpetuate itself, because thought leads to more thought, and then to action.

In the Tantrāloka, Abhinavagupta states categorically that it is thought-construct that binds the human being. He understood that thought is of the mind, and because the mind has a limited capacity for consciousness, it therefore has to get it wrong. While Śiva has the capacity to create in His mind without limiting Himself, we don't. We create a whole scenario with incredible scenery, the hero, the heroine, the love story, the sad story, and it has no end. We must learn to surrender thought before it forms by recognizing it as energy and understanding that we don't have to sustain it or allow it to crystallize into form.

You must not believe your mind. The mind cannot perceive its source; it isn't big enough. Accept that your perspective is wrong, or at least limited. This is how you'll understand what's right. Until we are free from our attachment to the mind, we will be bound by it. The problem isn't the mind but the attachment to the identity it creates and that we will fight to the death to sustain. We have to recognize that it's the limited aspect of ourselves (our ego) that's functioning in order to surrender it. It is only by surrendering our mind and the attachment to thought that we are freed from the constraints of thought-construct.

Most all of our thoughts create, sustain, and reinforce our experience of duality, and we are attached to those thought-constructs that reinforce our misunderstanding that we're separate. Rudi always said, "The mind is the slayer of the soul." He also said, "Take your mind and stick it in your heart." Allow your mind to fall into your heart, and when you find yourself stuck in your mind, look elsewhere.

Staying Centered in Higher Knowledge

If we don't look for liberation we will discover something else. We may have and do everything we ever dreamed of, and even be happy for a while, but if all of that isn't part of the process of discovering absolute, autonomous freedom and joy, then we'll be doing it for the wrong reasons and we'll get the wrong result. We will not come to the point of understanding that what we identify as ourselves and what we therefore like, don't like, need to get rid of, etc., is missing the point. It takes real convicted awareness to stay focused on discovering the highest truth in ourselves. We can't say we want to discover that and then continue to function from a lower truth.

In some ways it's all about what address we plug in to our GPS. If we plug in all our trauma and drama, we'll find it very quickly. If we plug in Śiva, it may be a longer trip, but we always stay on the path because we have a singularity of focus. When we know where we want to go, all the struggle and difficulty is part of the process of getting there. If we want to drive from Texas to New York, we plug it in to our GPS, get the directions, and follow them to our destination. We know where we're going. We don't just get off the road and say, "Here I am in Kansas. I think I'll stay here."

Why should our spiritual life be any different? Why shouldn't we be clear about where we want to go? Why shouldn't we have the discipline to stay focused on what we say we really want? So gas costs more than we anticipated. Maybe we'll even have to stop and work for a while to pay for gas. Maybe we could hitchhike. Who cares what the journey looks like? Why should we lose sight of where we're going because of the journey? What's the good of being God if we can't know we're God? This is why the Shaivite Tantrics say it is the journey *as* God.

Subtle Discrimination

We can think of the cosmic energies of will, knowledge, and action as the threads that create the fabric of life. Developing the sensitivity to those threads of energy and allowing them to show us the weave is what transforms our understanding of the ultimate truth. Real knowledge comes from discernment, the conscious capacity to feel the threads of Divine will, knowledge, and action weaving our life. If we're busy fighting with life, we will never perceive the weave.

While we must develop this discerning capacity through our meditation, through our capacity to feel the heart of God within us, if we can't open our eyes and engage life and have the same experience, then it isn't real. Anyone can discover Unity in their own heart if they look, because it's always there. Spiritual discernment is being able to open our eyes and see manifestation, duality, without losing contact with Unity. It is the recognition that duality is not separate from its source. This is why Rudi made his students open restaurants and bakeries and construction companies and become doctors and lawyers. He knew that spiritual freedom is freedom from duality, and that duality can only be transcended in the manifest world.

Consuming Our Misunderstanding

One of the most extraordinary gifts of Rudi is a practice he called the "double-breath." (For a description of the exercise and a link to an MP3 of the guided meditation, see the Appendix.) The essence of this exercise is that we must consume the life we project from our limited understanding back into ourselves, refine it, and then project it into a higher state of clarity and knowledge. With this exercise we can absorb the emission of our own lives—the manifestation of our own will, knowledge, and action—and consume it back inside. We do this over and over, perpetually re-internalizing our life force so that it can be refined into the subtlest of the subtlest. Only in its subtlest state can the *kuṇḍalinī* energy rise through the *suṣumṇa*, through the psychic body, and into higher states of consciousness.

We must seek and practice that experience in meditation, and we must also do so throughout our day. And when some misunderstanding arises from within us, we take a breath. If we get into a tight situation with someone, if we stop slinging our sledgehammer long enough to feel the underlying energy of the situation, all of a sudden it changes. Now there's a dialogue of energy, a flow. As we internalize the energy of the dynamic, we come to understand that there is no separation between us and the world; there is no separation between Unity and duality. We penetrate the appearance of duality by consuming the misunderstanding that it is such.

God's perspective—that highest, infinite knowledge—will not fit within the matchbook we call a heart. Tantric tradition is the rejection of nothing, and yet what's amazing, even for those of us who practice it, is that we reject our own freedom through an endless pursuit of happiness from a place of bondage. That's a heavy burden to carry. We have the power to reject God in our lives, and we use it every day. The point of *sādhana* is to develop the discipline to recognize when we're functioning from a limited consciousness within ourselves so that we can stop it.

We must become like the *haṁsa* bird, a mythical creature with the remarkable capacity to extract just the milk from a mixture of milk and water. Not only can it extract the milk from the mixture, it can extract the pure sweetness from the milk. Like the *haṁsa*, it is in the engaging and drinking of this concoction called life that we discover joy. It is in penetrating through and consuming God's emission that we make contact with its Source and Creator.

God didn't create life out of suffering. He created it out of His own effulgent joy. He just let it overflow. Why not try that in our own lives? And know this: Anytime we aren't functioning from that place, it is our choice. Even if we can't find that most expanded, unconditional state, we still always have the discriminating awareness and self-reflective capacity to offer whatever level of unconsciousness we're functioning from into the fire of Consciousness. This is the joy and the consciousness of *sādhana*. True knowledge is knowing that we create our own freedom.

KRIYĀ ŚAKTI: THE POWER OF ACTION

We've seen that *icchā śakti* is Śiva's Divine will to perpetually expand His freedom and joy. By the Divine energy of *jñāna śakti*, Śiva knows exactly what He wants to create to share that freedom and express that joy. Perfect in His understanding and bliss, He knows that all that emerges and manifests from His will is perfect. Thus when He acts, by the Divine power of *kriyā śakti*, He does so in order to express that same perfection. Śiva's action is simply the expression of His own energies and Consciousness, and this is the experience we seek, which will liberate us from the perception of duality and the binding of karmic patterns, and reveal to us the simple bliss of being.

Kriyā śakti is pure action. It is God's power to assume or manifest Himself in any form or shape, although in terms of the unfoldment of manifestation, He still hasn't done so yet. Remember, the highest powers of Śiva function completely and perfectly within His own field of Consciousness, without manifestation. It's critical to understand this because what it means is that we must be very clear about the source of our actions before we proceed to act. The constant dilemma we face is our uncertainty about whether we are about to act from consciousness or unconsciousness, from our highest Self or from some limited perspective, i.e., our ego. For example, we may declare that we want to know God, and then find ourselves behaving in ways that are contrary to that intention. That's where these Divine powers have to work in concert, because when they don't, we experience dissonance.

In particular, functioning unconsciously within the energy of action provokes so much misunderstanding within us because action is the grossest form of duality. It is the one specific energy that most veils the reality that all life is really just Consciousness and energy—and thus the one energy we most often get caught in. We experience our actions and our movement through the world as separate from the other energies of Consciousness. We think that we are doing something. This is the veil of duality called "I am the doer." Functioning within that veil, we lose sight of the fact that all action is simply Consciousness expressing Itself as energy, and we therefore lose sight of the purpose of action, which is Śiva expressing the joy of His own existence through us.

Divine action expresses the true nature of Śiva and is the result of His absolute freedom. Our life is the same. We choose our experience and reality, moment by moment. The difference between God and us is that His action is not directed toward anything or anybody; it is not aimed at the results of that action. It is the intrinsic joy of Consciousness perpetually expanding Itself. We need to ask ourselves, "What is our action directed toward? Is it coming from and expressing freedom?"

From the power of will, the inseparable energies of knowledge and action emerge. Likewise in our own lives: Our knowledge—what we believe and where we focus our awareness—is inseparable from how that knowledge expresses itself in our actions. Our will is expressed through the knowledge we function from and the actions that emerge from that knowledge. If we function from tension, we are tense. If we function from freedom, we are free.

In penetrating through the energy of action we begin to free ourselves from the misunderstanding of duality. As we engage the dynamics and people in our life, we can recognize that whatever binding we feel in those interactions is our own limitation and not inherent in the situation. In this way we can glimpse how these Divine energies endow us with the power and the choice to create our experience. Even if we have somehow misunderstood that in one moment, in the very next moment we have to opportunity to choose to do it differently.

Kriyā śakti is where the rubber meets the road, because will and knowledge without action are nothing. It is completely unreal if it isn't our experience. We experience our life in the manifest world. This is one of the secrets of understanding what the *maṇḍala* of Śiva's Trident is trying to teach us. While none of Śiva's powers is more important than the others, the power of action is the emphatic power of expression. We can have all the intent in the world, and we can know exactly how we want to express that intention, but it is only in the doing that it becomes reality. Otherwise it's a figment of our imagination. In both Śiva's experience and our own, good intentions aren't enough. Intentions must be expressed with clarity and freedom. We can't say that we want to live in service, and then act from total self-absorption. Commitment is only authentic when expressed in action.

Action and Spanda

Like a rocket ship revving before it's launched, the energy of *kriyā śakti* is revving within Śiva's own Consciousness, and it is continuously generating the world. As it revs up, the power it releases creates a chemical reaction and still more energy before it finally has enough power and momentum to project out of itself and release. Out of one single essence, multiplicity arises. That revving is *spanda*, the imperceptible movement that builds on itself from within itself—the recurring pulsation within stillness—until it finally just explodes into action.

In the last chapter, we discussed the Spanda tradition and its focus on the moment of energy arising. This represents the conscious choice we have whether or not to allow that revving to take form—even as a thought. We've considered how the critical requirement in making that choice is to discern where that vibration is arising from. This is a subtle thing to understand: In Śiva that revving is the creation of manifestation in its perfection. He knows exactly what manifestation is and therefore He can simply "make it so." In us, however, since so much of the time we're neither serving nor projecting freedom, we don't know what it's going to look like. Then we get angry when it doesn't remotely resemble what we thought it should look like when it finally manifests.

Śiva gets it right before He acts, something we ought to consider. Whenever there is the perfect will and knowledge to create, doing it is a snap. It just flows out of Him. This is important, because it means we shouldn't take action unless and until we know our true intention. And if we're not sure, we must consider very carefully and discern where the urge to act is coming from within us.

We assume that getting what we want will bring us happiness, but often it really only obscures the essential bliss of being. When we are limited in our knowledge and understanding, we function from desire, attachment, fear, and anger, which form a continuous loop of binding emotion. In the words of the Bhagavad Gītā, "Desire and anger abide in the mind as if to increase happiness, but in reality they exist to delude." When we are free from both attachment to pleasure and aversion to pain and suffering, we understand that the actions of chasing after one and avoiding the other obscure true knowledge of our highest Self and the joy of experiencing our own existence.

Karma

Typically what we do in life is act, react, and then say, "Oh, shit," because we realize we acted from a limited perspective, that we got caught in a threat to our perception of ourselves, and we've done or said something that does irreparable damage to our relationships with people in our lives. Karma is created when we act from an unconscious, limited place in us, a place of self-service and willfulness. This action sets in motion binding patterns of behavior within ourselves and with others. Action doesn't just happen in the body but in the mind. Perhaps the most insidious actions happen in the mind, which are our projections from misperception. So act from the highest perception, and if you're not sure, don't act. Surrender your limited perception in order to access a higher perception.

The best way to free ourselves of karma is to let it go, and when it starts to glom back onto us, to let it go again. At a certain point, burning it happens through not repeating the same pattern again. I love the saying, "the difference between a sinner and a saint is that the saint has stopped sinning." Padmasambhava and Milarepa, two of the greatest saints ever recognized within the Tantric Tibetan Buddhist traditions, had dubious histories and are said to have been murderers, yet they found their freedom. In order to surrender a pattern, you have to stop being defined by your mind and the fear of what you did or what you're going to do. Then there's no issue of karma anymore. Śiva doesn't create karma. If you really want to be free of your karma, stop doing for yourself. Open your heart, surrender your will, and become Śiva's agent.

Ending the Endless Loop

Only the individual creates karma. So even as we free ourselves from our identification with a sense of separate individuality, complete liberation is not available without the releasing of all our karmic patterns. When is it that we don't create karma? When we're not there anymore. When we are not the doer. When only Śiva is doing. Karma is the result of willful action, and every self-centered action we perform creates karma because it reinforces the sense that we are separate individuals who succeed through our own will. Non-action doesn't create karma. When we function from a thought-free state, free from desire and attachment, we no longer create actions that leave impressions in the mind, or *saṁskāras*, which become seeds for future thoughts, desires, and actions, i.e., karmic patterns.

From this state, actions and results will follow, but the result will be higher knowledge, not necessarily the material benefits and successes we typically chase. In remaining unattached to the fruit of our actions, we allow the highest result to show itself, as it won't be filtered through our own self-focused need. When we act out of service and freedom, the result is more freedom and the consciousness of that freedom—which is freedom from duality, from bondage, from suffering, and from rebirth. A true *sādhaka*, or spiritual aspirant, always acts from the highest knowledge (discriminating awareness), knowing that only action performed while established in the consciousness of freedom is not binding.

When we first begin to recognize and allow Śiva to be the doer of our life, there is the sense of not doing anymore, but that doesn't mean we are not in action; it means we are acting on God's will. When we understand and allow God's will to truly determine our action, it isn't that we don't have goals. It is that those goals are in harmony with what needs to be done. For example, at my center we have clear goals and ideas about what we want to accomplish, but those goals are within the broader context of our established purpose—to serve God in simplicity and unconditional joy. There is no conflict.

At some point we truly understand that God's will has nothing to do with *what* we do but the depth from which we do it. God's will is singular: the perpetual expansion of joy and freedom. We understand we are not the doer, and He is doing as us. We are free from the misunderstanding that there must be a result to our action. We see that all action is service to God and His will to expand freedom. Whatever we do is for that purpose. Whatever He gives us to do is for that purpose. It is only our limited misunderstanding that wants to translate the action into some specific form.

It takes tremendous stillness, commitment, and clarity to not take action until it is clear that it is God expressing Himself as us. It takes profound willingness to surrender our projections, which are based on our limited need, in order for the reality of a situation to show itself. Even though the mind insists that action takes us out of stillness, every action we perform from a place of stillness brings us further into the depth of our own awareness.

The sole purpose of action is to discover the truth, to know our highest Self. Knowledge and action are never separate, although knowledge is superior to action because action is only abandoned through knowledge (expressed as conscious choice and disciplined action). We can only understand the union of the two by getting out of the mind, into the thought-free state, and by not acting on any given thought, perspective, or need that arises from the mind, or limited knowledge.

ACTION IS EXPRESSED AS CHOICE

My greatest gift to myself has been the effort I've made to hold on to the commitment I made the moment I saw Rudi. I was a lost nineteen-year-old coming out of three years of drug stupor. I had no capacity to work or to function, yet somehow in that meeting, something opened in me, and I was able to hold on to that at every moment since. Even when I had resistance, through forty years of practice, I never doubted that I was doing what I needed to do. The resistance, the fear, the unwillingness to change, sacrifice, and serve, those moments come up for all of us—that's when you have to "just do it."

Don't focus on the resistance or the fear; focus on your wish to grow. Remember what it was that inspired you to make the wish in the first place. And remember that Rudi's mantra has a period at the end of it because it must be unconditional: "I wish to grow."

In our lives, *kriyā śakti*, the energy of action, is expressed through our choices. Even when we understand that we have absolute, autonomous free will to choose, sometimes we choose to not live in, or even pursue, the highest part of ourselves. This happens when we are attached to the outcome of a choice, to the fruit of our actions, thinking, "I will do this in order to get that."

Fundamentally, it is the fact that we are responsible for our own state that most pisses us off, but having that responsibility, we must make a conscious choice. Once we make a commitment to our own growth, the only choice that is wrong is the one where we refuse to grow. Choice can ultimately be boiled down to what level of consciousness we function from, because sometimes life seems to make some choices for us. In those cases, the choice isn't in what we do or don't do, but in how we respond to what life brings us—in the honoring and recognition that someone smarter than us is making the choices. We have the right to make choices in our lives, and that translates into action, but we must be conscious about what we choose. This is how Divine Consciousness boils down to the actions of our life driven by our choices.

Rudi's life was about one thing: growing spiritually and finding freedom. Why did he tell us to engage the world? He did so because there is no choice but to engage the world. Again, the issue is our level of consciousness as we engage. So often we are either chasing pleasure or trying to avert pain. Both chasing and aversion are the same in that they represent the perspective of the mind and our attachment to the fruit of our actions. Pleasure and pain show up in our engagement with the world, which is why the world is perfectly designed for us to engage it, because that's how we free ourselves from the appearance of duality. The issue is always how aware we are about what we are doing, and whether we are consciously choosing growth and freedom. This might even manifest as the conscious choice to *not* do something in the world, to surrender our need for a career, for example. I really wanted to be a rock star and instead I worked in a bakery. How perfect!

If we are deeply centered and understand that we engage in action for the purpose of Self-discovery, it changes the dynamic completely. It doesn't make a difference whether or not we work in a bakery. I really didn't like working in a bakery sixteen hours a day, seven days a week, yet I loved every moment of it. This was not because of the action of it, but because of what it was doing for me inside—the requirement for surrender and the learning of service. I was the head teacher in the ashram, yet I was the one working in a bakery all the time while everyone else was spending lots of time with the swami there. Who designed that lesson? I certainly didn't, but I learned it day after day. And even when some resistance started to surface within me, I understood what it was, and I was grateful.

The Highest Action Is Non-Action

Action is an aspect of energy; it's one of the ways energy expresses itself. Non-action is also energy. On one level, the consciousness of surrender gets translated into the action of letting go. Letting go is a conscious wish, and to surrender, we have to energetically let go of whatever dimension of our life we are holding on to. In this respect, the highest action is non-action. It is simultaneously an action as well as a consciousness and a wish that ultimately moves us into the state of surrender, where the letting go takes place.

In the Bhagavad Gītā, there is an incredible articulation of the yoga of action. Its entire message is that action must be based on knowledge. The whole epic is a conversation between Lord Kṛṣṇa and the warrior-prince Arjuna in the middle of a battlefield before the start of a war. When Arjuna sees all his relatives on the opposing side, he loses morale and decides not to fight. If he leads his army into battle, he is bound to kill his own kinsmen. Wouldn't it be better, he asks, to throw down his weapons and let himself be killed?

Responding to Arjuna's confusion and moral dilemma, Kṛṣṇa explains Arjuna's duties as a warrior and prince, stressing that he should perform his duties without attachment to the results. "Surrender all action to Me, with the mind resting on the highest Self. Freed from desire and the sense of "mine," abandon that you are the doer." Kṛṣṇa focuses Arjuna on the purpose of activity: "To action alone hast thou a right and never at all to its fruits; let not the fruits of action be thy motive; neither let there be in thee any attachment to inaction."

Kṛṣṇa teaches Arjuna that there are several paths to God, one of which is embracing one's duty in the form of action. As a warrior and a prince, Arjuna's role is to fight. Kṛṣṇa tells him that in doing his duty he mustn't worry about the results of his actions. When we act with a result in mind, we are listening to our own desires. Right action means accepting our duty and acting without personal desires. In this way, we learn that our highest Self has no desires or fears, and we are no longer attached to the fruit, or results, of our actions.

Kṛṣṇa tells Arjuna repeatedly, "Do your duty. Engage yourself in rightful action. But do not aspire for the fruit of your action." His intent is to turn all of Arjuna's actions into sacred actions, to align Arjuna's will with Divine will. This happens when Arjuna surrenders himself fully to the Divine, offers all his actions to the Divine, and gives up all his attachments to the results of action.

So much of what we hold on to is the subtle idea that if we offer our life to God, we'll get exactly what we want. Maybe we will, but maybe we won't. All the tension we feel around getting what we want is our individual will and our misunderstanding that there must be a specific result to our actions. This is how the veil of duality called "I am the doer" functions.

Surrendering to God's will while being pissed off about it is not serving God's will. Whatever life requests of us, if we don't respond from a state of openness and freedom, surrender and joy, then we're not expressing those qualities. Some kind of negotiation still remains or we're acting out of fear. If we let go when we come up against those moments, we know whether or not an action is really required. If we're not sure, it's best to not do anything but sit and ask inside for more clarity.

Engaging Action for its True Purpose

The energy of action is the place where the highest knowledge within us either gets expressed or gets lost. We should live the extraordinariness of life while recognizing that every situation in our life is there to free us from the misunderstanding that the condition or the dynamic is binding and can affect our state of awareness. This misunderstanding is the first thing we need to be freed of, and the way to do so is by engaging action for the purpose of discovering our highest Self. If we are attached to the result of action, we won't discover the highest truth in ourselves, because only the ego, the limited part of ourselves that misunderstands and thinks we need something outside ourselves to be happy, feels attachment.

Go back to bliss, the unbounded joy of our own existence. We must let joy translate into our actions, into what we search for in life. We must bring fulfillment to our life instead of seeking to extract it from our life. As we align our capacities of will, knowledge, and action with those of Śiva, we begin to express freedom and service in all of our actions. Climbing the cosmic ladder back to Supreme Consciousness, penetrating through and merging with God's emission, begins with action. We penetrate through action by choosing to be still and to remain aware and conscious before and as we act. This gives us the opportunity to access and understand knowledge, to recognize God's will, to live in the bliss of our own existence, and to truly experience Consciousness as the source, material, form, and energy of life.

THE VEILS OF DUALITY

In Kashmir Shaivism and in my practice we talk regularly about the three veils of duality: "I am separate. I am different. I am the doer." This is a parallel discussion because as we penetrate back through the powers of will, knowledge, and action, we begin to free ourselves from functioning from them in a limited capacity. We gain access to and allow those powers—in their unlimited perspective—to show us our life, and this is what dissolves the veils of duality. When Rudi told us that "life must be consumed whole, with all it's pain, joy, and sorrow," what he meant was that we must penetrate through the veils of duality and through God's emission, because on the other side of that is luminous clarity.

This powerful teaching by Rudi is an eloquent expression of the essence of Abhinavagupta's statement: that our *sādhana* is to penetrate back through what emerges out of joy in order to discover unconditional joy. We experience that emission most prominently as ourselves and as the world, and we experience those as separate from each other and from their source. And we get seduced and caught in it. We don't see the world as simply the emission of the powers of Consciousness in a perpetual expression of freedom and joy. Once we recognize that, we see that the whole point of that emission is the expression of freedom and joy, and we stop looking in the experience of manifestation and emission for something other than that. Abhinavagupta is telling us to open, receive, and to use the very powers that we receive to penetrate back through those powers in order to free ourselves—even from God's emission.

Parā, Parāparā, and Aparā:
The Goddesses of Will, Knowledge, and Action

The reason the Śiva's Trident *maṇḍala* is also referred to as the Parādevī *maṇḍala* is because emerging out of Śiva Himself are the three goddesses of His supreme powers of will, knowledge, and action: Parā, Parāparā, and Aparā. The three prongs of the trident represent those three Divine energies through which Śiva emits the entire universe. If we recall that the first energy that arises from infinite, supreme Consciousness is unconditional joy, we might ask ourselves: If that were our experience, would we need to do anything else? The answer, of course, is no, but we would anyway, because if we lived in the experience of bliss, we would want to express and share it. The three goddesses representing Śiva's powers of will, knowledge, and action are the means by which He expresses and shares His own perfection.

This emission, or *visarga*, is the result of Consciousness Itself and the bliss of Its own awareness exploding forth as God's will, which is nothing other than the perpetual expansion of the freedom and bliss He experiences as Himself. The goddess Parā is *icchā śakti*, the will of God, which is the intent to express freedom. The goddess Parāparā represents the clarity of that intention and the knowledge within it, which is also called *jñāna śakti*. It is by this power that Śiva already knows exactly what perfection and freedom are and what they feel like. As

He begins to imagine the creation of the world of multiplicity, He imagines it solely as an expression of His joy and freedom. Because He possesses *icchā śakti*, the power of will, and *jñāna śakti*, clarity of knowledge, when He ultimately decides to express His freedom He calls upon the goddess Aparā, who represents His fifth power of *kriyā śakti*, or Divine action, and He "just does it."

The reason that will, knowledge, and action are described as goddesses is because the term "goddess" is synonymous with *śakti*, or creative energy. The goddess at the very top of the trident, the supreme goddess Parā, is synonymous with infinite Divine will. The other two, Parāparā and Aparā, are the goddesses of knowledge and action. The trident depicts knowledge on one side and action on the other, but these two are never separate, and one is not higher than the other, because one leads to the other and vice versa.

The goddesses are depicted as a trinity, yet they are understood as one. Parā is always on top because it is from Śiva's own Consciousness and the joy of His existence that His Divine will to express the freedom of His own experience emerges. It *has* to come first. The initial intention is to create, to allow His experience to express itself; only then, knowing exactly what it feels like to live in that experience, He acts. This energy is personified as the goddess Parā, the supreme goddess at the top of the trident, the first of the three powers that arise out of the joy of Śiva's existence. She is the energy of Śiva's will to create, emerging from Him in order to express all of manifestation. This should give us a clue that the doorway into Śiva's heart is through His will.

From within His Consciousness and the bliss of His own awareness, Śiva expresses that Consciousness and bliss through His will, the goddess Parā. What's relevant to us is that through Parā, Śiva manifests His Consciousness and bliss *as us*. These goddesses are the deities of our own consciousness, and they are not separate or different from the Goddess Kuṇḍalinī. In my practice we speak about the awakening of Kuṇḍalinī and allowing Her to rise back to Her source, which is Śiva. In the context of Śiva's Trident, it's the same notion: we are attempting to awaken ourselves to the powers of our own higher consciousness. We are trying to make contact with the deities of our own consciousness, the levels of awareness that function within Śiva's heart. In making contact with those energies, we can open ourselves to live from and through those highest levels of awareness.

The three goddesses Parā, Parāparā, and Aparā symbolize the process by which Śiva expresses His freedom in creation. Will, knowledge, and action—the triad of energies through which the emission of the universe takes place—are emoted from bliss. It isn't the other way around, contrary to what we believe about our own experience of life.

At the same time, also embedded within the *maṇḍala* are the very practices and teachings to help us penetrate and move back through that emission. Abhinavagupta's quote is quite amazing in that even as it describes Śiva emitting the universe, there is the recognition that His own freedom and experience of Himself comes through the union with that which He emits. In other words, the emission of His own Consciousness is not separate from Him. He has absolute freedom because He is in union with His own emission. He didn't just emit and then lose His power.

The goddesses of will, knowledge, and action arise out of Śiva's freedom, and therefore out of our freedom. It is penetrating back through that which gives even Śiva His freedom. Guess what? We are responsible for Śiva's freedom! This is exactly what Abhinavagupta means when he says, "In the practice of Anuttara Trika, the *sādhaka* penetrates the energy of emission, becoming one with Śiva, the source and holder of the powers of the universe."

The three powers that emerge out of Śiva's Consciousness are the very same powers we use to have that infinite experience and to discover that joy. In discovering autonomous bliss, we can discover God. This is the practice called Anuttara Trika. *Anuttara* means "none higher," meaning there is no higher practice. "Trika" represents those three powers. The incredibly beautiful and conflicting thing to understand is that even Śiva considers the three goddesses that emerge from Him and His own bliss to be higher than Himself. This is because He knows that being full of infinite Consciousness and joy is meaningless if it isn't expressed, which is what He does through those three goddesses.

Śiva's Trident is explicitly telling us to penetrate through those three powers, because it is in doing so that we understand their source, Śiva. That's why He considers the goddesses to be higher than Himself. It is through those triadic powers that manifestation and the appearance of duality take place. To transcend the experience of duality, we must understand and function from those three powers. When we function from the stillness of our own will, mind, and desire we can hear Parā singing, and the notes are our life. The goddesses on top of the trident are the energies of Grace. The reason we must access those energies is because in accessing them, we can access the Consciousness from which they arose, which is Śiva Himself.

God's Powers Are Our Powers

God's Powers Are Our Powers

The five powers or energies of Divine Consciousness we've been discussing are our own capacities, which we use to create our lives at every moment. Recognizing this immediately cuts through all the binding thoughts we have, such as: "Somebody did something to me," "Somebody didn't do something for me," "I don't have what I'm supposed to have." We can hit the delete button on that endless list of things, because we create the life we want within our own experience.

Svātantrya, the state of freedom and autonomous joy, isn't something we create but something we discover in ourselves. Remember that what first emerges out of Supreme Consciousness is the unconditional joy of experiencing Itself. What naturally arises from that, even in the Divine, is the will to create and express that freedom. All of creation, everything we experience, is that Divine will expressing its own joy. It is our Divine right to discover that unconditional joy in ourselves.

Often, we don't understand what spiritual freedom is, and often, this is the very reason we don't seek it. As Nityananda says, "Your liberation seems so far away to you because you don't look for it. If you're looking for the hammer you hold in your hand, you must look in your hand." We must look for liberation, and we must look for it free from any idea we might have of what we think it is, which immediately limits it.

As expressed in Abhinavagupta's quote, our existence, and thus our experience, is the effect of those five powers, and it is the penetration through the emission of those powers that gives us the clarity to understand that. It is the penetration through the multiplicity of creation that arose through God's will, knowledge, and action that brings liberation. To review, those five powers are:

1. *Cit śakti*, the power of Consciousness Itself
2. *Ānanda śakti*, the power of bliss
3. *Icchā śakti*, the power of will (Parā)
4. *Jñāna śakti*, the power of knowledge (Parāparā)
5. *Kriyā śakti*, the power of action (Aparā)

These five powers are emoted within Śiva out of *svātantrya*, the absolute freedom of Consciousness Itself. The astounding understanding that the trident *maṇḍala* expresses is the recognition that freedom—even Śiva's freedom—exists only in His own union with that which is expressed out of Him. How powerful for us to understand this unity in our own lives. The discussion of these energies is really a discussion of our moment-by-moment experience. The reason it's not our experience is due solely to our limited understanding.

Just as Śiva does, we create the experience of our life. It is His gift to us that we have the innate capacity to choose our experience of life, moment by moment. While we may not get to dictate the details, how we experience any particular set of dynamics is always a conscious choice. If we can penetrate through the emission of the energies that have created our existence, we understand that we have the power to use that penetration to create our own experience of life. This requires profound, subtle awareness, the door to which is our own heart.

Abhinavagupta's words help us see that it is penetrating through that symphony—being able to hear every note without losing track of the concert—that develops within us the discriminating awareness to understand the dynamics of life, and how every dynamic is part of life's perfection. Those five energies are vibrant realities, levels of higher consciousness functioning always and forever, creating us and our lives. At the same time, those powers don't exist just within us; they exist in the world. Thus, there is always the twofold consciousness of living in ourselves and doing so as we create our life in the world, and finding that same awareness as we engage all the dynamics of our life that we do in our meditation.

A Legend in His Own Mind

Another way to think of these powers is as five different aspects of God, all still in union and entirely within the mind of Śiva. The expression of His powers is the will of God expressing His own joy. Ultimately, we can understand that Śiva's expression of freedom is entirely without form, that it all happens before form arises. In fact, form is so far down the road that it isn't relevant to God's experience, which is a clue that it needn't be relevant to ours. Even as He expresses bliss, will, knowledge, and action, Śiva hasn't yet descended into form. He has yet to become us, and He hasn't yet forgotten Himself. Śiva could even be said to be a legend in His own mind.

These first five powers, which function within the field of Consciousness before actual form or manifestation, are simply the different frequencies of Śiva's power. While there is the urge to act, the knowledge that allows for the choices and specificity of His action, and the energy of action itself, these are just the revving of the rocket, so to speak, in the realm of pure potentiality.

God was always there, even before the Big Bang. That Presence, that Divine Stillness, that vibrating reality begins to emote out of the imperceptible perception of Its own Self. What's important to note is that it is out of *cit śakti* and *ānanda śakti*, the dynamic interplay between Consciousness and energy, Śiva and Śakti, that the other energies begin to emerge. Śiva's will to create, His knowledge of how and what to create, and the action of doing it, all happen within His own awareness before any manifestation takes place. This relates to our experience because that is exactly how our awareness works. Our thoughts arise beginning with an impulse of our will, followed by specific ideas and choices, and finally coalescing in a particular direction or plan of action.

Pure and Impure

The five powers we've been discussing are referred to as "Pure Consciousness," in the sense that Consciousness is not yet tainted by any hint of confusion around differentiation. Śiva creates duality within Himself by separating Himself into five powers. This infinite Presence, autonomous within Itself, says, "Let there be many." Yet initially, that differentiation does not dim His light. Held within that differentiation, Śiva sees Himself as all of that.

One of the beautiful aspects of Tantric understanding is that there is never a denial of the experience of duality, but there is the recognition that it is only the *appearance* of duality. There is only, as Consciousness descends, how it separates Itself into those categories of Consciousness, called *tattvas*, which we will explore in detail in the next section of this book.

In traditional discussions of the *tattvas*, the first five, which are the levels of consciousness that correspond to those first energies or powers, are called "pure" *tattvas*, simply because they exist within Śiva's own Consciousness as potentiality, without form or manifestation to obscure them.

Everything below those first five *tattvas* is considered "impure" because duality manifests. Does that mean that the beautiful trees outside are impure? Of course not, but they would be referred to as "impure" because we perceive them as separate from us. The words "pure" and "impure" are simply the language the Tantric masters used to describe the concepts of Unity and duality. The reason that manifestation is "impure" is because our perceptions of it confuse us and dim the light to the extent that we are unable to perceive it in its luminous clarity. This is why duality is a problem.

As Consciousness continues to contract and descend into the lower *tattvas* of form, we perceive duality because we see form rather than the source of form. *Māyā* is the energy that conceals Unity and creates the illusion of separateness, or duality. Everything below the first five powers is considered "impure" because it is obscured by duality.

Those same five energies exist within us as individuals, yet they are limited by our own understanding and perception. The practice of Kuṇḍalinī Yoga is the awakening of that vital force within us, allowing it to rise up through our psychic body, to penetrate through the barriers of misunderstanding and the veils of duality. It is from within those veils that we perceive those five powers from a limited, individual, or "impure" perspective. The simplest way of describing our progression of experience toward freedom is moving from separation and duality to non-separation and Unity. We begin to understand that all of this form and manifestation is sustained because of its One Self. At a certain point, we no longer see any separation.

The Five Powers and Svātantrya

The purpose of life is to experience *svātantrya*, unconditional freedom and joy. Embedded within the iconography of the Śiva's Trident *maṇḍala* is the explicit instruction that we must penetrate through duality to experience and function from a unitive awareness and the highest expression of the powers of will, knowledge, and action. This alignment continues to move us back to Infinite Source. The field of that Infinite Source, the light of *prakāśa* simply shining and reflecting itself, happens in the field of *svātantrya*. The five powers are not separate or different from that freedom; they are *expressing* it.

When we don't recognize ourselves as the creative source of our own experience, and instead see ourselves as victims of external circumstances, we are bound. When we gain understanding of the five powers, we see the entire universe as a living reflection of our own powers; everything is brought into alignment and union with Consciousness Itself. This must be our experience. In perceiving Unity, the trees, the birds, the sun, other people, and Infinite Consciousness are all just One: *svātantrya*, the expression of freedom.

The wonderful thing about this understanding is that we're beginning to see how the highest powers of Consciousness create our experience at every level of our awareness, and that inherent even within the experience of being bound is the experience of freedom. The highest Consciousness is already infinitely present within us, and at some point we discover that living in and functioning from that Consciousness is nothing other than our own choice. Until we recognize that we will never be free, because the very conditions we inflict on ourselves in the attempt to affect our consciousness and experience are what prevent us from being free.

Joy is the doorway to God. Joy, unconditional freedom, is the access point to its own source. Simply said, if we aren't happy now, why would we think we'll be happy later? If we don't love our lives now, why would we think we'll love them when they change? That state of surrender is one of joy and unconditionality, of recognizing that life is perfect the way it is. It may be hard, but it's still perfect, because perhaps whatever difficulty we may be facing is our friend, our catalyst for growth. Perhaps what we perceive as a difficulty is really our own Self-awareness creating a dynamic that presses up against our misunderstanding in order to change us. Never lose sight of the absolute freedom and joy that is your Divine right. Surrender everything that keeps you from that freedom, instead of surrendering freedom itself.

Penetrating the Five Powers

The five Divine energies we've been discussing are real and powerful influences of our experience. They don't just describe how the cosmos was created. While that is one aspect of how these energies function, that is irrelevant if we don't understand and allow them to transform our own experience. These powers are not separate from the Consciousness that is aware of them. They are true energies that create the matrix of the structure of the universe and are powerful forces that move through all manifestation, including us as we think, feel, and operate in daily life.

Because these five powers are energies, we can feel them and tune in to each of them. As we become adept, we can discern the source of any energy. Abhinavagupta's keynote quote is telling us exactly that: Even these extraordinary Divine powers, from which all of manifestation is created, have a source. To discover that source, we must dissolve and penetrate through manifestation, through Śiva's emission. Our spiritual practice, and our liberation, is the penetration of the energies of emission that create the universe. Tantric practices clearly state that the discovery of the source of life is achieving union with Śiva's emission by penetrating through that emission. Unfortunately, what so often happens is that we get caught in the duality that emission creates.

It is important to note that in discussing and exploring these highest levels of Consciousness, we are not yet in duality, that is, the descent and contraction of Consciousness. This should give us a clue that all our struggles to transcend duality are really Spirituality 101, because duality emerges out of the five highest powers. It is the *descent* of those five powers.

The reason we decide to get serious about meditation is to develop the ability to actually recognize and make contact with those streams of energy as they move through life. We must be serious about spiritual practice and be willing to invest our energy and awareness in depth on a regular basis in order to penetrate through Śiva's emission, which is the manifest diversity that we experience as duality. Abhinavagupta tells us that Śiva becomes free again through penetrating His own emission—which is manifest diversity—and recognizing it as simply energy expressing Unity. At what moment of our life would that recognition not be valid?

Śiva's Trident *maṇḍala* represents both the emission of Divine Consciousness and the involution of our own experience. This is why Abhinavagupta also says: "The *sādhaka* penetrates the energy of emission, becoming one with Śiva." All manifest expression exists in order for us to penetrate back through it so we may understand its source, and to recognize that it is not different or separate from that source. The simplest way to describe this process is the transcending of dualistic consciousness. When we discuss the ascent of Consciousness later in this book, we'll explore the various methods and practices we use to arrive at that place, but the shortest path is to surrender everything. As Nityananda says, "Do not hesitate to sacrifice everything that keeps you from Śiva."

"Any Schmuck Can Do It with Money"

Rudi once sent one of his students away from New York with the instruction to start a new ashram in another state. After the student had spent several weeks crying at the thought of having to leave Rudi, he went to Rudi and said, "Okay, if you want me to, I'll do it, but I'm going to need some money." With a twinkle in his eye, Rudi turned to him and said, "Any schmuck can do it with money." Within three days of moving to another state, this student owned a house and a business, without any money.

We must develop the incredible discerning capacity to experience the state of freedom through our meditation, through our capacity to feel into the heart of God that is within us. If we can't open our eyes and have the same experience we have in meditation, it isn't real. Any schmuck can discover Unity in their own heart if they look, because it's always there. Spiritual discernment is the capacity to open our eyes and see duality without losing contact with Unity. It is the ability to recognize that duality—also known as creation, emission, or *visarga*—is never separate from Unity, but is, in fact, contained within it.

Spiritual practice, both in our meditation and particularly as we engage the world, is the transformation of our limited experience of that *visarga* into God's experience. This transformation hinges on the question of who is the doer. Either we be the doer or God be the doer. While both exist at the same time, which one do we want to choose?

Once we stop struggling with the world and trying to understand it on its own level, we understand that the world—all these people and all these conditions—are all simply energies, no different from us and from God. We discover them as energy instead of getting caught up in their form. Rudi's mantra to himself at the end of his life was: "I surrender all things: thought, form, matter, and sound. Everything." This was his way of penetrating through the energies of emission in order to recognize his highest Self.

Freedom Is Always a Choice

It is only by penetrating through duality that we discover and experience Unity. The teachings on the *tattvas*, which we will explore in the next section, make clear how easy it is to make a choice. We can choose to be involved in the level of our psychology, our emotions, or our this or that, or we can choose to simply open to the deepest, most profoundly simple, white light clarity the Self.

The incredible beauty of Tantric practices, and the direct lesson of Rudi's teaching and life, is that the conditions of life do not need to change in order for us to experience freedom. In fact, if we think we have to change something in our life in order to attain freedom, we are binding ourselves further. It is the very thought-construct, "this needs to be different," that is binding. It's not whether we have one partner or another, one car or another, one job or another that limits us. It is the thought: "I am not happy because of this, and I will be happy when that happens," that binds us. Ergo, as Abhinavagupta says, thoughts are the source of all bondage.

Our capacity to free ourselves begins with our willingness to do so, our willingness to truly surrender the world we create out of our thought-constructs, which, instead of bringing us joy and freedom, cause us to experience binding and suffering. This starts with a simple willingness to let go of how we think things should be. This willingness is, in fact, Divine will functioning within us and declaring, "I will create My freedom." God's will is the perpetual expansion of freedom. What is our will about? May God's will be our will.

God's Powers Are Our Powers

The five energies of Consciousness, bliss, will, knowledge, and action are the powers of Pure Consciousness, and because we are not separate we possess the exact same powers. The fundamental pivot point in spiritual freedom is the recognition of that, and the choices we make thereafter. Our freedom lies in the purity and the force of those powers. Ultimately, it is the aligning of those powers in us with those same powers in Śiva that brings liberation.

Haven't we used these powers on our own for enough lifetimes without such great results? If we continue to experience suffering as the result of our limited use of these powers, somewhere there is a disconnect. We all rail against the argument that it's that simple, but as Rudi so often said to us, "Life is profound only in its simplicity."

If we do not have the courage to be honest about the experience of life we are creating, we will never come to the place of surrendering, of saying to Śiva, "Free me from this." As we start to understand how these Divine forces function within us, we act from a different intention. As we turn back inside and offer our misunderstanding to Śiva, our life begins to change. Our *experience* of life begins to change. Our experience of things, people, and circumstances as good and bad takes on a whole different resonance. So often, the very moments that are uncomfortable and difficult and require that we change are the very moments of freedom. We cannot hold on to ourselves and change at the same time. We must surrender in those moments, and allow ourselves to be changed.

SECTION TWO
The Descent of Consciousness

The Tattvas, Part One: The Divine Reality

The Tattvas, Part One: The Divine Reality

The philosophy of Kashmir Shaivism embraces the entire world as not just the realm or domain of Śiva, but literally as Śiva Himself. By direct experience, the ancient Shaivite masters realized Consciousness as the sole substance of the universe, permeating all of creation at every level, and they meticulously described the process whereby this one undifferentiated Consciousness unfolds, descends, and manifests Itself as the universe. This process has thirty-six stages, or *tattvas*, which may be thought of as levels of consciousness or categories of existence. This model of the thirty-six *tattvas* that emerged in the nondual Kashmiri Shaivite tradition distinguished it from the earlier Sāṃkhya model, which expressed only twenty-five *tattvas*.

The thirty-six-*tattva* model represents a sophisticated layering of levels of awareness reflecting how Divine Consciousness descends into form. *Tattvas* means "that-ness," and the *tattvas* themselves may be likened to a road map.

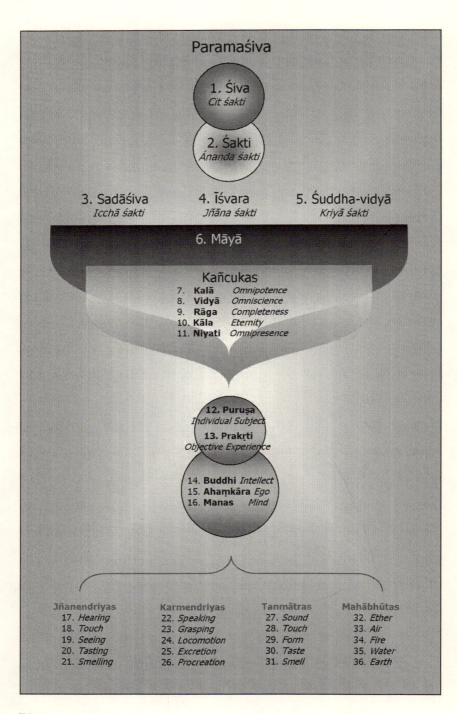

The *tattvas* describe the process whereby Consciousness contracts and condenses Itself from the highest level of supreme Pure Awareness all the way down to inert matter. The *tattvas* are the categories of Śiva's experience of Himself, and therefore they are also our experience.

Some teachings assert that there is a thirty-seventh *tattva*, Paramaśiva, which is understood to be *svātantrya*, the field of absolute autonomous freedom from which even Śiva and Śakti emerge. This hierarchy implies that even Śiva and Śakti are not as high as freedom itself! Paramaśiva may also be thought of as the Universal Heart, the place where Consciousness abides. Paramaśiva is the power of freedom inherent within Śiva that empowers Him to be Himself, to recognize Himself, and to express the joy of that being and knowing. Thus it is important to understand the model of the *tattvas*, as they represent our pathway to *svātantrya*.

Just as there are different levels of consciousness, there are different levels and qualities of energy. The model of the thirty-six *tattvas* demonstrates this same principle, with every level of consciousness expressed as a corresponding quality of energy. What's so incredible to understand is that as Consciousness expresses Itself as these categories of existence, manifestation simultaneously unfolds. At the same time, it is this very explosion into multiplicity in all its glory that begins to hide the truth, even though that explosion was emitted both from and within that truth: Śiva's infinite joy of being Himself. This is a paradox. It arose from Śiva within Himself, yet it somehow veils Him. That unfoldment, that explosion of freedom, is what creates multiplicity. This incredible manifestation of the universe is the same emission to which Abhinavagupta refers.

The *tattva* hierarchy is the explanation of how that emission—the powers by which Śiva emits Himself—creates every category of existence, from Infinite Consciousness all the way down to rocks. Śiva creates thirty-six levels of existence, all of which exist within us as individuals, within our own *suṣumṇa* or psychic body. Somewhere in the process of that unfoldment we get created, and unfortunately, our experience is that we don't know that we are Infinite Consciousness. In that sense, we're not much different than a rock. The most important point to recognize as we proceed with this discussion is that because each *tattva* contains the infinite whole within it, infinite awareness exists even in the densest state. It is therefore always accessible to us.

This diagram of the *tattvas* shows the descent of Infinite Consciousness from Its absolute state into manifest form. It is a graphic depiction of the autonomous freedom of Śiva, the unconditional state of awareness and the bliss that arises out of knowing one's own Self. This is the emission of the powers of Consciousness, the five energies—which are the first five *tattvas*—from which everything arises and that sustain all of existence.

The *tattva* chart is a road map to the Divine, a map of Unity and the inherent duality that's expressed as part of that Unity, all existing within a state of Oneness. What's important to us is that we have the capacity to recognize and experience that state of Unity within ourselves. This is the bottom line of all Tantric tradition: We can recognize and experience that God dwells within us as ourselves.

In Shaivite tradition, the exposition of the *tattvas* is not only the attempt to describe cosmology, but more importantly, how infinite, pure, unmanifest Consciousness becomes imminent, concrete matter. The *tattvas* are described in many places, but very succinctly in the eleventh-century Shaivite Tantric scripture Pratyabhijñā Hṛdayam, as the descent of Consciousness into increasingly contracted states. The fourth sutra from that text says, "Even individuated consciousness, whose essence is Consciousness in a contracted state, is a contracted form of the universe." The understanding it's imparting is how pure, Infinite Consciousness descends into duality. Like a set of Russian nesting dolls, the *tattvas* help us understand that held within even the most contracted state of life there is always that same Consciousness.

We can think of the *tattvas* as the elevator of Consciousness that travels from the penthouse all the way to the sub-sub-basement. We can think of our practice as the ride back up the elevator to the penthouse. I've used that analogy many times because if we're on level 13 and we've never been to level 14, we don't have a clue it's even there. Rudi always described that as people shopping for bargains in the sub-basement of Macy's, accepting the rejects that nobody else wanted, and never going up into the higher levels of quality and availability because they weren't willing to pay the price.

My family loved to visit me in Lafayette, Indiana, where my first ashram was, because there was a store nearby called Four Corners. It was a clearinghouse where places like K-Mart and Wal-Mart sent everything they couldn't sell. And you could buy twenty pure polyester shirts for ten dollars! So my family would come up once a year and load up their cars with all these great bargain-priced polyester shirts. This is what we do in life. Everything has a cost. Our freedom has a cost, and the currency is the surrender of our own suffering.

Every Level of Consciousness Is Always Accessible

One of the significant aspects of the discussion of the *tattvas* is the powerful and succinct clarification of the appearance of duality as manifestation, which begins to answer the questions, "Why? How did we get from there to here?" We've already touched on one of the more important answers to the question of why God did all this: out of the joy of His own existence. The joy of His own Consciousness just couldn't contain itself. From that, the will of God created all manifestation.

While the teachings regarding the *tattvas* attempt to explain why we suffer, they also tell us why we shouldn't. The *tattvas* represent the pathway out of suffering, which in Shaivism is understood as the transcendence of dualistic consciousness, the experience of being separate from our highest Self. This is why we suffer. All the things we think cause our suffering are just the effects of our misunderstanding.

The chart depicting the *tattvas* very succinctly depicts those five powers of Consciousness—the power of Consciousness Itself, and the bliss that arises from that, and the will, knowledge, and action to express that joy—as the top five *tattvas*. Then this little energy called *māyā* comes along and obscures the whole thing by creating a sense of duality within time, within space, and within infinite knowing, action, and power. *Māyā* is a sophisticated filter of how Infinite Consciousness creates—for the hell of it I guess, or at least for the joy of it—the appearance of separation and duality, because the discovery that it's not duality is just so incredible.

This is why Śiva sat there and said, "How can I create all these beings, and how can I make them happy? I got it! I'll make them unhappy so that they have a reason to search for happiness." So yes, we can blame all our suffering, pain, and agony on God. Just don't blame Him for very long, because He also gave us the way out.

Our duality is not real in the sense that we are an effect of the duality that Śiva creates in Himself. What we're trying to do is depersonalize manifestation and transcend ourselves, to penetrate back through the level of separation intentionally created by God. This allows us to understand that although we have the experience of duality, it isn't necessary, and our "stuff" is not the cause of duality. The *tattvas* are our personal road map of the awakening of our own consciousness into higher states of awareness that are inherently free from duality, pain, and suffering.

The inner scientists of early Tantric practices explored and realized this, and in outlining the *tattvas*, they tried to express their experience of the discovery of their own Divine nature. They used their own inner Hubble telescope to see and experience all of these levels of awareness. This isn't their theory. Through the *tattvas*, these incredible saints are relating their direct experience. Perhaps more importantly, they are explaining that it can be *our* experience. In fact, they are explaining that this *is* our experience—every second, every moment, every millennium. All we have to do is become aware of it. All of these levels of Consciousness or categories of existence, all these levels of that-ness, are always and forever functioning simultaneously. Because that's true, we have access to whatever level of consciousness and quality of energy we choose to connect to, always and forever.

While the *tattvas* are the emission—the *visarga*—that creates all form and manifest life, form doesn't need to disappear or change in order for our level of awareness to change. All awareness, all energy, all Consciousness that becomes manifest is all still drunk with Divine Consciousness. As Consciousness descends into denser levels of awareness, It takes on more and more form. Yet even within inert matter there is that same Consciousness. The important thing to understand is what level of consciousness we function from.

Tattvas 1 Through 5: The Divine Reality

As we move forward, it is important to reiterate that the five powers of Divine Consciousness we've been exploring are the highest levels of Consciousness. In looking at the chart, those same five powers are depicted as the top five *tattvas*, although they are called by different names.

The first five *tattvas*—Śiva, Śakti, Sadāśiva, Īśvara, *śuddha-vidyā*—are exactly the same five powers we've been exploring:

Consciousness, bliss, will, knowledge, and action. The entire nondual Shaivite philosophy is built on this notion: that Infinite Consciousness emits everything out of Itself, and no matter what level of awareness of Itself It functions from, that same Infinite Consciousness is held within it, and vice versa. The reason it appears to be in a contracted form is only because that particular level of Consciousness doesn't know that it is infinite. This is because the *tattvas* below the level of *māyā* are experienced in and as duality.

In considering the *tattvas*, the important thing is to think of the implications. Beginning with the highest, we'll discuss each of them, at least down to a certain level, where the *tattvas* become less relevant to understanding our true nature. In exploring these levels of consciousness, we begin to see how they immediately apply to our own experience, expressing what Rudi said to us so often: "Surrender yourself, and then you can change." Notice that he didn't say, "Change yourself, and then you can surrender." How amazing.

TATTVA 1. Śiva. In terms of the *tattvas*, *cit śakti* is called Śiva *tattva*. This is the top of the hierarchy of Pure Consciousness. Śiva is the highest of all *tattvas* and ultimately the only principle. At this level there is only pure subjectivity. The experience is simply "I am," pure and unadulterated "I-ness."

If the universe is the creation of God's own mind, the Supreme Intelligence, then the first reality or *tattva* is naturally God or Śiva Himself. This is transcendent stillness, unmanifest and formless. It is also *prakāśa*, the light of Consciousness. At this level, Śiva is Consciousness with the potential of power, as Śakti is not yet manifest.

TATTVA 2. Śakti. Bliss is the next *tattva*, and this bliss is not connected to anything except the experience of existence. Out of the power of Śiva *tattva*, Śakti *tattva* emerges. It is so wonderful to understand that the second-highest level of reality, of

Supreme Awareness, is joy, *ānanda śakti*, the dynamic power of pure, infinite, bliss, the power of the unconditional state of experiencing our own existence. This is the power whereby God experiences the boundless joy of His own existence.

Śakti *tattva* is *vimarśa*, blissful Self-awareness. At this stage in the descent of Consciousness, the cosmic energy of Śakti becomes manifest. It is never separate from Consciousness, as it is understood as the energy of Śiva. This is often indicated by the term "Śiva-Śakti," meaning that one is never separate or different from the other. How can one separate the energy of Śiva from Śiva? Thus the experience of Consciousness at this level is still simply, "I am."

How incredible to recognize that the effulgent expression of Consciousness is pure, autonomous joy! The word "autonomous" is important because what condition can we then choose to attach? What condition do we need? In talking about the second-highest level of consciousness that exists, we immediately understand how that functions within us. We're only at the level of joy here, and we're talking about how amazing, how joyful that experience should be, to just let it all go and be in that dynamic flow that emerges out of us and flows back to us. When, for whatever reason, we find we're not experiencing that state of simplicity, we can say, "Wait a minute. I am not functioning from the place I want to function from." Because we're aware of our own capacity and functioning, we always have the choice to change it.

In fact, it's *only* in those moments that we can really change it. It is only by changing a pattern in the very moment it begins to express itself in us that we can change the pattern. It is so important that we change when the change is there to change us, and if we're truly serious about our growth, those opportunities will always show up in our lives. This is why understanding the levels of Consciousness is important. The power of living in the state of joy and unconditionality, *ānanda śakti*, is the state of surrender. In functioning from there, there's no more "I gotta surrender this, I gotta surrender that." There's nothing left to surrender.

The big lotus in the middle of the trident *maṇḍala* represents bliss, and absolutely everything—every level of experience, manifestation, and unlimited or limited Consciousness— emerges from that. It is the penetrating back through all that emerges out of Consciousness and bliss that gives us access to that experience. Everything that manifests out of Śiva's unconditional freedom, joy, and love must be consumed, because that's how we truly become absorbed into the source. Although they are still considered "pure" awareness, it is from the powers of will, knowledge, and action (the next three *tattvas*) that the potential for the veil of duality surfaces.

TATTVA 3. Sadāśiva. Sadāśiva is another name for *icchā śakti*, or God's will. This level of reality is pure, infinite willpower, the power whereby God experiences Himself as an unlimited, independent force ready and able to perform any action He wishes. At this stage God forms the resolve to bring His power of creation into operation. Abhinavagupta describes Sadāśiva as "eternally Śiva," because as the universe begins to come into existence only as a impulse, the Absolute loses none of Its Divinity. Consciousness begins to create form out of Its own energy, although it is still unmanifest. The totality of creation is reflected within Himself.

As Consciousness begins Its descent, multiplicity begins to arise. Even at the level of Sadāśiva, which is still Divine Consciousness held within Itself without any form, there begins to be a subtle inclination toward something other. While Śiva's experience is simply "I am," Sadāśiva's experience is, "I am This." Although the emphasis is still on "I-ness," there is now the subtle hint "something-ness," of multiplicity. It is so fascinating to recognize that it is the descent of Consciousness that creates multiplicity, indicating that in Divine Unity, there is no multiplicity. At the same time, all multiplicity is already within Divine Unity.

At this level of awareness, there is only the slightest, subtlest differentiation between the Absolute and the universe It emits. This is the first movement of differentiation, away from total nonduality. Consciousness begins to create form out of Its own energy, although It is still unmanifest. The totality of creation is reflected in His own Self. Everything that emerges after this point is the will of Śiva expressing itself. This is pretty important, to recognize how close to the top God's will is.

Tattva 4. *Īśvara*. The fourth *tattva*, Īśvara, is *jñāna śakti*, God's power of pure, infinite knowledge whereby He is able to know all things, and to know Himself as all things. At this stage, God conceives in His mind the universe to be created. In that conceiving, He holds within Himself all the patterns and structures that will form the universe. Īśvara is the level of consciousness in which the world finally becomes distinct, meaning it is created, but only in an internal sense, within the Supreme Subject. Consciousness begins to exteriorize Itself. The "I" starts to see the "That" (the universe) as different, although still within Itself.

Īśvara is not really separate from Sadāśiva, but it maintains a definite emphasis on "This-ness." The experience of Sadāśiva is "*I* am This." At the level of Īśvara "This" becomes distinctly manifest, and the experience is now "I am *This*." However, there is still no difference between the Creator and the created.

Tattva 5. *Śuddha-vidyā*. This is *kriyā śakti*. At this level, the Divine power of pure, infinite action whereby God may assume or manifest as any form or shape comes into operation. At this level of reality, Consciousness still experiences Itself as the universe, without any differentiation between subject and object. Creation begins, but only as a vibration that produces the seed of the universe.

Already held within Śiva's mind is this subtle creation of not only recognizing Itself but creating within that recognition something that begins to feel like it's not Itself, that it's something separate from Itself. From these first five *tattvas*, this tendency emerges entirely on the field of awareness. There is still no form, yet there is the idea of form. There is the subtle experience of "I am This," instead of "I am." Yet within the experience of "I am This," there is no distinction between that experience and the experience of "I am."

Perfection Can Only Express Perfection

Abhinavagupta writes in the Tantrāloka, "Up to and including this stage, Creation is the ideal in the sense that it is very much one with the Mind of God, just as a thought or idea is one with the mind of the person who conceives it." These first five *tattvas*, the five powers of Divine Consciousness, connote Pure Awareness, in the sense that within Consciousness Itself, there has not yet been any experience of duality. The differentiation, diversification, and multiplicity into the triadic powers of will, knowledge, and action are experienced as the fabric of a total Unity, differing only in their perspective or emphasis. At this stage, there's simply the plan to expand freedom, without any detail. In Śiva's act of creation, His freedom is expanded, yet His freedom is not conditioned by that expansion, that emission. The energies of creation do not limit His experience. This is why the keynote quote by Abhinavagupta says that it is the penetrating back through those energies that brings us into union with Śiva.

These five powers all function within the awareness of the Divine before there's any externalization or manifestation. Let's imagine Śiva as the great engineer He is. As He designed the universe He did some inner testing and thought, "No, that doesn't work, this doesn't work." But at a certain point,

He realized that however it expresses itself must be perfect, because it's arising out of perfection. He probably thought, "I don't need to have everything controlled. I only need to remember that what I am doing in creation is expressing My own freedom and the joy of living in that freedom." So He flips the switch.

The teaching embedded in the *tattvas* expresses the understanding that there are many levels of consciousness that open and open and open, and that the highest level should be what we seek. The wonderful part is that we must live through, penetrate, and devour all of the emission of that Consciousness, meaning the world, duality, and all our perceptions of everything.

As we move forward, remember that each and every one of the *tattvas* is simply a description of Śiva's own perfection and His passion to express that perfection. Since we are not different or separate from Śiva, we also get to choose whether our life is an expression of the passion for freedom and celebration, or something different. In the nondual Tantric traditions, there is no rejection or suppression of any level of consciousness. There is only Consciousness and all Its different depths of awareness, all of which are available within us.

All of this discourse so far is setting up the Big Bang—creation—which, paradoxically, is also the obstacle to freedom. It's setting up the idea that we think that living in the world is what life is all about, which therefore becomes the obstacle to freedom. Understand that even Śiva's triad of Divine powers—will, knowledge, and action—can bind us, and in fact they do everyday. Because of the energy of *māyā*, which emerges from those triadic powers, we misunderstand them and therefore they bind us.

Śiva knows that what arises out of His powers of Pure Consciousness is the power of *māyā*, the appearance of duality and the obscuration of Unity. He already knows creation is perfect, so it is as if He flips the switch and says, "Won't this be fun if I turn down the light a touch so people have to search for Me?" This is because that discovery, that Self-referential capacity to recognize our Divine Source, is what life is all about. It is the joy of life. If it's too apparent and people don't have to really search for it, they'll take it for granted. They won't be deeply, devastatingly grateful in themselves, and they'll get distracted.

The Tattvas, Part Two: Maya

The Tattvas, Part Two: Maya

Nondual Shaivism holds that there is only one substance in the universe; each of the thirty-six *tattvas* is understood to be nothing but Consciousness, or Śiva, simply vibrating at different frequencies. The densest, lowest, grossest *tattvas* contain within them all previous, higher *tattvas*. Held within even the lowest resonance is all that light. Since all *tattvas* exist within the *suṣumṇa* of each human being, we always have access to the higher states of consciousness through our own awareness. Through the *tattvas*, Shaivism describes the transformation of Divinity into humanity and back into Divinity. As we continue our exploration of the descent of Consciousness, we will discover how Divine Consciousness creates the universe, oh, and us.

Kashmir Shaivite tradition divides the *tattvas* into the realms of "pure" and "impure," purity and impurity being a simple way to describe the appearance of separateness. We have explored how the first five energies of Consciousness (Consciousness Itself, bliss, will, knowledge, and action) connote pure awareness, since no duality is as yet experienced. This is pristine, unified Consciousness, with no form or manifestation to obscure It. Yet even at this subtle, pure level, differentiation and multiplicity are experienced as part of the fabric of total Unity, different only in perspective and emphasis. Those five energies represent the first five "pure" *tattvas*, as they exist within the field of Consciousness Itself, before any misunderstanding of separation. Everything below that, from *māyā*, the sixth *tattva*, all the way down is called "impure" consciousness. We can think of the analogy of an hourglass in which Pure Consciousness descends through a single *bindu* point and, as if through an eyedropper, expands into all this multiplicity.

We might also think of the analogy of a snow globe. Infinite Consciousness, out of the unbounded joy of experiencing Itself, has the urge to express that joy, knowing exactly how to do so, and taking action, all within Itself, without any form or separation, without any diminishing of the fullness of Its Unity. It all happens within the snow globe. There's no snow coming in from outside; the water doesn't leak out. It is full in itself. All that potency within Infinite Consciousness prompts It to just let it blossom out, and it is in the moment of blossoming out that the experience of two-ness happens. We now perceive ourselves as outside the sphere, and this is the experience of duality, of feeling separate and disconnected from our source. There's an imagined barrier keeping us from that contact, so we think, "I must be separate from that."

In the diagram of *tattvas*, the five pure *tattvas* are shown above the veils of *māyā*. It is at this moment, where *māyā tattva* appears, that we first encounter the beginning of impure perception, the veils of limitation and obscuration, which include every *tattva* from the point of *māyā* all the way down to the grossest expressions of Consciousness. This is the realm of duality, and it is the normal experience of human beings. This is the beginning of the end of the experience of pure, undifferentiated Oneness. It is here, at *māyā*, that the misunderstanding arises that Śiva and His creation are different and separate from each other.

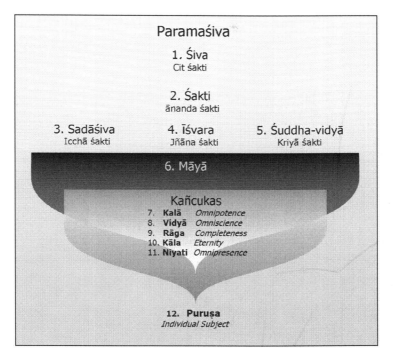

Tattva 6: Māyā

While the first five *tattvas* are the mechanism by which creation happens, at a certain point *kriyā śakti*, the power of action, contracts and descends into *māyā śakti*, the energy of veiling and limitation. As this incredible, extraordinary universe manifests from and within the single Consciousness of Śiva, He uses the power of *māyā śakti* to create the perception of duality, an essential step in the movement toward variegated manifestation. *Māyā* is the highest *tattva* of manifest reality. Everything after that is still part of One Thing; it just looks, feels, and acts like two.

From the nondual Tantric point of view, Divine Reality pervades the entire universe, all *tattvas*, including those from *māyā* on down. Abhinavagupta says, "Śiva is the light of Consciousness, present in everything. He displays his light identically in all the categories of existence (*tattvas*), all objective phenomena, and views them all as Himself in his Self-delight, which never vanishes." The limitation of *māyā*, the veiling of understanding, travels with Divine Consciousness all the way down through the rest of the *tattvas*. Further down, our individual life shows up, and after that our ego, which, because it is farther from Source, is even further away from the experience of its highest Self.

Like the five energies of Consciousness, *māyā* is also an energy or capacity. It is the power whereby Consciousness projects Itself into manifestation—space, time, and form—and by which the One becomes many. It is this very explosion of manifestation that creates the veil of limitation, the source of the three veils of duality—I am separate, I am different, I am the doer—because the recipients of manifest reality (i.e., us) see it, become seduced by it, and think, "This is all there is," not realizing there's a deeper source for all we see. Since we don't perceive that source, our experience in the world is dualistic. We don't see the forest for the trees.

Māyā, the sixth *tattva*, is the power to limit and divide Śiva's triadic powers (will, knowledge, and action) and create the misperception that they're separate from their source. It is that dynamic aspect of energy that Consciousness uses to simultaneously manifest and conceal Itself. Śiva creates those energies within Himself, but before He lets them do anything, He decides to conceal them, creating the illusion that even as they manifest creation they're somehow separate from Him.

Even though Śiva began the process of His own veiling from the very moment He emitted His own powers, it is here, in *māyā tattva*, that the veiling becomes complete. The "I" is observed as separate and different from Itself, duality arises, and Consciousness no longer experiences Oneness. While it is in the creative, imaginative, passionate power of Śiva to create multiplicity, it is by the limiting and concealing power of *māyā* that duality manifests and His light begins to be veiled. In us, *māyā* is our capacity to obscure our own experience to such a degree that we even forget that we forgot; we forget that we have a choice.

As we move down the *tattvas*, it is only after *māyā* that manifestation takes place, which suggests that all manifest form, the entire universe, is only *perceived* as being outside its source. Further down, that misunderstanding becomes denser and denser. As Consciousness condenses and descends, It moves further and further from the possibility of recognizing that It has a formless source. The levels of consciousness within the *tattvas* of duality are self-reinforcing, which is why we can't look for freedom and Unity in duality. It isn't there! This is why we must be willing to surrender duality.

Why Māyā?

Remember when you were a kid and you went on an Easter egg hunt, how exciting it was to look, and the thrill of finding that egg? It was about the thrill of discovery. This is the purpose of *māyā*, to create the possibility of discovery. As manifestation emerges out of Śiva's own bliss, He decides, "I've got to share this. Finding Myself through My own Self-reflective capacity is so exciting that I'm going to give that possibility to all of life." But in order for discovery to be possible, there must first be a concealing.

Śiva thought, "I like myself. It's groovy and joyful and I've got all these powers. I've got will, knowledge, and action, with which I'll create this incredible manifest universe." He already knew there would be individuals and individuated consciousness. In His pure awareness, Śiva understands that through the process of contraction—the descent of His own Consciousness and the emergent experience of separateness—that all these individuated expressions of Himself (i.e., us) would arise. In order to experience and enjoy and walk through the universe He created out of Himself, He limits Himself and assumes form. Divine Consciousness becomes us. Creation is thus a form of Self-limitation.

Out of His own *svātantrya*, His absolute, autonomous freedom, Śiva deliberately handcuffs Himself. His Divine will is the expressed intention of creating differences, so He limits His own will, which automatically limits His knowledge of Himself and His power to act. The power of *māyā* obscures Pure Consciousness and Its powers, resulting in the limited self: the individual human being. Inherent in that contraction is the opposite movement of expansion, which is how we have the capacity and the Grace to transcend and transform our individual experience back to its highest form.

In His infinite wisdom, Śiva has all these grand ideas, but He creates this layer of uncertainty about what this all is, simply because it will be fun. Even though He knows exactly what He's going to do and how He's going to do it, He also knows that He's going to obscure the process, because there is nothing greater than the joy of finding oneself. He thought, "I know that the bliss of finding Myself will be so joyful that even I will forget Myself. All creation will have a veil over it. The bliss of My Consciousness is so powerful that I'm going to throw it all away—because it will be even more powerful in the remembering. I will have some value for it. I'm going to surrender, and forget Myself."

Śiva's eternal mantra is *Aham*, "I am." In the first five *tattvas* there is a shift in emphasis from "I am" to "I am This." In the descent of Consciousness, in the veiling of Its own Self from Itself, Consciousness begins to see "I" as distinct from Itself. So this veiling is simply the expansion of freedom, the expansion of Śiva's will to create the universe out of His own bliss. He's thinking, do I push this button? Yes, because in that process, individuals will emerge, and they'll look for the Easter eggs.

Duality, which is simply multiplicity, is necessary in the scope of Śiva's plan. He doesn't see all those things as separate from Himself. But He tricked us, because in the process of unfolding manifestation, He intentionally turns down the light, deliberately limiting His own capacities and attributes in order to create us as individuals. This is *līlā*, the play of Consciousness.

THE FIVEFOLD ACTS OF THE DIVINE

Shaivism describes what are called the Fivefold Acts of the Divine: creation, maintenance, dissolution, concealing, and revealing—all of which are always happening all the time. These five cosmic processes apply to all of life at every level, and everything that is of the nature of form goes through the first three, including us: we are born, we are maintained for a period of time, and we die. By its very nature, *māyā* conceals the fact that reality is nondual, that it is Śiva. This is the concealing in the Fivefold Acts of the Divine. The concealing is the expansion into multiplicity, or *māyā*. The revealing, or Grace, is the penetrating back through that multiplicity to recognize Oneness. Grace doesn't show up in the *tattvas* as a category of consciousness, suggesting that Grace is omnipresent; it is Śiva. Life happens because of God's Grace, and Grace is not different than Consciousness.

The acts of concealing and revealing are the game of hide-and-seek happening to Consciousness from within Itself. The other acts, applied to human experience, are that we are born, we live, and we die. Everything we experience arises and subsides. There doesn't need to be much consciousness in the process of those three acts, and unfortunately, most often, there's not. Our experience of Śiva concealing Himself in our lives is the pain of feeling separate.

The descent of Consciousness does not mean a fall from Grace. In fact, it is Grace revealing and expressing Itself as form. It is the energy of Grace that creates manifestation, from which emerges the individuated expression of the Divine. Śiva takes on the form of you and me so He can move through the universe He created and live in the passion of that creation. Because He is all-knowing and all-capable, He intentionally limits His own capacity for perception so that we can discover Him. This is Grace, the freedom-bestowing power of the Divine, and It is the power and the point of *māyā*.

Tattvas 7 Through 11: The Kañcukas

Emerging from *māyā śakti*, *tattvas* seven through eleven are called the *kañcukas*, the coverings and limitations of Śiva's powers that reduce them to the limited forms of power we experience as individuals. *Māyā* is the root of these coverings, the cause of Unity dividing into multiplicity, creating all the limitations in experience. The *kañcukas* are the aspects of *māyā* that further reduce, separate, and conceal the highest and limit the unlimited. These are the limitations of omnipotence, omniscience, completeness, eternity, and omnipresence, respectively. These are the mechanisms by which Śiva conceals the fullness of Divine reality and "fractalizes" His entire Unity into the matrix and experience of manifest reality. Eternity, for instance, gets diminished into segments of time—seconds, minutes, hours, days, years, lifetimes, centuries, and eons arise. We experience our life in terms of time: this happens, and then that happens, and then something else happens. Śiva experiences eternity. There is no before or after, only ever-present awareness.

As Consciousness continues to contract and manifest as form, energy, and creation, not only does Śiva create the power of *māyā*, of apparent separation, He expresses it in incredible refinement. He decides, "Let's not just make duality. Let's get sophisticated about this. If we're going to separate things, let's really separate things. Let's create an experience of two-ness for the individuals that will emerge from this whole process. And this will be so much fun for them because this game of Clue I'm creating will be so extraordinary that they will experience unconditional joy even before they reach the state of it. They will experience that bliss in the recognition and discovery that they are not separate from Me."

Śiva takes his own attributes, capacities, and experience and limits and separates them. Out of Oneness he creates multiplicity. The experience of all power becomes limited power; eternity becomes time. Remember, the whole point of creation is for Śiva to rediscover himself through individual beings. He decided that it's such an amazing experience that it will require some effort and true surrender. His own bliss, the state of surrender He functions from, must be inculcated into these individuals as they are created. As Śiva subjects Himself to the limiting aspects of *māyā*, His powers become reduced. His bliss, will, knowledge, and action all become limited; He becomes us: individuals caught in place, time, and desire.

TATTVA 7: *Kalā*. This is the limitation of Divine action. Śiva is omnipotent, but by the power of *kalā tattva*, that all-powerful capacity becomes limited. Lacking full access to Divine energy, individuated consciousness is limited in its actions, and omnipotence becomes the limited capacity to do. What we seek through all the confusion, multiplicity, and apparent diversity of manifestation is one simple experience: that all of it is Śiva, the play of Consciousness, the perpetual expression of freedom. Our own experience is that we have limited power and limited capacity to act, and it pisses the hell out of us. This is everyone's experience, and as we'll see, it gets worse. As we descend, experience becomes still denser and more fractured.

TATTVA 8: *Vidyā*. The next *tattva*, *vidyā*, is the limitation of Divine knowledge, *jñāna śakti*, which is Śiva's omniscience. Śiva takes His all-knowing capacity and limits it. It's what He's doing every moment of our life: Our experience of the highest knowledge is being limited. Due to this particular veiling of Infinite Consciousness, our inherent omniscience is reduced to limited knowledge of ourselves and the world around us. Because of this misunderstanding, we have limited awareness of what is really happening, and we forget that all this is Śiva.

In the Fivefold Acts of the Divine, the powers of concealing and revealing are not destructive powers. Supreme knowledge never gets destroyed, only concealed or revealed. At *vidyā*, the pure knowledge of *jñāna śakti* gets dissipated and constrained. One of the ways this happens is through the perception of movement as separate from Source. We see a mouse running across the floor and somehow think it's separate from us. This is the appearance of duality. One of the most significant ways that concealing happens is through action, through movement, the appearance of something happening outside ourselves.

Tattva 9: *Rāga*. *Rāga* is the limitation of Divine will. As we further descend, the experience of "I am" begins to wane, and we feel incomplete. Not understanding our own completeness, we begin to experience desire. Because of this contraction of awareness, we think we are now the doer; we feel separate and different, and therefore need something outside ourselves to feel complete. Fullness, abundance, and satisfaction become a sense of lack, and the desire to know and acquire other objects than the Self arises. This is how Divine will, *icchā śakti*, becomes limited individual will, otherwise known as desire, attachment, and aversion. Desire is the natural result of not knowing yourself, of thinking you are separate from your highest Self and that you therefore need something else to be complete. As

Śiva and Śakti begin to unfold and overlay this illusion and limit their capacity for consciousness, they forget who they are and begin to think, "I am not whole. I need something. I need a BMW." Desire is born out of limited knowledge that tells us we are not the entire universe and therefore not complete.

Being all-knowing and possessing the capacity to understand His own state, Śiva chooses to limit even His own will. This is how *icchā śakti,* the Divine will to perpetuate freedom, gets limited through this process of contracting and descending and becomes limited will, which, in turn, makes possible the indvidual. In us, within that limitation, the desire for something arises: Will becomes desire. Instead of understanding our will as the perpetuation of freedom, we experience it as desire for something outside of ourselves. So we can blame Śiva for everything we think we need in life to make us complete. He doesn't mind. He loves us unconditionally, even if we blame Him.

TATTVA 10: *Kāla.* This *tattva* represents the limitation of eternity, which becomes time. Past and future—and all the thought-constructs surrounding them—arise. One thing happens, then another thing happens, which leads us to believe in causation and to see things in linear, chronological terms. Within the limitation of time, we experience birth and death, arising and ceasing. The constant flow of Presence disappears, and eternity becomes time: seconds, minutes, hours, days, lifetimes. When we perceive our life in time, we leave the state of Presence, of infinite unfoldment. We somehow think something has to happen even to get back to infinite unfolding. Because there's time, we have the idea that there's life and death, that there's one idea and then the next.

The gap between trying to satisfy a desire and not having it fulfilled continues the process of looking, which is what time is all about. To be in Presence is to be devoid of all thoughts regretting the past or projecting the future. It is being whole now. When we are fully present, there is no desire. We are so filled, what else could we want?

TATTVA 11: *Niyati*. *Niyati* is the limitation of Śiva's omnipresence, which becomes space and causation. As Consciousness becomes subject to the limitation of time, the thought process arises, which always develops in time. As Consciousness becomes dependent on location and circumstances, It loses Its freedom and independence. Not only are we caught in time, we are trapped by the identification with an individual body, with specific circumstances, located at a particular point in space.

Niyati is the covering that allows for cause and effect, or karma. Unlimited, infinite, boundaryless-ness becomes limited space: this room, that room, Brazil, Berkeley. Because of limited time and this limitation of space and circumstances, we perceive life as causation: in this place, this happened at this time. Then we start creating thoughts around that, thinking things should be different, and reacting. We start doing things; and when we start doing things what generally happens is karma. Because we act and react from limited understanding, we've stepped back to feeling incomplete and we start doing things to complete ourselves, and often, we don't care who we mow down in the process. Patterns of tension, thought, and behavior arise, and we become trapped in the chain of cause and effect, action and reaction, that is karma.

"FREEDOM IS SEEING THE ONE IN THE MANY"

Through Śiva's awareness and the bliss of His experience, He chose to express His freedom in creation. In Tantric Shaivite tradition, the reality of manifest form is understood as the appearance of duality because our human experience arises in form, which obscures the *source* of form. This is why Nityananda said, "Freedom is seeing the One in the many."

Tantric understanding never denies the experience of duality that other traditions acknowledge, only the reality of it. The Tantrics said there's only the appearance of duality. Dualistic philosophies present the manifest world as being outside of God. Tantric tradition explains what happens within God. There is no duality, only the experience of it. Never in Tantric tradition does it say that those levels of experience are unreal. The beauty of Tantric understanding is that it's not denying that this is all real. It's saying manifestation is just a level or frequency of reality, and we get to choose the level of reality we want to live in.

The thirty-six-*tattva* model of Kashmir Shaivism is a beautiful explanation of how manifestation happens, but somehow we get caught in the expression of it rather than experiencing its source. We get caught in thinking that the expression of manifestation is different than its source. That's apparent duality, and because we experience our life from that place of separation and misunderstanding, we suffer. Duality is the consciousness of suffering. It is the surrendering of duality that moves us back into higher states of consciousness, the consciousness of freedom.

We experience life as separate from us because of *māyā* and the *kañcukas*. On one side there's duality, and on the other side there's Unity. It is the penetration, the dissolving of those perceived limitations, that moves us back into that experience of Unity, where we begin to understand the veils of duality. The condensing of our experience happens because we misunderstand and think that we're separate. Worse, in most cases, our activity in the world only reinforces that experience of separation.

Manifest reality is not an illusion, and it doesn't go away once we see it as arising within Divine Consciousness and understand that Divine Consciousness is its source. Our individual feelings, thoughts, and fears are part of that reality, and they don't go away because we move to a bigger understanding. We simply learn to recognize them in their limited capacity, and say, "Okay, I can live from my own capacity, or I can live from God's capacity." Our experience of love, gratitude, and joy isn't the same as Śiva's experience of love, gratitude, and joy. That's the distinction. When we are not connected to Source, our understanding and capacities are limited. As we free ourselves, our capacities and perspective expand.

In our *sādhana*, we're trying to get from our mind to Śiva's mind. There is a doorway that you walk through, which is *māyā*, the sixth *tattva*, the line between pure and impure Consciousness. On one side is the experience of Unity, and on the other side is the experience on non-Unity, which is painful. When our awareness functions below the point of *māyā*, we can't perceive the experience on the other side of the door. Our spiritual practice is getting past that door. While our typical experience of our existence is suffering, on the other side of the door is the unbounded joy of our existence: bliss, unconditionality, the state of surrender. This is because those Divine energies of Consciousness, bliss, will, knowledge, and action are experienced completely differently on either side of that door. On the other side is Śiva's experience, and because it is His, it can and must be our experience. The only reason it hasn't been our experience thus far is because we haven't yet recognized that we have a choice.

Penetrating Māyā, Transcending Duality

The *tattvas* are not just a description of the creative expression of Consciousness. They are also a sophisticated way of describing Śiva's journey. The Divine's journey consists of the unfolding and contracting of Its Consciousness to as dense as It can get, and then just breathing It back in, back through every level of awareness all the way to Pure Consciousness. That is also *our* journey. Inherent in the journey is the possibility of forgetting, which is the fourth of the Fivefold Acts, concealing. The merry-go-round of creation, maintenance, and dissolution goes around and around and up and down. It is the concealing and the forgetting of what it's all about and why it's happening that is Śiva's choice. *Māyā* is the limiting principle that produces our state of limited experience. At the root of our misunderstanding of our true nature are our impure perceptions that lead to a sense of separation, difference, and individual doership, which are the veils of duality. Piercing those veils is how we gain access to Pure Consciousness and energy.

It is the penetrating back through duality—not just though our duality but through God's duality—that brings liberation. The *tattvas* are important to understand because they are the progression of our experience. Whatever level our *tattva* is at is only relevant if we *accept* it as relevant, if we don't look deeper and recognize all of this manifestation as simply Śiva's breath.

It is rare that a person is able to consistently see through *māyā*, through manifestation, all the way to God without some internal practice. Spiritual practice is the release of Spirit from tension, which is best defined as the appearance of duality and the misunderstanding it provokes. What we are attempting to do in our spiritual life is to free ourselves from tension and misunderstanding. As we'll discuss in the third section of this book, there are many different practices we can do in order to accomplish that. In the *maṇḍala*, the trident represents what Rudi called "the spiritual vertical." As we move up through the *suṣumṇa*, our central energetic channel, we free ourselves from all those levels of misunderstanding. As all *tattvas* exist within the *suṣumṇa*, all levels of misunderstanding are burned up by the rise of the *kuṇḍalinī* back through the *suṣumṇa* to its own source, back to Śiva. In terms of spiritual freedom, it all starts with *māyā* and the *kañcukas*, the veiling power of duality. This is the pivotal moment of achieving our freedom, when the true possibility of penetrating through the veils of duality really begins.

It is in piercing through manifestation and duality that we find Unity, as long as we're looking for Unity. *Māyā śakti*, and the veils of duality that it creates, is the doorway to freedom. Transcending duality is the doorway to Unity. It's impossible to understand Unity from duality, so as we seek to transcend duality and begin to penetrate through it, our experience of life is very different because it is no longer our limited experience. We begin to have the unlimited perspective of Śiva, and we being to function predominantly from within the unlimited experience of Unity.

We always try to fit higher experiences into our limited experience, which is why we are slow to figure out what is really happening. The incredible power of *māyā* limits the capacity for perception. In our own meditation, and in our life, when we find a place of greater understanding, we finally stop trying to define and understand life based on our previous experience. This is one way of surrendering. As soon as we try to take expanded awareness and fit it into the framework of our own limited awareness, it gets diminished. It doesn't fit. It is the surrendering of our individuated perspective that allows us to have a non-individuated perspective.

Māyā is perception. Our mental thought-constructs are the effect of *māyā śakti*, but we personalize this experience instead of understanding it as a universal phenomenon. We have to get past personalizing it first. The point of engaging the world is to learn that there is no separation between the Source and the manifestation of the world. We must find Unity in both. As we do that, we're dissolving the impurity of understanding within our own consciousness, within our own *suṣumṇa*. Our capacity to surrender in the context of our engagement with the world is how we begin to dissolve that impurity. As we do, we let go of our individual will, our individual knowledge of what or who we think we are, and our self-serving actions that arise from all that.

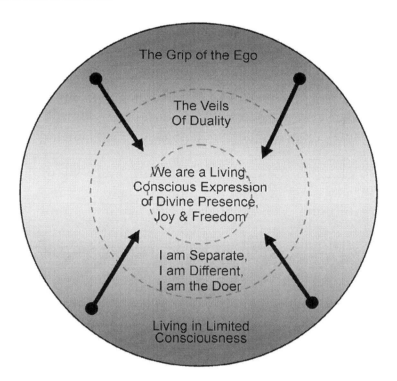

Another way of visualizing this penetration through *māyā* is to imagine three concentric circles. The outer circle is what I describe as the grip of the ego. It's the nonsense stuff. We're so obscured we just don't know, and we're fighting with life. As we penetrate through that first circle, we begin to comprehend that all of our struggles are just the effect of the pain of our separation, the misunderstanding of the veils of duality, the second circle. If we know there are twelve blankets covering the light, and that the outer eight are irrelevant to discovering the light, it becomes easy to dispense with this stuff. We begin to penetrate through the levels of misunderstanding in ourselves and create the possibility of higher awareness, indicated by the central circle of the diagram.

When we finally find Śiva, we should ask Him, "Couldn't you have kept it simple?" Of course, He would answer, "I did; you didn't." This whole adventure of penetrating back through the energies of emission and the apparentness of duality is all part of Śiva's plan, emitted from His Consciousness and will, to play hide-and-seek. Why did He decide to play hide-and-seek? For the same reason you did when you were a child, because it was fun, and you had nothing else to do. You weren't worried yet about getting laid or making money or finding security in the world. You were just out there, it was getting dark, your mom was calling, and you were playing hide-and-seek for the joy of it. What does that say about our experience and all the things we have to do as part of our life and spiritual *sādhana*? That it should be fun, that its purpose is the discovery of joy. Yet we will never discover joy from suffering; we must bring joy to our life by discovering it within our own existence, within our own expression of ourselves.

The progression of our experience should be from perceiving and living in duality, to ultimately experiencing diversity in Unity, and recognizing that it all has one Source. We must recognize that there is no diversity, only Unity, and there is no conflict. We cannot experience Unity from a mind-set of duality, nor can we transform duality into Unity, but we can experience the Unity from which it all emerges. Spiritual practice is not just sitting on our cushion but seeing through the apparent duality of "you" and "me" as we interact in the world and recognizing that there's a deeper source to all we see. Suddenly the fight starts to drop away. We no longer need to control life, or anyone in our life. It's beautiful because we are moving back through *visarga*, back through that emission to discover the Unity from which it arose. And the very powers that created it are what we use to move back through it.

The Tattvas, Part Three: The Human Experience

The Tattvas, Part Three: The Human Experience

As Consciousness descends and contracts from Its highest state of infinite freedom into multiplicity and form, Śiva, the ultimate principle of the first *tattva*, now emerges as the individual, or *puruṣa*, at the twelfth *tattva*, with limited awareness and limited capacities. It is through the sophisticated obscuration and limitation of *māyā* and the *kañcukas* that the first five pure *tattvas*—the unlimited powers of the Divine—become Self-limited and personalized, creating the individual or *jiva*, each one of us.

TATTVAS 12 AND 13: *Puruṣa* and *Prakṛti*. The map of the thirty-six *tattvas* depicts how Śiva's Divine powers and all His infinite awareness boil down to one single point, *māyā*, and out of that eyedropper we emerge as individuated expressions of that Divine whole. Only further down that map do we get egos, minds, and physical bodies—and everything else that goes along with those.

Through the extraordinarily refined process of *māyā*, Śiva's experience becomes limited and obscured, and individualized experience arises. Śiva, the supreme, universal subject, creates out of Himself the individual, or *puruṣa*, with all His same glory but with twelve blankets over the light. There's been enough descent of Consciousness, the fracturing of Its powers, and the arising of time and space, that the process of Consciousness forgetting Itself is now complete. At the twelfth *tattva*, *puruṣa*, awareness is contained within the experience of the individual self, separate from Source. From this point on, we are caught in limited time and space, and we live in, function from, and understand life through the veils of duality: I am separate, I am different, and I am the doer.

The thirteenth *tattva*, *prakṛti*, is the fundamental operative energy of *puruṣa*. Like Śiva and Śakti, *puruṣa* and *prakṛti* are interdependent. They are, in fact, the reflection of Śiva and Śakti within the realm of *māyā*. While Śiva and Śakti are infinite and nondual, *puruṣa* and *prakṛti* are limited and subject to duality. What Śiva and Śakti do on a cosmic scale, *puruṣa* and *prakṛti* do on a limited, personal scale, possessing the same energies of will, knowledge, and action, and performing the same Fivefold Acts of creation, maintenance, destruction, concealing, and revealing. While *puruṣa* is the individual subject in all limited states of consciousness, *prakṛti* creates *puruṣa's* objective experience. Often understood as nature, *prakṛti* is the source of all the *tattvas* that follow it, from intellect (*buddhi*) and ego (*ahaṃkāra*) all the way down to the earth element, creating external reality.

When Śiva exercises His power of *māyā* he becomes contracted. As *puruṣa*, He experiences limited will, knowledge, and action, as well as limited bliss, which is conditional happiness. He is now subject to desire, attachment, and aversion, pain and pleasure, which create thoughts and emotions that bind Him. While Śiva is always the only subject, through our own individuation we experience ourselves as the subject and experiencer. We move out of the awareness of our individual life as an expression of God and His will, and begin to say, "I can do this. I'm the creator." This is a slippery slope that lands us in the hellhole called ego, a few *tattvas* down.

Only after there is individuated consciousness (*puruṣa*) and objective reality (*prakṛti*) comes *buddhi* (our higher intellect, or capacity for discernment), *ahaṃkāra* (ego), and *manas* (mind), which are *tattvas* 14, 15, and 16. This suggests that our fear of losing our individuality is unfounded, because identity arises after individuality. Our attachment to our identity as a separate entity happens even after that. We are individuals before we have an ego and a body! This means we can experience our individuality without an ego or a body and simply recognize ourselves as individuated expressions of the Divine, or *kuṇḍalinī*. Even though we are individuated expressions of that whole, because of the descent of Consciousness that has come before us, we experience differentiation and separation from the moment we emerge. We are born already entangled within the veils of duality.

Tattva 14: *Buddhi*. *Buddhi* is discriminating awareness, or intuitive understanding. It is the highest capacity for reflection and subtle awareness within the individuated human being, the superior mind, which can rise above ego and the senses. Nityananda uses the term *buddhi* interchangeably with "consciousness," "discernment," and "subtle discrimination." What's important to recognize in terms of the descent of Consciousness is that *buddhi* is above and is a more subtle level of awareness than mind and ego, so it's less limited than mind and ego. In other words, our discriminating intellect is free enough to be able to look up and see higher levels of awareness. *Buddhi* is Consciousness that has not yet become encumbered by the limitations of mind and thought, and therefore has an intrinsic freedom not found as Consciousness further descends. *Buddhi* functions from a higher level than thought-construct because thoughts are always about one thing: distinction.

TATTVA 15: *Ahaṃkāra*. *Ahaṃkāra* is the Sanskrit word for "ego." *Ahaṃkāra* means "I-maker" or "I am me." Śiva doesn't need to say, "I am me." He just says, "I am." Ego comes from *māyā*—Śiva's obscuration of himself—thus it is a complete misunderstanding of our individuality as separateness. Because we're attached to that misunderstanding, we now have to defend it and attack people who suggest it's not really what we think it is. This is where thought-construct is created. Our ego is how we experience, concretize, and hold on to duality. It is the black hole of Consciousness. Light moves at 186,000 miles per second, but it still cannot escape the density of a black hole. Consciousness moves without the constraints of time and space, yet it cannot escape the density of the ego, which will fight to defend itself and its perspective—and it will die trying. The ego doesn't even know it's confused. It's wrapped so tight it can't see anything but itself.

As the diagram of the *tattvas* shows, before we ever have a physical body, we have an ego. It's not our body that we have to be free of. In fact, we can rest assured that God will take care of that for us. That's planned obsolescence. All the lower *tattvas*, including our perceptions, thoughts, actions, and physical bodies, emerge out of ego. The ego exists entirely within the sphere of duality, in a state of identification with the physical body, its needs and desires. Because it identifies with only this small part of creation and rejects all else as "not me," it is subject to negative thoughts and emotions such as pride, competitiveness, and jealousy, which is why all struggle is of the ego. Its mantra is the Mantra of Stupidity: "What's gonna happen to me?"

Once we begin to ascend back up the ladder of the *tattvas* (the subject of the third section of this book), even when we get past our ego, we still have to transcend duality. Having said that, let's get past our ego first and then deal with transcending duality. The ego is no less Divine than Divinity Itself, but the ego will never know that. Functioning from this *tattva*, or level of awareness, we cannot perceive our own Source. The ego isn't big enough, and there are too many blankets over it.

TATTVA 16: *Manas*. As Consciousness continues to descend, It loses both Its perspective on wholeness and Its infinite capacity to be aware, but It's still always Consciousness. Otherwise known as the mind, *manas* is the instrument of duality, because it creates thought and subjective perception. Since *manas* interprets everything in terms of distinctions, attraction, and repulsion, it acts only on condition, desire, and fear, and it is fraught with contradictions: doubt, shame, desire, and fear. Like a computer, it is programmed to seek pleasure and to avoid pain.

In Tantric understanding, the mind is understood as thought-construct, not intelligence. The reason Abhinavagupta describes thought as the source of bondage is because thought is always the attempt to define something. It is a level of awareness that needs to define and separate. The thought "I am separate" can only do one thing: bind you. There's no denial of thought, simply the understanding that thought is Consciousness having descended into a more limited state.

The mind is a contracted form of Divine awareness, and inherent in its experience is limitation, and thus the obscuration of true reality. The thoughts, feelings, and perspectives of the mind are the very activity that obscures its own Divinity. Our experiences of happiness or unhappiness—and of all of our emotions, in fact—are fluctuations of the mind. Emotions could be described as the goo that binds all of our thoughts together. The problem is that we believe our thoughts, emotions, and perceptions to be reality.

This level of consciousness is an outgrowth of ego. We might even say it's a cancerous growth within ego. When Consciousness descends into thought, we lose the capacity to experience our life as perfect exactly as it is, because perfection is never defined in form, only in unconditional awareness. We have misconstrued Śiva's will, which is simply the expression of freedom and joy, in whatever form it takes. Śiva doesn't think about whether or not everything is perfect. No thoughts arise in His experience, only the bliss of being, the impulse of will, the highest knowledge, and the actions of freedom.

TATTVAS 17 TO 36: Every *tattva* below *manas* is related to physicality—our body, sense perceptions, and our engagement with the world. Breathing, tasting, and excreting are described as levels of consciousness, the densification of Supreme Consciousness functioning simply as our bodies and our awareness of our bodies in relationship to the physical world.

Tattvas 17 to 21 are the senses. Called *jñanendriyas*, or the powers of perception, these are the capacities by which the Self gains knowledge of the outer world (hearing, touch, seeing, tasting, and smelling). *Tattvas* 22 to 26 are the *karmendriyas*, or the powers of action (speaking, grasping, locomotion, excretion, and procreation). The *karmendriyas* represent the active functioning of *manas*, and as their name suggests, actions performed at these levels of consciousness have karmic repercussions. *Tattvas* 27 to 31, the *tanmātras*, or subtle elements, are the bands of information (sound, touch, taste, form, and smell) that form our experience of the physical world.

The last five *tattvas*, 32 through 36, are the *mahābhūtas*, the gross elements (ether or space, air, fire, water, and earth). The *mahābhūtas* are the DNA of all form. These are the ingredients of the physical world and the elements of the physical body that represent the final point of manifestation, where *prakāśa* condenses into matter, at the same time remaining identical with Śiva. Even the psychic body—the *suṣumṇa* and *cakra* system—has some materiality to it, mostly in experiencing itself as separate. We were created and given a body so Śiva could walk through His own universe. Even though we have a body we somehow think we are just this separate, physical body—we're walking and doing and playing tennis and hopefully winning more than losing—but it's really only Śiva moving through the universe He created from within Himself to celebrate His own existence.

Understanding the Tattvas in Terms of Our Own Experience

A very interesting thing to recognize in terms of the descent of Consciousness is that the body and its functions are last on the totem pole, the very densest form of Consciousness—although it is composed of and animated by the levels of awareness above it. It is our individuality expressing itself, no more or less real than any other part of us. The problem is that we somehow think we *are* our body; we think we are alive because we have a body. Yet our life, embodied in this moment, is our means to liberation. The body is the Divine incarnate.

When Rudi died, I saw this mass of flesh lying there with no apparent Consciousness in it. It felt to me like a black hole, the gravity was so dense, in profound contrast to the sheer non-density that was Rudi when he was alive. Yet Rudi's energy, in fact, was still palpable. Death and birth are the same experience; it is simply energy transforming itself. That was an amazing recognition for me. In terms of the *tattvas*, the physical body is the farthest from Source, yet it is the place we start our journey back home. Without our body and the inherent Consciousness within it, we couldn't start or make the journey back home.

In many spiritual traditions, final liberation is understood to happen after leaving the body. In Tantra it is understood that this same liberation can be experienced *before* leaving the body. The manifest world is Śiva's body, and He created it so that He could walk around in Himself. *Jīvanmukti*, freedom while alive in individual human form, represents a fundamental distinction between Tantric traditions and other orthodox traditions that say you must die before you know God. The Tantric point of view asserts, "I know I am Śiva. I experience myself as not separate from God. I am all of this. The fact that my body might fall away is irrelevant."

The descent of Consciousness so eloquently described in the teaching of the thirty-six *tattvas* reveals the process that gives us a body so we can find our freedom. It isn't necessary to shed the body in order to find freedom, but we must shed the misunderstanding that we *are* our body, and that we are alive because we have a body that breathes. Form never limits Consciousness. It only appears to do so. Don't be quite so attached to your body as yourself, but be very attached to your body as the *vehicle* of yourself. Take care of it, but don't be confused thinking that you are nothing more than your physical body.

As we free ourselves from levels of limited consciousness and recognize that there's a higher awareness with a broader perspective, we truly begin to experience ourselves as God walking on earth. To arrive at that point of view we must have already moved past the idea that our body is relevant to that experience. This is how saints like Rudi and Nityananda walk around on the face of the earth every day without the body as a limitation. Nityananda, for example, was even known to appear in several places at once.

The Tattvas, Simplified

In his book *Consciousness Is Everything: The Yoga of Kashmir Shaivism,* Swami Shankarananda simplifies the full teaching of the thirty-six *tattvas* in a very eloquent way, with a minimalist version of the *tattva* chart consisting of just three *tattvas*:

- **Tattva 1**: Universal Consciousness or Śiva/Śakti (God) = Pure Awareness of I Am
- **Tattva 2**: *Māyā* (duality, apparently separate and different from God) = There is me and there is God
- **Tattva 3**: The individual and the outer world = My experience is self-created

First is Universal Consciousness, Śiva and Śakti in their infinite freedom and joy. Next is *māyā*, the veil of limitation, obscuration, and separation. On the other side of *māyā*, Śiva and Śakti emerge as *puruṣa* and *prakṛti*, the human individual and his objective world, bound and diminished. What this so clearly demonstrates is that the spiritual path, the recognition and experience of Oneness, is about moving through *māyā*, our perception of separation, duality, and individuality. Everything below that is gymnastics; everything above is living in, from, through, and as God. That's the simple, skeletal nature of it: There is unlimited Consciousness and limited egoic consciousness. In between there is this thing called duality, which is simply the perception that there's pure and impure, limited and unlimited.

Shankarananda's explanation is beautiful because it really describes our experience, in that mostly what we are aware of is ourselves and the world. We live our lives bound within that level of awareness. This is the way most people live—there's me and there's the world—not realizing there's one Source to both. The only thing that separates us from our Source is the misunderstanding that there's us and the world and then there's God. So this model is a beautiful, simple way of thinking about the teaching of the *tattvas* and the purpose of spiritual practice.

The struggle between our individual self and the world doesn't ultimately determine whether or not we penetrate through *māyā*. If we struggle with ourselves and the world, we're simply struggling with ourselves and the world instead of understanding that the true struggle and pain is our separation from God. All struggle is the ego. God doesn't struggle. If you find yourself struggling, know that it is your ego, and just stop functioning from the place that can't function from any other place. Don't try to drag your ego with you. It doesn't want to go. The ego never in a million years gets enlightened. It gets left in the dust. As the infamous Tantric Buddhist master Chogyam Trumpa explained, "Enlightenment is the greatest disappointment of the ego." The ego creates any kind of fear, distraction, or thought-construct that it needs to sustain itself.

We change jobs, partners, houses, not realizing that changing conditions does not change our state of happiness, except perhaps for a short time. The problem with changing conditions is that it distracts us from seeking permanent joy and creates a pattern: "I'll get rid of my partner and then I'll be happy. I got rid of my partner, I'm not so happy. I'll find another partner and then I'll be happy. I'm not happy with this partner either." We create repetitive patterns of misunderstanding and never learn from them.

God's will is the expansion of freedom. There is no form in freedom. There is no condition we're trying to change. When we push to change something with the idea that changing it will change our experience, that's our will. That's being willful and functioning from a place of incompleteness. Our need to define God's will into some specific thing is just us functioning from the lower *tattvas* of "It's all about me!" and "How does this affect me?" instead of understanding we are simply God manifest. People often say to me, "I don't know what God wants me to do." That's because they're not listening. What I understand they are really saying is, "I'm not happy with what God is saying He wants me to do. I'd rather be doing something else."

There is not one condition that can ever bind us unless we choose to allow it to bind us. Multiplicity, creation, and expression are not binding unless we misunderstand them as such. The whole discussion of the *tattvas*, the sophisticated layering of how Consciousness descends, is showing us that just because multiplicity happens, that doesn't mean that there has to be any binding. How amazing!

WHAT GOES DOWN MUST COME UP

The diagram of the thirty-six *tattvas*, and its corollary, the Śiva's Trident *maṇḍala*, is a map of diversity and Unity, and particularly, diversity within Unity. It is a map of duality and Unity as they exist within a single state of Oneness—Paramaśiva. What's important to us is the recognition of that state of Oneness within ourselves. As the *tattvas* make clear, individuated human consciousness is none other than God's own supreme and unbound Consciousness, albeit in a contracted and limited form. The purpose of spiritual practice is to ascend back through the *tattvas*, through God's emission and multiplicity, and achieve union with our Divine Source. The purification of the *tattvas*—which is the purification of our understanding of Consciousness Itself—is the practice of Kuṇḍalinī Yoga, the raising of that dormant vital energy and Consciousness back to Its source.

The descent of Supreme Consciousness from Śiva all the way down to the elemental levels is the process of manifestation, the creation of the universe. Ascending in the opposite direction is the process of spiritual evolution, which culminates in merging back into Śiva. It's important to remember that the highest principle, Śiva, is always present throughout the entire descent. As Consciousness descends, each *tattva* represents a grosser level of awareness, a slower vibration than the one above it; yet each still contains all the *tattvas* above it. Every level of consciousness that's articulated within the *tattva* system exists within our *suṣumṇa*, the central channel of our psychic body. This means that the highest principle is always present within and available to us.

Before (and after) we have a body or thoughts, we are simply our *suṣumṇa*, a streak of light. We must find that streak of light, that illumination, within our awareness. What's the first thing we do when the lights go out? We look for a light. Maybe we walk into a wall or two in search of that light, and okay, fine, we get a few bruises along the way. Why wouldn't we use that same metaphor in the way we live our lives? Why wouldn't we look for the light instead of constantly slugging it out in the darkness?

In nondual Tantric understanding, Consciousness is everything. Nothing is separate; nothing needs to be rejected. We only need to understand what dimension of consciousness we function from. If we are locked in our mind and our limited thought-constructs, if that is the level of consciousness we function from, then we're locked within that stratum of density. However, this doesn't mean the full spectrum of consciousness isn't always immediately available to us.

The *tattvas* assert that everything in life exists at the same time, always and forever, pulsating in and out as the *spanda* of the universe. Emerging from the highest powers of Supreme Consciousness, creation and form take place, never losing contact with unmanifest non-form, both transcendent and immanent. This is why we can drive a car, pay attention as we're driving, and listen to God at the same time. We can function in different dimensions of awareness simultaneously. *Vimarśa*, the God-given Grace to know our own state, allows us to discriminate between those levels and to choose.

Freedom for the individual is freedom from individuality, which is synonymous with duality. We must free ourselves from the experience of duality. That means we must be free of our own attachment to our individual identity. As the teaching of the *tattvas* shows, we become an individual before we even have a separate identity. Think of the implications! We are individuated expressions of the Divine. That notion is the very definition of *kuṇḍalinī*. There is no body, mind, or ego; there is simply Śiva breathing, pulsing in and out. Achieving freedom and union with God is penetrating through the emission of that same source, and we are the emission. Let me rephrase it: Who and what we think we are as part of that emission is what we must let go of.

In the descent of Consciousness, at the point of individuality, there is as yet no body, mind, thought-construct, or ego. We use our ego to identify ourselves, and unfortunately we identify ourselves as separate from our own individuated experience of Śiva. We can function from and serve within that individuated capacity without an ego, without thoughts, and without a plan. In fact, if we have any of those, some part of our ego has either begun to manifest (Consciousness descending) or hasn't been dissolved yet (Consciousness ascending).

Every Level of Consciousness Is Limiting, Except the Ultimate

In the course of our *sādhana*, it doesn't matter what level we're at as long as we're moving up and freeing ourselves from our own experience of contracted Consciousness. The treachery of *sādhana* lies in our capacity to be seduced by our own elevated states of awareness. When we start to grasp the power of Śiva in our hands, we must never forget whose power it is. There is only one freedom, and any trace of a separate "me" that thinks it has all this power at its disposal is still not Śiva. It is our ego.

It's important not to get too caught up in understanding our spiritual experiences from the perspective of our limited ego. The whole point of the ascent is to free ourselves from our limited perspective. The *tattva* model is a map of choice. While we shouldn't get caught up in which *tattva* we're in, the goal is to be immersed in all *tattvas* at all times, and to remain established in the source of the *tattvas*, which is the source of existence. Freedom, *jīvanmukti*, is the experience that all of life emerges from God's heart. This is something to remember.

SECTION THREE
The Ascent of Consciousness

Trident Man: Kundalini Rising

Trident Man: Kundalinī Rising

In the last section we explored one of the most important aspects of Shaivism, the *tattvas*, the sophisticated articulation of how the entire universe emerges from Śiva's own freedom, Consciousness, and joy, and His will to express and share that. In this section we will explore the reverse process—the ascent of Consciousness back up through the *tattvas*, from the dumbest of the dumb to the subtlest of the subtle. This ascent toward spiritual freedom is a conscious process, and one that is available to all human beings. By virtue of our power of *vimarśa*, we can rise up through every dimension and density of "that-ness" until we pierce the veils of duality, and experience and live from Śiva's five Divine powers.

The ascent through the *tattvas* expresses what the progression of our experience of life can become: the state of autonomous freedom, which is the ultimate goal of our *sādhana*. From the top, it's easy to see all the way down, but from the bottom, it's not so easy to see the top. Imagine you're in ancient Egypt, and that you're King Tut sitting on top of a pyramid with thirty-six levels. From that vantage point, you can see everything. You can see the horizon. You can see the kingdom of God. Down on the bottom level, however, you can't see that much. The refinement of our own consciousness is the process of vertically moving up through each level of awareness so that we can see all the levels below: the full landscape of reality and our own life.

If the *tattvas* represent the descent of Consciousness, spiritual practice is Its ascent. The practices of the Trika as refined and described by Abhinavagupta support this process and experience by incorporating as a central part of their meditation and ritual practice the visualization of Śiva's Trident within one's own body, which is really the realization that all levels of awareness (the thirty-six *tattvas*) already exist within our *suṣumṇa*. The diagram we'll refer to in this chapter is an image of this practice and visualization, created by the modern scholar Alexis Sanderson through his careful extraction of details from the Tantrāloka.

I call this image "Trident Man," because it is a graphic depiction of Śiva's Trident, which contains all the *tattvas*, within a human being. This diagram describes how we can penetrate, rise back through, and become one with the same powers of emission that create us. As we do so, we come to understand that every level of our consciousness has a higher source, until we ultimately rise high enough to dwell in Infinite Consciousness. To repeat the quote from the Tantrāloka:

> *The highest insight of Anuttara Trika is union with Śakti, the triad of energies of will, knowledge, and action. This is Śiva's Trident, the three aspects of his absolute nature and freedom, which he possesses by virtue of his union with the power of his own emission. In the practice of Anuttara Trika, the sādhaka penetrates the energy of emission, becoming one with Śiva, the source and holder of the powers of the universe.*

Trident Man: Kundalini Rising

What Abhinavagupta is so eloquently stating is that life is energy, and that we must consume it. As long as we are focused on the outer form of our life, we miss the fact that our life is an individuated expression of Divine energies. In penetrating through the misunderstanding of life as form and recognizing it as simply energy, we begin to comprehend the source of that energy as Consciousness Itself. This is the totality of spiritual *sādhana*.

As we will explore, it is the rising of the *kuṇḍalinī* up through the *suṣumna*—depicted in the diagram as a column or tube bisecting the human being—that ignites the reverse process of the descent of the thirty-six *tattvas*. Trident Man is a depiction of how we as individuals, beginning thick as a rock, can begin to transform the descent of Consciousness into an ascent. As the diagram shows, we have been given the capacity to free ourselves from our limited understanding so that we might awaken to and live from the highest levels of Consciousness, and ultimately, to exist in the penultimate of those.

In spiritual practice there are many ways we approach this process of ascending the *tattvas*. These include our service, our practice of surrender, and our meditation. It's also in the receiving Grace, the awakening of the *kuṇḍalinī*, and the discovery of the internal breath—the breath within the *suṣumna*—that the veils of duality begin to dissolve. We transcend those obscurations and limitations by awakening the *kuṇḍalinī* energy within us, allowing it to rise up through the psychic body, open the *cakras*, pierce the *granthi* (the knots of tensions and karma within the psychic body), and reveal Unity.

In the Tantrāloka, the visualization of Trident Man appears in the section of practices called Anuttara Trika. *Anuttara* means "none higher," stating one thing: There is no higher practice. What the image of Trident Man represents is the transformation of limited understanding and consciousness into Divine understanding and Consciousness, even as we're in this body. In fact, it is *because* we have been given this body and our individuated experience of life that we can turn our attention inside to become aware of the powers that create us. In understanding how our individuality is created in the descent of Consciousness and energy, we recognize that it is the ascent back through those levels of consciousness and energy that frees us from our individuated experience in order to merge with Śiva. This is the highest possible experience, to become the ultimate experiencer and the source of all experience. This is liberation, and it is our Divine right and ever-present possibility.

Trident Man: The Road Map to Freedom

Like the chart of the *tattvas*, the Trident Man diagram is also an amazing road map, describing how Consciousness—which has descended and become denser and more manifest—turns back in on Itself. This is *vimarśa*, the capacity of Consciousness to know Itself and discover Its own source. As we continually refine our awareness, we awaken to the beautiful discovery that life is simply and only Consciousness.

There are several moments in the ascent where we will struggle to let go, but if we don't play the game, we have no possibility of winning the next level of awareness. If we're afraid to play the game, we just forfeit. We mustn't forfeit our life or our liberation because we're afraid to be changed or to let go of the things we think we need to be happy. We sacrifice our happiness by holding on to the very things that make us unhappy. It's not a very smart equation, but we still do it.

The simple answer, which we will explore in depth in Chapter 10, is to surrender, no matter what level of awareness we achieve or don't achieve. Even as we begin to approach a higher state within ourselves, if we don't continue to surrender we will miss the point that those powers are not our own. While we might discover extraordinary freedom within duality, it's still just freedom within duality.

One of the ways we can transcend our separateness is to simply give up our separateness, including our need to control, and all our judgments and conditions about how we think life should be. In fact, the conditions we find ourselves in are the very conditions that manifest from within us to show us that we're caught in condition: "I'm happy because I have this. I'm unhappy because I don't have that." We begin to understand how precious the difficulties of our life are because they are designed to transform our consciousness. Rather than trying to change conditions to make us feel better, we change in ourselves, and then we understand.

The things we reach for in our misunderstanding that they're going to make us happy are the very things that prevent us from rising through the higher levels of consciousness to experience unconditional joy. We may achieve happiness by hitting the best forehand of the day, buying the nicest dress, or even getting a pedicure, but don't confuse that happiness with the simple, profound, unconditional joy that says, "You know, I didn't hit one good forehand today, and it was still great."

The powers that emerge out of Śiva's Consciousness are the same powers we use to discover that joy. In discovering that autonomous bliss, we can discover God. What does that say to us, clearly and simply? If we're not happy, we're not going to find joy. If we can't truly love our life and find the simplicity of happiness for the opportunity to discover the highest, if we're caught up in our suffering over this, that, and the other thing, we're just unhappy instead of recognizing that we have everything we need at this moment, always and forever. We need nothing to live in joy. This is not a rejection of having, but it should tell us that when we find ourselves reaching for something because some part of us feels incomplete, we can choose to stop reaching and find that fullness inside. Then everything that's part of our life is part of that same fullness.

This map shows us that it is the transformation of our limited understanding—the penetration through the emission of Divine powers—that brings freedom. Since that emission is what gives rise to our experience of duality and separation, it gives rise to our misunderstanding that there's God and then there's everything that He created. Our *sādhana*, which is every breath we take, is to surrender that limited experience and perspective deeply enough, over enough time, so that those energies rise back to their source, and we begin to experience them in a higher awareness. We come to understand that we walk on this earth because of God's will. Our entire *sādhana* is to surrender until we have that experience, and then, as Śiva, to surrender ourselves again.

Trident Man and the Fivefold Acts of the Divine

Tantric philosophy maintains that all of creation is the effect of the Fivefold Acts of the Divine—creation, maintenance, dissolution, concealment, and revelation—which happen continuously and eternally. To review, the first three acts can be described as follows: God's presence is a vibration that perpetually arises and subsides. Welling up from that vibrant effulgence, from the joy of being, God creates the universe as Himself—within the field of Himself and made from Himself.

Through His own *vimarśa* or capacity for Self-awareness, God maintains His own existence, and He dissolves created existence back into Himself. In terms of the *tattvas*, it is the liberating of Consciousness from Its Self-imposed degrees of density that dissolves the *tattvas*. Along the path of the *suṣumṇa*, each *tattva* dissolves into the preceding one until the experience is one of resting in supreme, undifferentiated Consciousness.

Underlying those first three acts is a Consciousness and energy that either conceals or reveals the reality of life. Within the processes of creation, maintenance, and dissolution, there is both concealment and revelation. In Shaivism, concealment is understood as the covering up of the truth. God created the universe as an act of concealment, consciously surrendering His awareness of Himself. This is *māyā*; the perception that there are two conceals the reality that there is only One. The *tattvas* express Śiva's act of creation, which, at the same time, is the act of concealing. Pure Consciousness descends into all of manifestation, including us as individuals, where It conceals Itself. How amazing to recognize that God conceals Himself by becoming the very stage that duality is enacted upon. Revelation is Grace, the revealing of the truth. Trident Man is a depiction of the fifth act, revelation, the awakening of Consciousness, Its ascent back to Its highest state, and Its expansion back into Its universal Self.

We've seen that because the Divine is always present, always within us as ourselves, we perform the same five acts as God at every moment of our lives. We live these same processes: expanding, contracting, and repeating patterns. All our experiences can be understood in terms of this pulsation: something arises, we experience it, and then it subsides. Creation, maintenance, and dissolution are present all the time, but the nature of our experience is determined by whether we are focused on the act of concealment (*māyā*) or the act of revelation (Grace). When we focus on revelation, we consciously allow Grace to guide our lives.

The Power of Kuṇḍalinī

Trident Man depicts the process of recognizing our Divine Self. It is the penetration back through the *tattvas*, all levels of limited consciousness, all the way back to God. The dissolution of dualistic consciousness happens through the path of the *suṣumṇa*. As all *tattvas* exist within the *suṣumṇa*, this means all thirty-six must be purified. How do they become purified, all the way back to Śiva? By burning them up through the rising of *kuṇḍalinī*. This is why Abhinavagupta states: "This is done through the practice of Kuṇḍalinī Yoga. There is no other Divine fire able to consume the whole of duality than *kuṇḍalinī*."

Within the diagram, the trident itself represents what Rudi called "the spiritual vertical." This is the upward movement of *kuṇḍalinī* through the *suṣumṇa*. Every level of misunderstanding is burned up by the rise of the *kuṇḍalinī* through the *suṣumṇa* back to Śiva. The practice of Kuṇḍalinī Yoga is the Divine fire that raises the energy back up to its source, which is described in scripture in many ways. Nityananda referred to it as the "heart-space." In Sanskrit this energetic center is called *dvādaśānta*, the abode of Śiva's powers of will, knowledge, and action. This is where duality is transcended, allowing the understanding of those Divine forces to become the field of Consciousness from which we operate.

The rising *kuṇḍalinī* can be compared to the formation of blowholes often found along a lava-covered shoreline. They are the effect of energy, in this case waves, penetrating through solid lava and opening it from the bottom up. The repetition of the upward-moving energy dissolves the density of the lava, creating an opening. All of a sudden, there's a little blowhole, and then a bigger blowhole. Just as in this example, within us, the *kuṇḍalinī* energy has increasing freedom to move up and through, because the solidity of our experience of duality begins to dissolve, allowing *kuṇḍalinī* to rise back to its source.

This is a purification of our experience of life, palpable both in our interaction with and awareness of life, and in terms of feeling a flow of energy within us. Trident Man is a depiction of the awakened *kuṇḍalinī* burning from within itself, within the density of karma, and dissolving it from the inside out.

The Psychic Body and Granthi

The practice of Kuṇḍalinī Yoga is the refinement of energy within our psychic system and, specifically, within our central channel, the *suṣumṇa*. You can think of the *suṣumṇa* as a glass tube, and the impurities—our tensions, patterns, and karma—as so much sand and debris clogging it up. Along the path of the *suṣumṇa* there are seven *cakras*, or energy centers, from the base of the spine to the top of the head. As we clear out the impurities, the consciousness and energy held within each *cakra* get released in our awareness.

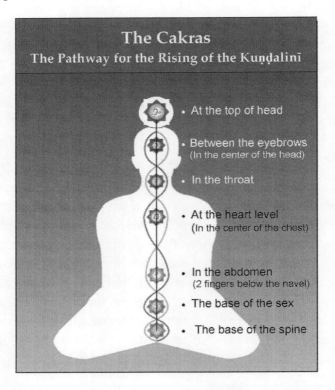

While it is not explicitly expressed within the Trika tradition, within our *suṣumṇa* there are also three *granthi*, or knots: the *brahmā granthi* at the base of the spine, the *viṣṇu granthi* in the center of the heart, and the *rudra granthi* in the center of the head. These *granthi* are the coalescence of lifetimes of trauma, tensions, self-serving patterns, karma, and *saṁskāras*, the impressions or scars left from past experiences. The *granthi* are like big boulders that block the flow of energy in the *suṣumṇa* as it tries to rise back up to the center of Consciousness.

The *granthi* are the densification of our *vimarśa*, our ability to know ourselves, and realization is not possible until the *granthi* are dissolved. This happens first in the base of the spine, then in the heart, and finally in the center of the head. The practice of Kuṇḍalinī Yoga focuses on opening the heart, receiving a higher spiritual force from the teacher (*śaktipāta*), and allowing it to flow through the psychic body, flushing out the impurities. The stronger the flow within a person, the more permanent this process becomes, and the more capacity this energetic flow has to burn through and dissolve the *granthi*. This is why flow is so critical to our experience of awakening, because flow washes away the debris of limited understanding and penetrates the *granthi*, allowing the *kuṇḍalinī* to rise from the base of the spine to the top of the head, bringing freedom.

One of the greatest gifts of Rudi was his understanding of flow, which he called "psychic Drano." In practicing his double-breath exercise (see the Appendix), we consciously circulate our own life force through our psychic system so that it can be purified. We draw in a higher, finer force, channel it through our psychic system, and allow it to dissolve the inherent tensions and impurities. As the *kuṇḍalinī* rises through the *suṣumṇa*, it burns away all impurity: our limited understanding, the actions we perform as a result of that limited understanding, the karma we create through those actions, and, ultimately, the veils of duality. The Shaivite yogis of old understood this. They experienced and described it as the gathering of our individuated life force and returning it to Śiva. In the process, our separate identity dissolves and realization shines forth.

The *granthi* represent our attachments to our limited perspective, because around those attachments to our misunderstanding, an accumulation of density and murkiness builds up. As we uncover the higher creative force within us and it begins to surge up and create openness, all of the tension, misunderstanding, and karma that created the *granthi* in the first place begin to surface in our awareness. The *granthi* are bound by our patterns, which are the bands that bind all of our tension, karma, projection, and self-rejection. As the energy opens in us and begins to loosen those patterns, they inevitably show themselves. The difference is that now we have the self-reflective capacity to be aware of our patterns, and hopefully a teacher who keeps pointing them out to us, so that we can change.

As we establish ourselves in flow and free the *suṣumṇa*, our *kuṇḍalinī* is awakened and begins to move up, opening us to a deeper consciousness within ourselves. While it isn't exactly a linear process, the simplest way of describing our progression is that we start from a place of experiencing pure diversity (i.e., the *brahmā granthi* at the base of the spine, which represents the biological imperatives to eat and reproduce). Once we break through that first *granthi*, we open our hearts to experience our own source and unity in diversity (the *viṣṇu granthi* in the heart). This is where we begin to recognize ourselves as individuated expressions of the Divine, and we innately understand that we emerge out of that wholeness. This allows us to pierce the *rudra granthi*, where our experience shifts from being an expression of that whole to recognizing: I *am* that whole. This is the experience of complete Unity, which only occurs once the *rudra granthi* in the center of the head is broken through.

In breaking through the *rudra granthi*, the experience of higher consciousness becomes permanent. Until this *granthi* is dissolved, the powers of will, knowledge, and action are limited within an individual. Once that *granthi* is broken, those same powers are expressed through the individual in their Divine capacity.

In my view, there is no difference between *māyātattvam* in the Trident Man image on page 146 and the *rudra granthi* in the center of the head. This knot extends from the upper palate of the throat, which is the base of the *granthi*, up to the center of the head. Dissolving the separation between our individual self and our universal Self begins here. We consume the density of that misunderstanding from the bottom, starting with the upper palate, extending through *māyātattvam* up to *śuddhavidyātattvam*. This knot must be broken before duality can be fully transcended.

As you do your meditation, feel the flow of energy moving vertically within you, and try to become immersed in and consumed by it. From the center of your being, within the central channel of your psychic body, become aware of that vertical flow at all times, and then extend that flow horizontally into your life. What I mean by that is to stay centered in that energetic flow as you engage the people and dynamics in your life. This way, instead of being pulled out of your center, you are constantly reinvesting this energy from your engagement with your own life back into your psychic system. Developing the capacity to feel and be aware of this flow at all times is what leads to the flowering of Consciousness.

Abhinavagupta tells us in the Tantrāloka, "All *tattvas* must be purified." Spiritual practice is the purification of the contracted, descending energy within us. There is a purification all the way back to Supreme Consciousness. Even Śiva and Śakti, the power of Consciousness and the power of joy, are part of the *tattvas*, so even those need to be purified. Even the experience of oneness with God needs to be purified, because inherent in that experience there's still a subtle perception of separation.

As our awareness ascends through our psychic body, we use the energies of manifestation, the energies of our own experience, the energies of our mind and emotions, our karma and trauma. We use all of that energy, internalizing it back within ourselves and moving into ever more refined, more unlimited states of consciousness. In ascending the *tattvas*, we penetrate through the powers that created the universe to get back to the infinite, simple joy that created creation.

Dvādaśānta

The particular discussion in the Tantrāloka in which Trident Man appears is focused around an initiation called "installing the throne." This throne is none other than Śiva's Trident, and it is the throne of the three goddesses—Parā, Parāparā, and Aparā, the Divine powers of will, knowledge, and action. Installing the trident and the throne of the goddesses through this practice is to become aware of and give home to those Divine powers within us. Embedded within the ritual and practices of Anuttara Trika are lots of visualization and mantra all leading to what I call the *dvādaśānta* meditation. (A link to an MP3 of this meditation is in the Appendix.) The practice of this meditation leads to the recognition and experience that our individuated experience is at the Grace of those goddesses.

Dvādaśānta, the abode of the three goddesses, is a space located about twelve inches above the head. This is part of our psychic body, which doesn't end at the top of the head, because it's not contained within the physical body. That space is the eyedropper from which we emerged, the level of consciousness from which all manifestation is expressed. The purpose of the meditation is to learn how to move back through that space. Śiva's Trident is a psychic structure that holds Consciousness, and when this trident is fully established within us, we have the very structure within our own awareness to hold the Infinite.

When we have surrendered duality long enough, our life force and consciousness become refined enough to move through the subtle gateway into *dvādaśānta*, the palace of Parā. She is the energy of Śiva's Grace, and it is through that Grace that manifestation takes place: the will to create, the knowledge embedded within Śiva's own Consciousness, and the action of creation.

The *dvādaśānta* exercise is Trident Man in its essence. It is also called the "*triśūla* meditation," the meditation of Śiva's Trident, because it is installing the throne upon which the goddesses reside within us. Guess who sits on the throne? Not Śiva, but Parā. The meditation embedded in the practice is designed for one thing: to create within us the structure to receive Grace. In fact, that structure is already embedded within us, so "installing the trident" is really the recognition of that which already exists within us. Through that recognition, we gain access to the awareness embedded within it—the highest Consciousness in us.

The *triśūla* meditation is described in the Tantrāloka as one of the highest in Tantric practices because it represents the ascent of Consciousness through all the *tattvas*. The installation of the *tattvas* in the *suṣumṇa* culminates in the visualization of the Goddess Parā at *dvādaśānta*. Parā is the Supreme Goddess, holding within Herself the powers of Śiva's will, knowledge (Parāparā), and action (Aparā). She is the energy of Śiva's Grace. Śiva created Parā from within Himself to express His own Consciousness and bliss. She is not different from Śiva. She is Śiva's energies.

In practicing this exercise, we begin to truly establish ourselves in those Divine energies, which emerge out of the power of Śiva's own Consciousness and unconditional bliss. Tantric tradition asserts that the experience of Unity is only possible through the internalization of our own consciousness and the rising back through the veils of duality. This meditation requires practice, as it is only through diligent, regular internalization that we develop the subtle awareness and stillness to ascend through the *suṣumna*, to penetrate through separation, and to tune in to *dvādaśānta*.

The practice is recognizing that the *suṣumna* is not just within our body. It is the extending of awareness from our own heart directly into that space. It is not separate from us, and we don't project out of ourselves to connect to it. Rather, we extend and open the same way a lotus flowers. The *dvādaśānta* exercise is not just the opening of that flower but the discriminating capacity to feel the distinction of every petal. These Divine energies are one emergent quality of Śiva's power, yet through our discriminating capacity we can understand the subtle distinctions between those three powers. We can then function from them as a whole but understand the different resonances creating the symphony. We know when we experience God's will; we know when we know what God knows; and we know when we act as God.

Dvādaśānta is the resonant space in Śiva's own awareness of His powers, still unmanifest. When we extend our psychic body through the top of our head out to *dvādaśānta*, we connect to the powers of creation above us, the unmanifest force from which we are dropped out. In the meditation we make contact with those Divine powers in their own level, and begin to establish ourselves there.

As we do the meditation, we are turning our life force back into the channel of transformation called the *suṣumṇa*, creating the possibility that we will reach the penthouse where the goddesses live and we can ring their doorbell. We can then invite them to come out and play. But just remember that in the game we play we must do their bidding, because we are at once their guests and their servants.

Reaching that doorbell is the result of the purification of our own awareness. Reinvesting our life force back inside clears out the debris of lifetimes of misunderstanding and opens that channel of light. As we become more still and more in tune with these different resonances, we begin to truly experience ourselves as the powers of Consciousness in that space. We can then become aware of the *bindu* in the center of *dvādaśānta*, which is the doorway to an expanded world of Consciousness.

We can't take our thought-constructs — our mind, emotions, drama, or trauma — through that space. While some part of us may rise through, some particles of us are so dense that we can't be lifted all the way through. It is only by Grace that at least one small part of us gets through and we begin to make contact, but if there's even one atom of us remaining beneath the veil of duality, then there's still one atom of separation.

Rising into the abode of the powers of Śiva is an internal process of surrender and the external expression of that surrender in our life. Ultimately, it requires the surrendering of our individuality, which scares us because "we" won't be there to experience it. Well, hallelujah! If we connect and surrender to that illuminating consciousness then clarity arises, because it's functioning in and of itself. This is where our decision to live in some depth of stillness is really important. We will never make it through that space with all our noise. It has a noise baffle: the *granthi* in the center of the head. Nothing gets through except pure energy and stillness of Consciousness.

As we begin to make contact with those higher levels of awareness, we're able to penetrate and open into that space that holds the energies before manifestation. We begin to understand, experience, and function from those powers. We transcend our duality and experience Śiva's Consciousness emitting Itself as those powers. It is the surrendering of our limited power and identity, both in our meditation and in our life, that gives us access to Śiva's Consciousness and powers.

Dvādaśānta, Trident Man, and the Tattvas: The Building Blocks of the Ascent

Let's explore the rising of the *kuṇḍalinī* and the ascent of Consciousness to *dvādaśānta* in the context of installing Śiva's Throne through the Trident Man visualizations and practices. In the image on the next page, we see all of the *tattvas* expressed along the axis of the *suṣumṇa*. At the top, it trifurcates into the trident, upon which the goddesses of will, knowledge, and action abide in their home: *dvādaśānta*. It's important to understand that this is not simply a meditation or practice but an all-encompassing focusing of consciousness—the internalization of our life force and directing it back to Śiva, "the source and holder of the powers of the universe."

Tattvas 36 Through 32: The Kaṇḍa

The bulb shown at the base of the *suṣumṇa* is called the *kaṇḍa*, which contains the lowest five *tattvas*, the *mahābhūtas*. The *kaṇḍa* is the union of the energies of the *cakras* in the base of the spine, the sex, and the navel. This includes the *brahmā granthi*, the lowest knot in our psychic body that keeps us bound and which must be broken to initiate the ascent. In the very moment we receive *śaktipāta*, that *granthi* is broken open, if we open ourselves to it. From that moment, the fire of *kuṇḍalinī* begins burning its way up the *suṣumṇa*, burning through and

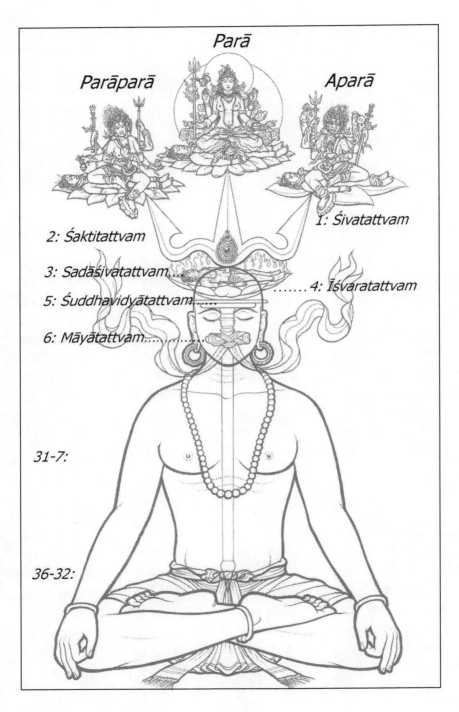

dissolving all *granthi*. The Trika image of Trident Man assumes that the *brahmā granthi* has already been broken open and the dormant *kuṇḍalinī* is at least waking up. It assumes that our awareness is not bound at and dominated by the grossest levels of life, the biological imperatives to eat and reproduce. In bringing our awareness there and consciously gathering and raising those energies, we release the vital force within us to begin its ascent through the *suṣumṇa*.

Tattvas 31 Through 17:
The Powers of Our Engagement with the World

These levels of consciousness (the *tanmātras*, *karmendriyas*, and *jñanendriyas*) are designed by Śiva for *bhoga*, or enjoyment. These are our capacities to savor and celebrate the effulgence of sensory life and to appreciate aesthetic beauty. We can experience and enjoy the full Monty—the sweet taste of a piece of ripe fruit, the fragrant scent of a gardenia, the melodies, harmonies, and rhythms of music—all as part of the concert of life. In other words, we can live in the fullest manifest expression of the emission of Śiva's powers!

We purify these *tattvas* by consuming our identification with the world and with ourselves, and thus our experience of life perceived only through our senses and bodily functions. We understand that this level of life, while unbelievably beautiful, is simply the manifestation of Consciousness on a material, physical, and sensory level. Our total experience of life is enhanced but not determined by our physical and sensory capacities. As we transcend these limitations of our interaction with the world, we simultaneously change the relational equation of our life as one of simply subject and object. And we can move up to free ourselves from the more binding levels of limited identification, namely mind (*manas*) and ego (*ahaṃkāra*).

Tattvas 16 Through 12:
The Matrix of Human Experience

Ascending through the *tattvas* up to the level of *manas* (*tattva* 16) is not the primary work of spiritual *sādhana*. This is because those lower levels of consciousness are not particularly limiting to the ascent of consciousness back to Divine Source, although it is amazing how many people never leave those sensory levels of the shopping mall. The real work begins when we address the levels of awareness that truly create and sustain our experience of separateness. They do so because they have the capacity to do so. They perpetuate that limiting experience in an attempt to sustain themselves as the levels of consciousness fom which we function.

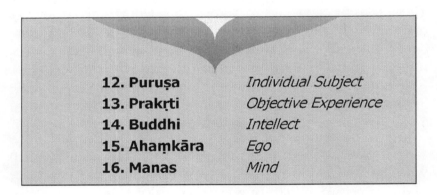

12. **Puruṣa**	*Individual Subject*
13. **Prakṛti**	*Objective Experience*
14. **Buddhi**	*Intellect*
15. **Ahaṃkāra**	*Ego*
16. **Manas**	*Mind*

As we discuss these levels of awareness—*manas, ahaṃkāra, buddhi, prakṛti,* and *puruṣa*—it will become clear that their confluence is an intricate, interrelated weave. The degree of separation between them is only measurable by our experience and choice! The back and forth in the discussion of them in upcoming pages is representative of the warp and weave of the fabric of our human experience. These *tattvas* are a soup of misinterpretation, what I call the "Bass-O-Matic" of human experience.

In the early seventies, *Saturday Night Live* was one of the most popular comedy shows on television. One of the many great skits they did was called "Super Bass-O-Matic '76," a fake T.V. commercial in which a garish, hyper pitchman played by Dan Akroyd touts a food blender that turns whole, raw fish into liquid pulp, ready to drink. To demonstrate, he takes an entire bass, drops it into the blender, and pulverizes it into a liquid. And then he drinks it! The last line in the skit is, "Now *that* is good bass!"

In the skit of our life, it is the blending of all the energies, consciousness, and experiences of being alive in the "Bass-O-Matic" of our *sādhana* that creates the very fuel to power and propel us toward freedom. In consuming that mixture, which is our own custom blend, we should exclaim, "Now *that* is good *śakti!*" In his inimitable way, Rudi said it perfectly, "This is the perfection of life. When you take all the quantities of life, both negative and positive, throw them in the blender with a glass of water, and drink it, you are a free person."

TATTVA 16: MANAS

We've seen that in Tantric understanding, *manas* (the mind) is understood as thought-construct, not intelligence; and our emotions are the glue that binds all of our thoughts together. Thought-construct always seeks to maintain the belief in separation, which is why Abhinavagupta asserts that thoughts are the source of all bondage. Liberation is only possible if we can free ourselves from the incessant chatter of the mind. In doing so, there's no denial of thought, simply the understanding that thought is Consciousness having descended into a more limited state.

To reach *nirvikalpa samādhi*, the thought-free state, the first thing we must do is stop reacting to the fluctuations of the mind. We have to stop believing the mind and its conclusions.

What we want is to be able to see the impulse of thought-construct as it arises and to let it go at that point. Usually, we don't. Usually, it's only after our thoughts have created some external form that we say, "Oh, I see what my thoughts created. It's a mess." Freeing ourselves from our own thought-construct is one of the critical points of *sādhana*. One of the most powerful tools we can use to do this is Rudi's double-breath exercise. (See the Appendix for a description of the exercise and a link to an MP3 file with the guided meditation.) Instead of allowing our thoughts to take us out of our center, we draw that energy back into ourselves and channel it into our physic body, where it can refine that density of consciousness. In this way, we transmute our own thoughts into fuel for growth.

This is why the concept of *spanda* is so important to understand. Once we are centered enough to witness our thoughts and emotions as they begin to arise, we can choose to surrender them then and there. Watching thoughts as they arise is like watching waves on the ocean. One wave is not any more or less important than another. Our thoughts have validity only because we give them validity. From a place of stillness, we can see what starts to arise in the mind, and we can consciously choose whether or not to engage it. Again, there's never a rejection of thought as unreal, only the understanding that it is real within its own context.

If we want to rise into higher levels of consciousness we must stop believing our mind and our thoughts. We must not let our experience up to this point in life determine the future of our experience. Through our disciplined inner practice of channeling the energy of our thoughts into our physic system, we free that energy to rise. We become freer than our mind and stronger than our emotions. We begin to see that our thoughts are simply the fictitious story that the ego uses to sustain itself and its limited capacity to perceive. The bottom line is this: Let go of your thoughts.

TATTVA 15: AHAMKĀRA

*All through the day
I me mine, I me mine, I me mine.
All through the night
I me mine, I me mine, I me mine.
Now they're frightened of leaving it,
Everyone's weaving it,
Coming on strong all the time.
All through the day I me mine.*

These insightful words written by George Harrison invoke the internal song we sing all day and most of the night, yet we never stop and ask ourselves where that song is coming from inside of us. It is the song of the ego, perpetually creating and sustaining its self-image and reality. The problem is that the ego always gets it wrong, as it cannot perceive its own source.

Notice that in the diagram of the *tattvas*, *manas* (mind) is shown under *ahaṃkāra* (ego), although they are as close together as the two sides of a coin. This is the egoic mind, not God's mind. We have come to the moment in our ascent of Consciousness where we must choose to continue to head up the ladder in order to get to the point where we recognize ourselves as individuated expressions of the Divine. This is why I always tell students: Stop fighting with and trying to change your ego; just free yourself of it. Until we move from the constricted understanding of ego, we can only experience our lives from that confinement and limited capacity to understand the truth of reality. We have not freed ourselves from the endless cycle of limited perception and cannot find a new place of awareness in ourselves. Spiritual life should be a stream of rebirths of consciousness, each absorbing us more deeply into the luminous clarity of Supreme Consciousness.

Freedom from the ego is at once the most difficult challenge of *sādhana* and the easiest. If you want to be free of your ego, simply stop functioning from it. Surrender who and what you think you are. Surrender the suffering you experience living in the ego by refusing to accept it. Consciously reach inside and make contact with a more expanded place of awareness in yourself. Do that by reaching deeply into yourself during meditation and making contact with a more profound openness and flow of energy in yourself.

The ego is just contracted consciousness and energy. Throw it into the fire of your own wish to grow and know God. As you do that, you'll understand that there's a higher consciousness you can function from. Instead of using your life force fighting and struggling, you can free yourself from the grip of the ego and use your energy to move toward the experience of being an individuated expression of God. From there, you can move up to Pure Awareness.

Tattva 14: Buddhi

Buddhi, the *tattva* just above *ahaṃkāra* (ego), is a significant point in the ascent of our awareness because it is at this level that we more fully realize we have a choice. *Buddhi* is the place where our own self-reflective capacity begins to truly function as choice. We either sustain our awareness of life from the point of view of the ego structure, or we have the discriminating insight to say, "Oh, I can go up. I can expand my awareness." Most people don't realize there's a distinction between their ego and the consciousness of *buddhi*. At every level of consciousness, at every *tattva*, there's the choice, to use Rudi's words, to stay horizontal or to move up vertically and expand our awareness. Speaking very directly on this, he said, "When the spiritual energy is stronger than the mind, what is said and done become the reflection of higher energy. At that point, the intellect speaks through the Spirit instead of through the tensions of mind."

If we aren't able to perceive that there are levels of capacity and awareness above limited ego and mind, then we don't know. Sometimes it's our own discriminating awareness, and sometimes it's the hand of God that shows us. Either way, that's Grace lifting us up, revealing to us that we have a choice. It is an important moment in our *sādhana* when the discriminating awareness that we have a choice allows us to move toward those pure *tattvas*, toward higher consciousness. It is also where we begin to truly function from non-attachment, because we finally get it—we are not limited by what we need, we are not driven by desire, and we don't try to control or hold on to life from our limited perspective.

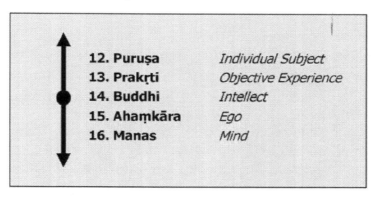

As the *kuṇḍalinī* rises, *buddhi* is a significant moment in the ascent and our spiritual evolution. Enough of our inherent, internal light starts to shine through that we can see. So when you want to make a decision, if you can't make it from the highest Infinite Consciousness, understand there's a place in between that point and your own limited self-serving ego from which to make the decision. Inherent in the choice to function from a higher state of awareness is the willingness to surrender the perspective that comes from thought-construct, and to not act based on what you think. What you think you know, and your attachment to your thoughts, limits you. True *sādhakas*, therefore, seek to have everything they think they know disproved.

If we really want our freedom and some true experience of joy in this life, we must stop looking anywhere other than within. It is our endless pursuit of something outside ourselves to make us happy that is the cause of our unhappiness. Because we have been given the self-reflective capacity to know our own state, we have a choice at every moment of our life. Once we understand this, we stop blaming life for our life. We free ourselves from the need for life to be something different than it already is. We endlessly sleepwalk through life not digesting and understanding all our experience as the perfection of life. Whatever struggle, karma, and density of understanding we face, we ought to thank God for it, because that is our path to work through whatever misunderstanding has accumulated.

So let's get over our mind and our ego and the endless loop they create, which is all our "stuff." Let's get through our own duality as quickly as we can so we can proceed to the true essence of spiritual practice: penetrating through God's emission and duality, of which we are an effect. If we stay on the merry-go-round of mind and emotion, over and over and around and around, we may clear up all our stuff only to understand that it's not our stuff that keeps us from Unity but the expression of multiplicity from Śiva Himself. It is *buddhi* that gives us the clarity to choose to get off the merry-go-round once and for all. And, as you may have guessed, the theme song at this level of consciousness goes like this:

> *Everybody, get on the floor, let's dance!*
> *Don't fight the feelin', give yourself a chance!*
> *Shake shake shake, shake shake shake,*
> *Shake your buddhi! Shake your buddhi!*

Tattva 13: Prakṛti

Recall that the thirteenth *tattva*, *prakṛti*, is the fundamental operative energy of *puruṣa*, the individual subject. *Prakṛti* creates *puruṣa's* objective experience because it gives rise to materiality, meaning that matter and energy take on the nature of form, including the human body. By the operation of *prakṛti*, we experience ourselves and others as objects, all separate from each other.

In transcending *prakṛti* through our *sādhana*, all perceived objects—including the structure of our own body-mind—are dissolved, in the sense that our consciousness is no longer bound by any identification with them. But don't worry; it doesn't mean your body disappears! As we ascend, we are, in fact, moving beyond the boundaries of physicality, discovering ourselves as nothing but individuated Consciousness. Truly, the fun starts here!

Tattva 12: Puruṣa, the Pivot Point

As we ascend to *tattva* 12, we are moving up through and freeing ourselves from our ego and all the struggling we do from within its grip. While we must make the effort to free ourselves from that binding, the only purpose of that is to get to *puruṣa*, the place of experiencing ourselves above our own ego, as an individuated expression of the Divine. Once we do that, we can surrender even that individuated experience and become one with Śiva.

As the *kuṇḍalinī* rises, we are freed enough from the grip of ego to recognize that we must free ourselves from that level of misunderstanding. In doing so, we come to the point of seeing and experiencing our separation from God. At this point on the elevator of the *suṣumṇa*, we're already free of so much of our need, misunderstanding, and condition. We no longer translate our suffering into not having this or that. We understand our suffering is simply our separation from God. We understand that we suffer because we've used our own individual will—given to us as a fractal of Divine will—to serve ourselves instead of serving the highest, because we believe we are the doer.

You will note that the *cakra* in the center of the heart and the *viṣṇu granthi* are not highlighted in the image of Trident Man, though I think they ought to be. What the Trident Man image suggests is that even the experience of beginning to truly function from the realization that we are simply God's agent doesn't completely free us. Becoming aware of the experience of the individual subject dropped out of Infinite Consciousness through the eyedropper of *māyā* is the point at which we can truly begin our ascent. From there, we can begin to surrender even *that* experience of ourselves, because even that is a separation. Thinking, "I am an individuated expression of the Divine," is still thinking, "I am this," instead of simply, "I am."

As the *kuṇḍalinī* rises, our individuality, which we most often experience as our mind and ego, gets consumed. We move above mind and ego, and function from the non-attachment attained through the discriminating understanding that although we have them, we are not our bodies, our thoughts, or our emotions. We experience individuality from a much bigger place; we are simply living as an individuated expression of higher consciousness within us.

Puruṣa's Heart Is God's Heart

The Pratyabhijñā Hṛdayam is a sacred text written by Kṣemarāja, a student of Abhinavagupta. The title means "recognition of the heart." This heart, the heart *cakra*, is where we become self-aware. We experience *vimarśa* in the center of our own heart and from here we can connect to God's heart. In reality, our heart and God's heart are one resonant space. Nityananda describes this as the heart-space, and he specifically states, "Freedom happens in the heart-space."

Puruṣa is the individuated experience of the heart of the Divine. It is where we feel God. Once that happens, the struggle is over. We let go of the idea that we are our body, mind, and ego without any fear because we understand we are an individuated expression of Divine Unity, not something separate from that. Yet, right above that, there's still *māyā*, the veil of duality. This is the pivotal moment in the elevator where we decide to either go up or get off. At this point, it's not a question of giving up our personality or individuality; it's the understanding of becoming more.

Once we discover our own heart we recognize that even our awareness of that heart is by Śiva's Grace. This is Śiva's own *vimarśa*, Consciousness doubling back on Itself. As the teachings on the *tattvas* make clear, that highest Consciousness is embedded within every level of awareness, so at this level of our own individuated experience, we begin to see, "I am me *and* I am all that."

As I always tell students, your heart is where you feel God. The particular emphasis I place on opening the heart is about freeing ourselves from the limited experience of being an individual subject, and having it flipped around so we can recognize ourselves as individuated expressions of Divine Unity. That experience is what allows us the capacity to further move up from there. As soon as we experience ourselves as an individuated expression of God, we have access to our direct connection to God.

Because we are individuated expressions of Śiva, feeling our heart means feeling God within us. It isn't just our individual heart but the heart of the universe. This is where we start to know God and His capacities as *prakāśa* and *vimarśa*. *Prakāśa* is the light that illuminates life, and *vimarśa* is our capacity to have and know that experience. Our heart is where we discover that we can live from that self-reflective capacity to know ourselves. It is from this point, where we experience God as ourselves, that we can move up through the heart, through the center of the head to transcend the *rudra granthi*, the veil of separation, and move through to the top of the head to *dvādaśānta*, where the triadic powers of pure will, knowledge, and action are unmanifest.

This is how we connect our manifestation as individuated expressions of that whole back to that unlimited, un-individuated expression. We've just connected the cables. The flow we've spent years developing in ourselves doesn't stop here. It is a conscious, discriminating connection to this thread that moves up through and connects us to our Self before we're manifest. As Ken Wilber elegantly states, "We know what our face looks like before our parents were born."

We become established in that flow, and our experience is infused with the recognition that we are not the doer. We are not separate or different. We are not experiencing; we are *being experienced*. We are not breathing; we are *being breathed*. This is the discovery of the internal breath, the breath within the *suṣumṇa*, which is the recognition that our existence is the result of Śiva's breath. Śiva is doing as us. This is liberation. (See the Appendix for a description of the Internal Breath meditation and a link to the MP3 of the guided meditation.)

If the highest principle is always present, then that same Infinite Consciousness is held within every individual. That same self-reflective capacity, infinite Divine *vimarśa*, is held within the individual *puruṣa* as it is dropped out of and through the eyedropper of *māyā*—the *bindu* between pure and impure consciousness. The challenge for us as individuals is our interpretation of that experience. *Puruṣa* is the pivotal point of the experience of separation and therefore critical to either living in that separation or moving through it. This point where individuation takes place marks the portal back into Supreme Consciousness.

WE EXIST BECAUSE OF GOD'S WILL

As we consider infinite Divine Consciousness, having descended to the moment where the individual becomes manifest, there are some important points to recognize. First is that we exist because of God's will and Grace. As we ascend back through the *tattvas*, all the turmoil and struggle we make in our lives isn't worth a damn if we don't get back to this point and recognize that we are individuated expressions of the Divine, by God's will and Grace. It is at this moment, when we transcend the categories of egoic consciousness that say, "I, me, mine," that we can begin to truly experience freedom.

To arrive at the awareness that is *puruṣa*, we must first free ourselves from egoic limitation and recognize that we are simply the effect of God's breath. We are simply God manifest. Not only do we melt in gratitude, we have the strength of Śiva because of the clarity and responsibility of that understanding. *Puruṣa* is the point where God's will has descended to create individuals to express and walk in His own freedom. The responsibility is the understanding of what we're here on earth to do, to live God's will and perpetually expand His freedom. The gratitude for that Grace in our lives pervades all of our actions.

Thus *puruṣa* is not just the beginning of our experience of misunderstanding; it is at one and the same time the beginning of our experience of freedom—depending on whether we are looking down or up. It is the rabbit hole, and the rabbit hole is up not down. It is our *bindu* point into heaven. Our individual experience and our freedom from that experience are not separate or different. In recognizing Śiva as the doer, it was Śiva who pushed us down the rabbit hole, and it is His Grace that pulls us back up through that *bindu* point.

At the level of *puruṣa*, we're talking about ascending and descending the *tattvas* at the same time because this is the nexus, where they meet, where we either ascend or we don't. If we allow our awareness to become stuck in any particular pattern, then we're creating density, which, as it gets heavier and heavier, causes us to sink and descend into lower levels of awareness—back into ego and mind.

It is in this moment in our journey as God that we must decide whether we will live as an expression of God's will and Grace, or whether we're going to hold on to our own will. This is the moment they meet. Our *sādhana* boils down to right here for each of us. This is where we free ourselves from the idea that there's duality, or that we're doing anything at all. It is only in surrendering the idea that we are the doer that we begin to penetrate through duality. At the level of *puruṣa*, we experience that we are simply an individuated expression of the Divine, free from any misunderstanding that we are the doer. This is a significant step in freedom from duality. The action of our life is no longer tainted by individual desire, and is action as Śiva.

THE JOY OF RECOGNITION

If being an individual is the gift of freedom, we could say that the highest Grace in our life is that God made us ourselves. In the process He concealed the fact that we are not separate from Him, because it's all about the joy of recognition, of opening our heart and experiencing unconditional freedom. It's such a powerful, liberating moment in eternity in which Śiva says, "I'm going to make individuals because I want to remember Myself. Even knowing Myself, I want to forget in order to have the possibility of remembering. What if there are billions of Me, all remembering?" What happens when there are billions of points of light? *Prakāśa*, the light that illuminates life.

Salmon swim upstream for one reason, to get back to where they were born so that they can be part of the process of creation. If a fish can do it, why can't we? How big is the brain of a fish? And that's the point. A fish doesn't function from its brain. It just lives in the creative flow. It's born, it gets pushed downstream, it struggles to get back upstream, it does its duty, and it's free. It doesn't take vacations along the way. It doesn't build a house on the shore. It just swims upstream. It listens to God saying, "Come home, come home." It doesn't use its will to do anything else. It doesn't identify itself as something outside that Divine will and Grace. It functions as that Grace. A salmon swims home because it knows where it came from.

In our individual journey back to where we were born, this critical point of choice is clearly expressed in the structure of the *tattvas*. The level of *puruṣa* is where we get to choose whether we truly want to live in God's service, or whether we're still going to push and shove to have something happen the way we think it should. The reason we do that is because we haven't quite discovered that what happens in our life is pretty much irrelevant to our liberation. How much money we have, where we live, what career we're engaged in, or which partner we have is not relevant to the state of awareness we function from.

At this moment in our individuated experience, we can choose to live in that simple clarity, that luminous light of bliss. We've penetrated through the density of our egoic misunderstanding, and from here on up, we're just rising. Really what's happening is we're being helped along; God is able to lift us up because there's no boundary or identification with some limited part of us holding on. It only takes one billionth of a second of our holding on to our identity as we think we know it to deny Grace's attempt to raise us up.

As Kabir so eloquently put it in his poem:

Friend, please tell me what I can do about this world I hold on to, and keep spinning out!

I gave up sewn clothes, and wore a robe,
But I noticed one day the cloth was well woven.
so I bought some burlap,
But I still throw it elegantly over my left shoulder.
I pulled back my sexual longings,
And now I discover I am angry a lot.
I gave up rage,
and now I notice that I am greedy all day.
I worked hard at dissolving the greed,
and now I am proud of myself.
When the mind wants to break its link with the world
it still holds on to one thing.
Kabir says: Listen my friend, there are very few that find
the path!

God is gentle. He continually tries to lift us up, but it can only happen when we offer ourselves in freedom and service. As God inhales, He lifts us back into Himself. This is the purpose of our individual experience. This is why Śiva walks around masquerading as us. This is worth remembering, because in not doing so, we deny the highest will of Śiva: the perpetuation of freedom.

SURRENDER IS HOW WE ASCEND

It is interesting to note that it's precisely because we've been given the Grace and gift of experiencing our individuality that we begin to think we're separate from the source that gave it to us. This is important to understand. All of our nervousness about giving up our identity is just our nervousness about giving up our identity. We cannot pass through the *bindu* point of *māyā* holding on to our identity.

It is this simple: Transcending our own individuality is the point in our ascent of consciousness where we decide to simply live in that joy, and to not allow anything, anybody, or any condition to take us out of that space, because as soon as we do, we accept the duality of our existence. It's impossible to understand Unity if we never let go of the idea that something else is the cause of our own state. It's impossible for limited consciousness to understand unlimited Consciousness. Only by surrendering our will deeply enough, over time, do we see that it isn't even the aligning of our will with God's that brings freedom. It is simply the allowing of God's will. This is why the first instructions I always give students are: take a breath, open your heart, feel the flow, and surrender everything.

This is the moment, at *tattva* 12, that individuals have so much difficulty transcending, because they try to fit it into their own individualized experience. We must decide at some point to live in a state of surrender, because the part of us that won't surrender is the very part that limits us and will never allow us to recognize there was nothing to surrender in the first place.

In terms of rising through the *tattvas*, how do we get, for example, from ego to *buddhi*? By surrendering our ego. When everything in us is saying, "I know this is right; you can't tell me it's not right," that's ego. If we let go of it, all of a sudden another blanket is removed, and there's some light by which to recognize, "Yes, I see that I function from my ego, and I don't want to do that anymore." The same surrender is even more critical as we attempt to move above the level of individuated expression to merge with Divine awareness.

Puruṣa is where we decide whether we are willing to surrender ourselves completely, to become Śiva, to not need to do anything but simply be God. The highest practice, the highest meditation, the highest way of living our life, is living in surrender. We come to understand that no matter how much it hurts and what it costs, we must let go of our limited, individuated experience in life if we want that higher experience.

Suffering Is Part of the Process

As we ascend, we understand that even our suffering is part of the process. Suffering is God's *bandha*, putting a little pressure on us, because the purpose of a *bandha* is to yoke, contain, and "intentionalize" energy so that it can move up. In the Fivefold Acts of the Divine, concealing and revealing are the hide-and-seek. Our experience of Śiva concealing Himself in our life is suffering and contraction.

We suffer because of the pain of that separation. But if we are Śiva doing this to ourselves, and the process of concealing creates pain, what is the purpose? To wake us up. Sometimes our biggest movement toward the light is from the darkest place, so even suffering is an act of Grace. This is why Rudi said pain is God loving you.

The pain of being a separate individual is God loving us. Our idea of pain is not having something, or losing a million dollars, or losing our boyfriend or girlfriend. When we grow up spiritually, we come to understand that true suffering is our separation from God. True suffering is having lost our completeness and therefore needing and desiring something outside ourselves in order to feel whole.

Instead of getting horizontal with our pain and suffering and defining it in terms of form, thought, and condition, we need to recognize that this is simply part of how our consciousness is trying to swim back home. Okay, we bump into a few rocks as we ascend. Sometimes we even get knocked unconscious. But we shake it off and continue to move up because we understand the process that is trying to unfold.

Even if we don't understand, we're willing to surrender our struggle and our tendency to reinforce our limited perspective. We let go because some part of us knows where we came from and is trying to get home. Remember, it is the heart, the fundamental, vibrating core of the *puruṣa*, that knows where we come from, and knows the way home. As Nityananda said, "The heart is the most sacred of places. Go there and roam."

Tattvas 11 Through 7: The Kañcukas

The five *kañcukas*, the coverings or forces of limitation, are fractals of *māyā*. They are the various ways in which *māyā* limits the five Divine energies of Consciousness, bliss, will, knowledge, and action. Although the *kañcukas* themselves are different levels of awareness, they are always experienced as an integrated matrix. As soon as we move through and above the level of *puruṣa*, we actually begin to experience the unbounded awareness that the *kañcukas* limit: omniscience, omnipotence, omnipresence, completeness, and timelessness, as opposed to experiencing those powers in limited awareness, from the contracted perspective of the individual.

The *kañcukas* are the sophisticated means that Śiva uses to contract his unlimited powers to limited powers, ultimately to the point of absolute limitation, all before manifesting the individual. Having recognized at *puruṣa* (*tattva* 12) that we are an individuated expression of Śiva, we now understand that in surrendering that individuality, we are also surrendering the limitations of that level of consciousness. The *sādhana* that achieves this transformation is the surrendering of doership. In allowing Śiva to act through us, His powers are no longer limited by our individuality. Amazingly, the most important use of those unlimited forces is to direct them upward, to raise our consciousness high enough to penetrate through *māyā*, the mother of all the *tattvas* of obscuration and limitation.

Tattva 6: Māyā

In the context of the *tattvas*, *māyā* is one level of consciousness within which is a level of power. Because it is energy, and because the appearance and illusion of separation is simply the effect of energy, it can be accessed and used to penetrate through that energy to find its source.

As we ascend through the *tattvas* and begin to move through the *bindu* point of *māyā*, nothing fits through except Pure Spirit. Our Gucci bags full of our stuff will not fit through that point as we enter back into the infinite field of Consciousness from which we came. Our stuff is just our sense of separation and all the paraphernalia we use to hold on to our egoic identity. To ascend to the highest states of awareness, we must shed all that—even our experience of separated individuality—which is consumed in the fire of the *suṣumṇa*, in the fire of flow that is the *kuṇḍalinī* rising.

Moving from the upper palate in the throat to the *cakra* in the center of the head is penetrating through duality, through *māyā*, the *tattva* of obscuration. Only an incredibly refined discriminating capacity allows us to move up and through. If the *rudra granthi* isn't dissolved, only a little bit of our awareness gets through. This is how the space is opened in the center of the head, allowing the individuated energy to find its source.

We must focus on finding and continually opening that space, and consciously surrendering our limited perspective and understanding so they are consumed, reabsorbed, and become part of the pulsating ocean of Infinite Consciousness. What happens ultimately when the blowhole gets bigger and bigger? At some point there's just open space, and the energy is free to do its thing. Bit by bit, our limited understanding is dissolved. That's why, in its simplest terms, Kuṇḍalinī Yoga is described as the awakening of that vital force within us and its return to Śiva.

When our consciousness, resonance, and vibration are light enough, when enough of our density has fallen away, we can penetrate straight out the top of the head and connect with the very forces that created us, never experiencing them as separate. This takes extraordinary subtle awareness. Through our *sādhana*, we are transforming our own awareness and refining our mechanism so enough of our energy is rising, meaning it is not creating density and separateness. All of a sudden, it's flowing upward, and we're just lifted. Our awareness is lifted through the *bindu* point of *māyā*, and we experience the pure levels of awareness within ourselves.

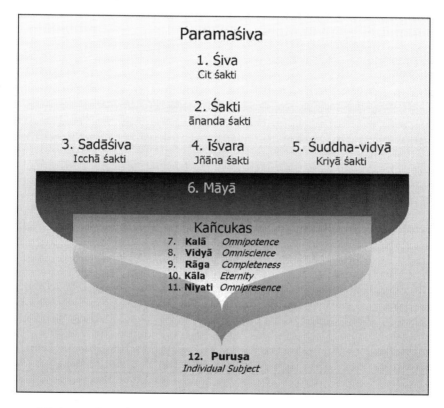

Ultimately, all *sādhana* is to bring us to the point of freeing ourselves from *māyā*, the quintessential veil of duality. *Māyā* is the doorway to freedom; transcending duality is the doorway to Unity. Don't get caught in anything that keeps you on the dualistic side of the door. Tune in to the highest, and let that illuminating light permeate the darkness, making all things clear. While you're doing that, do the dishes. Be conscious. Engage in life. There's no conflict between highest and lowest. This is how we experience that we are simply God manifest.

Moving into the Tattvas of Pure Awareness

As we ascend through *māyā*, we gain access to the *tattvas* of pure awareness. This is the big one—living in the levels of unlimited Consciousness. On the Trident Man diagram on page 146, these are labeled as *Śuddhavidyātattvam*, *Īśvaratattvam*, and *Sadāśivatattvam*, *tattvas* 5, 4, and 3, respectively. As we ascend to this point, we now have access to those powers in the sense that we begin to function from them without the limitations of our individuality or the illusion of separation.

Tattva 5: Śuddha-vidyā, or Kriyā Śakti—Pure Action

Having penetrated *māyā*, we come to the level of *śuddha-vidyā*. At this level in the Trident Man diagram, there are two horizontal bands or plinths shown in the center of the head, which can be thought of as two manhole covers, each with a hole in the center of it. These plinths are not different than the *rudra granthi*. Normally, these plinths, and the openings in them, are not aligned. As the *kuṇḍalinī* rises, the internal vibration causes the plinths to align, creating an opening for the energy to rise even higher. In the Trident Man visualization and practice, there are mantras given just for that purpose.

Interestingly, this was also Rudi's time and space work. He had an exercise that involved moving up through one of the plinths and shifting one over, so that you couldn't go back down, and could then move up. He never read about the *tattvas* or saw a picture of Trident Man, but he was talking about transcending the experience of time and space created by *māyā*.

Rudi experienced and understood those plinths as real, as psychic density. They are the granite slabs of duality, the final coverings between pure knowledge and limited knowledge. The drawing of Trident Man depicts those plinths—which are so transparent as to be nonexistent—as a solid barrier. What this describes is that as we penetrate through duality and our experience of separateness, we begin to have access to the five powers we've been talking about. On the diagram above the plinth is *śuddhavidyātattvam*, pure action, *kriyā śakti*, which we now have access to without the limitations of our own individuality.

This is not theory. This is the true transformation of our own experience. We truly begin to become free of the notion that we are the doer and we recognize ourselves as Śiva doing. We recognize that the Divine powers of action, knowledge, will, joy, and Consciousness Itself are really the only thing ever happening, through us and as us. Moving through this level of consciousness allows us to fully access Divine Śakti, instead of limited individual energy.

Tattva 4: Īśvara, or Jñāna Śakti—Pure Knowledge

As the energy rises to this level, we have access to higher knowledge and understanding of our true nature. Śiva's will is only one thing: the intention to express joy. From that clarity, knowing we are that Infinite Consciousness, knowing we can rest in that stillness, our actions become extensions of that knowledge and clarity of will. There's no longer any conflict between what we do and what we say we want to do. So often there's a disconnect between what we say we want to do and what we actually do, which demonstrates the relative weakness of our own will compared to the immense power of Śiva's will, which at this very moment is expressing us and our lives in all their perfection. Imagine how amazing our experience would be if this was the level of consciousness we connected to and allowed to express through us. On a scale of one to ten, I suggest it would be an eleven, because we can't imagine how amazing it would be. Rudi used to say that the biggest problem people had with their spiritual lives was that they couldn't imagine them. In the luminous clarity of pure knowledge, we see that things are perfect exactly as they are.

Tattva 3: Sadāśiva, or Icchā Śakti—Pure Will

In the Trident Man diagram, we see Śiva in the form of Sadāśiva lying prone on his back. Emerging out of His navel are those triple powers He creates from within Himself, the three goddesses. As His upward gaze creates those energies, all the while He bellows out an ecstatic howl of laughter from the joy of creating from within His own Consciousness. He is subjugating Himself to the goddesses because they are the powers of creation, the powers by which He expresses His own freedom and joy, demonstrating that the *expression* of freedom and joy is more important than just having it. Sadāśiva subjugates Himself to the powers of Parā, Parāparā, and Aparā within the field of His own awareness. At this point Śiva is depicted as a corpse with the trident emerging from His navel, surrendering Himself, even though He is the highest. When you are all powerful, Supreme Consciousness, you can do anything you want—even create something higher than yourself. This applies to our experience as well: Those of us who think we're all-powerful and all-knowing can also decide there's something higher than ourselves.

Thus there are actually two corpses there: you and Śiva, and He is a corpse for the same reason you are: because He surrendered and gave Himself up out of His own bliss. Out of His navel, depicted as emerging straight out the top of our head, the goddesses appear: His Divine will, His Divine knowledge, and His Divine capacity to act. He gives himself up to those powers. This is a depiction of Śiva sacrificing Himself. Since we are also Śiva, it's also our sacrifice. This image represents Śiva giving up His own freedom in order to express creation, yet He never diminishes Himself in the process. He surrenders Himself out of the joy of His own existence, saying, "Let there be life. Let there be the expression of My own joy." In that process of creation He forgets Himself, and this is the concealing in the Fivefold Acts of the Divine.

Tattva 2: Śakti, or Ānanda Śakti—Pure Energy and Autonomous Bliss

Śiva empties Himself and gives Himself up into creation, into emission, based on His own Self-awareness, and creates the universe, forgetting Himself in the process. Emphatic in this drawing is that the powers that create the universe are shown above Him, because it is by penetrating through them that we discover Him. This is *dvādaśānta*, the space where those goddesses abide.

While we experience Parā, Parāparā, and Aparā as distinct powers of will, knowledge, and action, ultimately they are one power, the power of bliss emerging out of Consciousness Itself. Thus Śiva is saying, "If you want to live in unconditional bliss, penetrate the powers of emission. Become one with, merge with, and function from My powers of will, knowledge, and action. As you become one with them you will experience Divine bliss. And in the experience of Divine bliss you will know your Self. Those three energies, which are not separate from Me, have a source. To discover Me, penetrate through those energies and arrive at the simple awareness, I am." In that state, whatever comes or goes is simply part of the flow. There's no grasping. We're not there to attach. This is the state of unconditionality and surrender.

Every day we should make contact with the Grace of our lives. Every day, ask Parā, beg Śiva, "May my will be Your will. May I know You as myself. May all my actions serve You. Free me from myself." This is the joyous offering of our limited self. Even when we begin to function as God's will, we're one step closer to God, but we're not yet God Himself. That's why we must penetrate through the emission of God's powers to discover God Himself.

At this level of awareness, which is Śakti, Śiva's energy, we move from living in conditional happiness to autonomous bliss. We simply live in the flow of life. When you come in contact with that sweet resonance, stop for thirty seconds and just feel it, so you can remember it. When you wake up in the morning, make that the first thing you tune in to. Start the day savoring the *rasa* of your own heart. Get in contact with the joy of your own existence—this is bliss. Okay, so you've done that right. Now, there's nothing else to do but to allow the Pure Consciousness from which that bliss arose to shine forth.

Tattva 1: Śiva, or Cit Śakti—Pure Consciousness

Immersed in the highest Self, we experience the Oneness of life in Divine Presence. This is the undifferentiated heart of pure awareness, which is our awareness. We have accomplished the purpose of Abhinavagupta's statement: "In the practice of Anuttara Trika, the *sādhaka* penetrates the energy of emission, becoming one with Śiva, the source and holder of the powers of the universe."

This ultimately all leads back to *svātantrya*, absolute, autonomous freedom, which is sometimes referred to as the thirty-seventh *tattva*. This is Paramaśiva—complete Oneness. The five powers of Consciousness, even the power of Consciousness Itself as an energy, all arise from that infinite, autonomous freedom. This experience is the highest liberation, and we never even get to experience it. Only Śiva gets to experience it.

Life is only Consciousness. If *visarga*, the emission of all manifestation, is the expression of Śiva's own Consciousness and joy, what part of it could not be perfect? This is the awareness we seek, and the awareness we choose. When you find yourself making some other choices, simply say, "Hold on there," and choose freedom. Choose clarity. Choose to get still and not let the hurricane of mind and emotion extract you from yourself. What if you completely let go of all control and all demand? What would happen is that you'd be a spiritually free person. As you loosen the vice of your own grip around your life and simply let it show itself, you'd say, "Wow. How amazing is that? How sweet it is." Until we are prepared to let go of all control, we live under the tyranny of our incessant need and relentless demand, and just like sliding down a fireman's pole, we can land back in those lower levels of awareness incredibly fast.

Ascending the Throne:
The Transformation of Consciousness

Śiva expresses His freedom through the emission of the supreme goddess Parā, who is the energy and power of Śiva's will and Grace. The three goddesses atop Śiva's Trident are the goddesses of His triadic powers of will, knowledge, and action: Parā, Parāparā, and Aparā. They are depicted as three, yet celebrated and understood as one. The most important thing to understand about them is that they are the deities of our own Consciousness.

The levels of consciousness of *śuddha-vidyā*, Īśvara, and Sadāśiva are at once within Śiva and emitted outside Himself. Śiva doesn't have an inside or an outside, and He has the power to express Himself in all dimensions at once—the capacity to be in two places at once while being nowhere at all! That is why in the image of Trident Man those levels of awareness are depicted both underneath the trifurcation of the trident and above it, creating the lotus seats for the goddesses. Everything happens in the Oneness that is Paramaśiva!

The three goddesses atop the trident are not separate or different from the Goddess Kuṇḍalinī. In classic definitions of Kuṇḍalinī Yoga, the latent *kuṇḍalinī* is described as a cobra coiled three times around the base of the spine. The three coils are the energy of our physical life, the energy of our mental and emotional life, and the energy of our spiritual life. As the energy awakens, it releases those coils so that the cobra stands up and fans out, which represents those Divine powers showing themselves.

In the context of our ascent of the *tattvas*, it is the same thing: We are awakening to the powers of our higher Consciousness. Unfortunately, within many traditions, externalized ritual practices that celebrate these goddesses often take prominence, so that practitioners get confused and mistakenly believe they are worshipping deities outside themselves. But the very reason internal practices were embedded within external ritual is to make clear that God's awareness is everywhere. It's in us and in the deity we may be worshipping. In its highest sense, externalized ritual is simply the doorway for moving into that internal space, which is where we experience and recognize those levels of consciousness in and as ourselves.

When Rudi taught his time and space work, he spoke of the horizontal, the vertical, and the spiritual horizontal. The latter is the infinite expansiveness of Pure Consciousness that holds within It all things, all form, all energy, all potential form, all potential energy, including all dimensions of *māyā* and of time. In the state of pure awareness, those things are all understood as part of one Consciousness, even though there's a different shade of expression to each. Spiritual practice offers the possibility of finding, discovering, and living in that experience.

What amazing Grace it is that we have within our own capacity the opportunity to discover that absolute Oneness in ourselves, to discover that we *are* that absolute Oneness. We are Parā. We are Śiva. The Parādevī *pūjā* that we perform in our practice is a sophisticated process whereby the awareness of all thirty-six levels of consciousness are installed within the psychic body of participants. There is both an exterior *pūjā* and practice and an internal practice. Both are valid and beautiful. When practiced from a place of understanding, there is no real difference between the two. This is yet another powerful example that there is no duality except in duality, and no separation between inner and outer.

That particular practice, which is the installation of Śiva's Trident within us—the extending into and allowing the light of *dvādaśānta* to show itself—is the maturation of the practice of Kuṇḍalinī Yoga. It is truly our response to Grace, in stillness, that allows us to extend our consciousness into that dimension.

Parā (will), Parāparā (knowledge), and Aparā (action) are the energies of Grace. In accessing them, we can access the Consciousness from which they arose, Śiva Himself. This is the purpose of *sādhana*, discovering that energy and the Consciousness from which it arose as never separate from each other. That is the essence of all Tantric practice. In accessing, living from, and penetrating through those energies, we become living expressions of the sacred sound of Śiva repeating His mantra, *Aham*, "I am."

The five powers of Śiva discussed at length in the first section of this book—Consciousness, bliss, will, knowledge, and action—are vibrant, alive realities, levels of higher Consciousness functioning always and forever, creating us and this life we have. The installation of Śiva's Trident creates within us the structure to access those energies. And yet, because they don't exist just within us but in the world, there's the twofold consciousness of finding that same awareness as we engage our life that we do when we meditate.

Transcending the Duality of Individuated Experience

The reason the *dvādaśānta* meditation is given is for us to be able to move back through that *bindu* point, which isn't an end point but a beginning point. This is the supreme *bindu* point between individuality and Divinity. Individual identity does not move through it; only Spirit moves through it. Individual identity is merged into infinite identity in that space.

The most important thing to understand about the exercise is that in making contact with that space, we are connecting with the same Divine Consciousness from which all creation emerges. We're making contact with the energy of manifestation before it manifests. As we master that experience, we tune in to the Divine powers that created us. This is not different than Rudi's time and space work because we are moving into a realm before the manifestation of time and space. We are being absorbed and emitted from that place, before duality. As we make contact with that source and allow it to overflow and awaken our own state, we move through duality into Unity.

By making contact with the Divine energies in *dvādaśānta*, we slowly transform our own will, knowledge, and action into Divine will, knowledge, and action. The radiance that flows back over us begins to dissolve the awareness of duality and our sense of doership. Our life flows through us from that Divine space and manifests itself in its perfection. *Dvādaśānta* is only accessed as we transcend our own duality. As it overflows, that Unity flows back through and informs our experience of duality as not separate from itself, but part of one whole, duality simply being the expression of manifestation. This is how we transform our experience, while alive, while having a body, and begin to experience Unity.

In practicing the *dvādaśānta* meditation we are asking to receive and be absorbed into those energies, inviting those higher forces to become prominent in our awareness. We must then allow them to express themselves as our awareness, otherwise we're calling on the Divine to render all Its power to us so that we can do something other than surrender in the service of that power. We are accessing extraordinary power, the powers of creation, and we must understand the Grace and the responsibility of that. We must deeply accept and commit to the transformation of consciousness that is available and activated as we access those powers.

Unless we consistently engage in this exercise we won't make contact with that place of access. This meditation requires the focused awareness to feel into the levels of consciousness all the way back to their source. You won't necessarily experience it the first or second or hundredth time that you do it, but if you are diligent it will become your permanent experience.

Becoming God's Agent

In the diagram you'll notice Śiva, the little guy lying across the top of the head. This is the aperture at the top of your head, the opening to *dvādaśānta*. As we connect to that radiant space, we are connecting to ourselves before we are born, to our source, the eyedropper. Permanent awareness of that contact dissolves our individuality, which we no longer perceive as separate from the eyedropper. This is how we become God's agent. We no longer function from individual will because we are freed of it. We've traded up: our individual will for God's will.

As we come to comprehend duality as an expression of Unity, we must express and function from that understanding as we engage our life. There is no inner or outer work. You can't be a master of *kuṇḍalinī* energy and not use that energy to serve its purpose in the world. The two are never separate.

When we free ourselves from our ego and surrender our will to the Divine, the supreme goddesses that are the emission of that Divine sit above us and direct our life. It isn't that we create the Divine flow that manifests through us and expresses perfection; we simply recognize it. It's always happening; we're just not quite aligned. It is through our consciousness as we engage life and through our deepest capacity to meditate that we become aware of those energies and allow them to inform our consciousness and express themselves through us without the filter of duality or any identity of separateness.

Those three powers are accessible to us in the *dvādaśānta* meditation and in our life. They're accessible as we engage the world and understand that all these people and conditions are energies. We can discover them as energies instead of getting caught in the form of them. To use Rudi's language, at every level of development there are always tests, so as we begin to have this inner experience, when we open our eyes the test will be there. Any experience we may have in our meditation, no matter how profound, is not real if we can't then function from it. We must use the same capacity of consciousness in our meditation as we do in the world, and vice versa.

This is the highest meditation offered within the Tantric practice of Trika, and it gives access to extraordinary powers and consciousness. You won't understand it all right away. It will take years to discover it, to let it unfold. Don't define it at any point. Let it reveal itself to you. This is the revealing Grace in the Fivefold Acts of the Divine. When you open your eyes, allow it to reveal the nature of creation. Your capacity to experience unity in life is directly connected to your capacity to experience unity in yourself. You're surrendering and extending from your own sense of separate individuality to universal Self. Let it grow and mature in you. Let it reveal itself. Isn't that what everything in life is about, letting it show you itself?

As Abhinavagupta says, "Śiva is the light of Consciousness, present in everything. He displays his light identically in all the categories of existence, all objective phenomena, and views them all as himself in his self-delight, which never vanishes." He says further, "The thirty-six *tattvas* are to be purified. The purifier is Supreme Consciousness. The means of purification is the triad of will, knowledge, and action. This is the highest initiation." The means of purification is making contact with and functioning from those powers in *dvādaśānta*. This is the point of the meditation. You access and are absorbed back into those powers in their Divine state. As you begin to function from that place, you truly experience Śiva's light in all things.

It is only Consciousness that can penetrate through the emission of those powers: this life that we perceive to be a battlefield. The real battle, however, is always to see the One in the many, to transcend form and free ourselves from dualistic awareness. This is the *only* battle. Why would Śiva in all His wisdom make it so hard? He didn't; we did. Through all that multiplicity and all those levels of consciousness, Śiva knows Himself: "I am." Śiva knows who He is even when He walks in our shoes. Like the entire Tantric exposition, the *dvādaśānta* meditation reveals one thing: There is only God, and this incredible, mysterious celebration of Himself. Our individuality has been Divinely offered to us in order to have that same experience. This is the Grace of Śiva: that we already know who we are.

The Upayas:
The Means to Liberation

The Upayas: The Means to Liberation

As discussed in the last chapter, Trident Man represents the process by which we as individuals begin to see the light and ascend the levels of the *tattvas* until we are reunited with Pure Consciousness. The Kashmir Shaivite masters didn't just say it's possible to achieve spiritual liberation. They're telling us exactly how it's possible, with multiple levels of practice from ritual to the highest, most refined meditations, giving us the means to transform our experience, which are called *upāyas*.

Upāyas are means or spiritual methods, the efforts we make to climb the *tattvas* and dissolve the veils of duality. There are four formal *upāyas*, and my own secret unofficial *upāya*, each representing a different aspect of focusing our consciousness back to Its highest Self. Beginning with the highest, they are:

- *Anupāya*: no path, the path of Grace
- *Śāmbhavopāya*: the path of awareness
- *Śāktopāya*: the path of energy
- *Āṇavopāya*: the path of individual effort

Like the *tattvas*, the *upāyas* are traditionally discussed from the highest down—from the subtlest and most direct to the most laborious and physical—categorized according to an aspirant's capacity for *sādhana*. In brief, *anupāya* is no path; there is nothing to be done. Someone like Nityananda functioned from *anupāya*, or absolute Unity awareness, from a very early age, if not from birth. *Śāmbhavopāya*, the path of awareness, is similar. All we have to be is aware. For those who can't be aware, there is *śāktopāya*, the path of energy; we create a flow of energy in ourselves. If we can't do that, we move to *āṇavopāya*: we serve; we make an effort.

You can think of the *upāyas* as a Mobius strip because they're not linear, there is neither a beginning nor an end point, and they're never separate from each other. One is never in conflict with another, and one is never really higher than another. While none are more important than the others, one or more may be more predominant in your experience at any given point in your practice. At any given moment you may be functioning from one or all of them at the same time. It is the joining of the descent of Grace from the Divine with the effort and devotion of the individual—the expression of his or her own *svātantrya*—that brings about realization and true freedom.

The *upāyas* are methods of *sādhana* that represent the focusing of consciousness. Because of *vimarśa*, the self-reflective capacity, we know what effort we need to make, and where we need to focus our awareness. You might say to yourself, for instance, "I'm wrapped too tight for New Orleans today. I'd better get quiet, keep my energy internalized, and use the double-breath." The *upāyas* represent our awareness of our own state and the focusing of our own energy and consciousness within that state in order to expand it.

Within each *upāya* there are many different dynamics and aspects and practices, and they all lead to each other. If we think of the *tattvas* and the *suṣumṇa*, we can imagine the *upāyas* as wrapped around them, creating the warp and weave holding together the fabric of our own existence and pathway to freedom. As yogic methods, the *upāyas* represent a matrix of understanding and *sādhana*, like intersecting circles of consciousness that support one another.

The *upāyas* are a simple yet powerful way of looking at the means of ascent, of liberation, of transcending duality and penetrating through *visarga*, Śiva's emission. The three paths of effort, energy, and awareness all function simultaneously as a single, integrated awareness. The *upāyas* are our capacity to work, to focus our awareness. Even at the dissolution of the thinnest veils, all three are functioning, but which method or path we predominantly function from is generally a result of depth over time, the maturity of our consciousness and our practice. Even *śaktipāta*, the descent of Grace, happens in different levels depending on the *upāyas*, on the capacity of a seeker's awareness.

Anupāya: The Pathless Path

While the *upāyas* are not hierarchical, they are hierarchical in experience. *Anupāya*, also called the path of Grace, is considered the highest means because there's no means necessary. It is a state of being, not attainable by any effort. *Anupāya* means simply being melted by Divine Grace. In one moment of receiving *śaktipāta*, with one glance or word from the guru, or directly from Śiva, freedom happens. In one flash we recognize our highest Self. There is no path required. There's no meditation required. There's no service required. *Anupāya* is simply and directly experiencing that I am Śiva. *Aham*. I am. This is the highest path.

Anupāya, the state of *svātantrya*, is the state of unconditional surrender—not the effort, the act, or even the awareness of surrender, but simply the state of freedom. In the Tantrasāra, also written by Abhinavagupta, he beautifully describes *anupāya*:

> *The very highest divinity, the self-manifest light of consciousness, is always already my very own being. When that is the case, what could any method of practice achieve? Not the attainment of my true nature, because that is eternally present. Not making that nature apparent, because it is constantly illuminating itself. Not the removal of veils, because no veil whatsoever exists. Not the penetration into that, because nothing other than it exists to enter into. What method can there be here when there is an impossibility of anything separate from that? Therefore, this whole existence is only one reality, consciousness alone, unbroken by time, uncircumscribed by space, unclouded by attributes, unconfined by form, unexpressed by words, and unaccounted for by the ordinary means of knowledge. For it is the cause through its own will alone, by which all of these sources of limitation, from time to the ordinary means of knowledge, attain their true nature. This reality is free and independent, a mass of bliss, and that alone am I. Thus the entire universe is held as a reflection within me.*

This is such an extraordinary, elegant expression of the state of *svātantrya*, the state of liberation and illumined clarity. This is the highest experience, and it is our Divine right. Our *sādhana*, the capacity to do *sādhana*, is the Grace that lifts us into that. That simple line that says you end up where you began is certainly true in our spiritual freedom, because it is ultimately in the state and awareness of *anupāya* that we recognize that Śiva alone is reality. As we climb the ladder of the *upāyas* and move closer to that experience, we begin to see glimpses of that. We begin to free ourselves of our limited understanding enough to see that there's more to life than me. Somebody with a bit more intelligence than myself designed all this perfection. That recognition is also Grace.

This lovely, poetic experience of freedom is available to us through the continual surrendering of our own limited consciousness, the perpetual willingness to get bigger than ourselves, whatever the dynamic. We have this idea that in our meditation we can let go of our perspective and become bigger, yet we can't express that in simple interaction with the people around us. There's never a conflict between your inner capacity to truly let go and live from a deep state of surrender and your capacity to express that as you engage your life. The world is a perfect testing ground, and it is our opportunity to express our understanding.

To live in unconditional surrender is the highest *upāya*, and all of us have access to that level of focusing if we choose it. As we function from that understanding, we stop struggling with life. Instead of trying to change life we change ourselves, which immediately changes our experience of life.

The reason *śaktipāta*—the descent and transmission of Grace—and the relationship with the guru are understood as *anupāya* is that the guru is the manifest agent of Grace. If for one moment we could authentically receive that Grace, we would be free. *Anupāya* translates as "God is." Not "God is doing," but "God is."

This is the realm of the five Divine powers of Consciousness, where there's simply God's pulsation, and all of the form and creation and manifestation hasn't happened yet. Its full glory, however, is all already there, held within God's own experience. *Anupāya* is the direct, integrated recognition that God is. I am. As it says in the Śiva Sutras about *anupāya*: "The realized yogi becomes Śiva. All of his actions are worship of God. Knowledge of the Self is the gift that he disseminates. He has acquired mastery over the *śaktis* of emission."

Anupāya might be thought of as the mastery of all *upāyas*. It is also both the goal and the source of the other means. Only the rare human being can simply open their eyes and function from that realization. The achievement of that awareness, the recognition of that Divine Heart, is what's being described there. How we enter into that awareness is through the other *upāyas*: *śāmbhavopāya*, the path of awareness; *śāktopāya*, the path of energy; and *āṇavopāya*, the path of effort.

Śāmbhavopāya: The Path of Awareness

As the Tantric masters described it, for the schmucks who aren't able to function from *anupāya*, the next *upāya* is *śāmbhavopāya*, the path of awareness, of being aware of the joy of our own existence. In this level of practice there's no meditation or chanting. It is simply the focusing on the Pure Consciousness that lies beyond thought and is free of all thought-construct. Thus the practice of *spanda*, of arresting thought-construct before it even arises, is part of *śāmbhavopāya*. It is simply functioning from the awareness of Śiva's will, which is the perpetual unfolding of freedom and joy. Abhinavagupta says of *śāmbhavopāya*: "The entire universe shines forth within the Self, consciously articulating the universe as an expression of the nectar of sweetness of Its own Self-existence."

The delineation between *śāmbhavopāya* and *anupāya* is so thin it's almost nonexistent, and really that's the case between all of the *upāyas*, because they're neither linear nor separate from each other. *Śāmbhavopāya* is the recognition, "I am aware that I am Śiva. I function from the Consciousness of Śiva, the only doer." The highest meditations given within Tantric practices awaken and unfold Consciousness from this state of awareness. As we progress through our meditation career, we must arrive at that capacity. Having been freed from limited consciousness, we function from unlimited Consciousness.

The mantra for *śāmbhavopāya* is Śiva's own mantra *"Aham,"* or "I am," repeating you. If there is a practice, it is to live totally from Grace, in unconditional surrender and unbounded joy. In meditation it is the complete letting go into Presence and stillness. In the world, it is allowing that Presence to show you your life.

Śāktopāya: The Path of Energy

As our capacity for practice descends, we come to *śāktopāya*, the path of energy and flow. In traditional scripture, *śāktopāya* is often described as the path of mind, because it is the transforming of the contracted energy of the mind into pure energy and flow. The mind is just energy. It's a little out of control, but it's still energy. The level of consciousness called *manas* (mind) is the instrument of duality that creates thought-construct, which creates definition and separation.

Śāktopāya is the purification of thought. As Abhinavagupta says, "For those whose minds are not purified, even continuous practice will not bring freedom. Even those initiated into the Shaivite mysteries and [who] possess a meaning of attaining enlightenment fail in their efforts as a result of mind. The mind must be purified." Even more directly he states, "Thoughts are the source of all bondage." Rudi said the same thing very beautifully: "The mind is the slayer of the soul." Once we understand this, we can recognize the mind as a pathway back to higher consciousness because it is by consuming the energy of the mind that the density of thought-construct gets converted into flow and energy.

One powerful way to transform the energy of mind is by using the double-breath. Through this exercise, we internalize our energy into the psychic body. We pull our awareness out of the level of mind and ego into the psychic body so it can refine that density of consciousness. As a thought starts to arise, we absorb it and convert it back into energy. Only as energy can it rise to a higher level of consciousness. It is through this inner discipline of arresting that contraction of consciousness—which is all a negative thought is, a contraction we engage in and react to—that we have the capacity to transmute it. As we dissolve the blockages formed by thought-construct and emotion, more energy can move up through the *suṣumṇa*, through the *tattvas*, and dissolve the *granthi* and the veils of duality, opening us to the highest levels of consciousness. That flow ultimately leads to stillness and surrender. As long as our identity is wrapped around our mind, we are bound. When our identity is wrapped around God's heart, we are free. There are no thoughts in God's heart.

Śāktopāya, the path of energy, is not just the understanding that life is energy but truly experiencing it as such. We can discover the source of that energy, which is Consciousness. When we can truly function in *śāktopāya*, there isn't the hardness of distinction between activity and form; we experience and are established in that flow of energy. This is, in essence, Rudi's work: Open your heart, feel the flow, and function from the awareness of that flow at every moment. In doing so, you will have pulled yourself out of the limited experience of the mind and emotions and separation, and you will begin to live in that flow. You will be able to rise "straight out of Dodge," as Rudi would put it, to the understanding of energy as the expression of Consciousness within which no separation ever takes place, even though multiplicity arises.

The mantra for *śāktopāya* is, "Throw another shrimp on the barbie," meaning, throw another limited part of yourself onto the fire, because it is in *śāktopāya*, the path of energy, that we transform and release awareness trapped within the density of our own limited awareness. Only a burning log emits heat. We begin to truly understand that life is energy—including all of this form, all these individuals, and all our experiences—and that energy is the pathway to the source of energy, because energy arises from Consciousness.

ĀṆAVOPĀYA: THE PATH OF EFFORT

Āṇavopāya is the path of effort, the path of the individual, and it is foundational. For a person who lives in the awareness of the lower *tattvas*, the consciousness of "I am my body," to get from that level of experience to "I am" requires a great deal of effort. *Āṇavopāya* therefore is the cultivation of right actions on the level of the physical body. It is the effort to meditate, to serve, to develop a disciplined inner practice, to participate in worship, ritual, and asana practice. It is the wish to grow. It is the very first thing taught in my particular practice: Open your heart.

Rudi would always say to us: "Open your heart; feel your heart; take your mind and stick it in your heart; take all your tension and stick it in your heart." This is a daily practice, and a lifetime of daily practices. When we have established ourselves there long enough and deep enough that we can truly function from our heart, we can then begin to consciously establish a flow, which is *śāktopāya*. The incredible refinement of that Grace we receive as energy can begin to burn through our misunderstanding and the impurities of our psychic system.

In traditional times when a seeker came to a guru and asked for instruction, the guru would say, "Fine. See my taro fields out there? Well, start digging, and in twelve years I'll talk to you, but only if you've dug for twelve years." This was the traditional training in spiritual practice. Why would they do such a thing? To see if an aspirant was serious. *Āṇavopāya* is the effort of demonstrating the willingness to serve in order to receive what we believe we need. How much surrender would have been required to do that for twelve years? *Āṇavopāya* is the path of individual effort, and the effort is to surrender. You thought they were just rejecting you and telling you to dig, but what they were really teaching was surrender. Even though what we're learning to do is just to function, to breathe, to feel our psychic body, these things are never separate.

THE SECRET UPĀYA

We can correlate the veils of duality—I am separate, I am different, and I am the doer—with *śāmbhavopāya*, *śāktopāya*, and *āṇavopāya*, respectively. The secret is that there is actually a fourth veil, and a fourth *upāya*. The fourth veil is called "I am the talker." This is when we take the experience of feeling separate, different, and that we're doing something, and decide to talk endlessly about it. This is how we spend so much of our life force: talking. Most of the time we talk to control, to create demand, or to defend some situation. The rest of the time we talk unconsciously. We must understand where that chatter comes from. Or we can just apply the secret *upāya*, called "duct tape *upāya*," and wrap it tightly around our mouths.

The practice of duct tape *upāya* is to stop talking, or, as Rudi would say, "stop talking like a horse's ass." We talk because we don't know how to be still and allow our inner awareness to show us that we're talking to try to control something—to create or change or defend some condition. So often when a difficult situation happens, the first thing we do is pick up the phone and vent. We immediately react from our misunderstanding instead of getting quiet, waiting, and allowing the urge to react and attack to subside. This is not about becoming morose but being conscious. When we get quiet, become centered, and establish a flow inside, there's much more possibility for communication to take place. Communication is simply flow, a dialogue of energy.

When somebody talks to us, before they finish the first sentence, we're already saying something back to them about us. Not only are we not listening, we're making it about us. What is the first thing we usually hear when we hear ourselves speaking? "I." That's a clue to what's coming next. If we're willing to get quiet instead of immediately needing to talk about our own experience—the experience we didn't have or should have had or could have had and didn't have—we're beginning to let go of the need to control.

What if the next time we ask someone how they are, we let them finish before we start telling them how we are? How much more energy would we have to free ourselves of the very thing we think we need to talk about? Can we offer a day, a year, even a lifetime of not talking about ourselves? Can we offer ourselves in surrender at every moment? If we can do that, what is there to talk about? Nityananda stopped talking because he realized, what is there to say?

Understand how much we reinforce our perspective by talking about it. There is a time and place: a) with our therapist, b) with our psychic, and I can't think of a third. What if every word out of our mouth was expressing joy and gratitude for how amazing life is? That would be a fairly different experience for most of us. Even in our difficulties, if we feel a need to share them, let's share from the perspective of, "Look how amazing this opportunity is!" How can we free ourselves of our misunderstanding and the suffering it causes if all we ever do is talk about it?

The real problem is when we use our energy to project and defend a limited place in ourselves. Be conscious of where you're talking from. Engage in life, and if somebody talks to you, talk back. Just be aware of yourself and of the purpose of talking. Let's talk about serving and giving, about something other than ourselves. When you are in conversation, be aware whether or not you're fighting or defending yourself or trying to demand something. Making the effort to duct-tape our own mouth is actually *śāmbhavopāya* because it comes from the awareness that we probably don't need to say a thing. In *śāktopāya*, not talking would be not extending from a place of tension, keeping the energy inside, putting it into the flow, and burning it. In refining that energy, we allow it to transform into a higher state.

I would go for walks with Rudi for two or three hours in the morning. He rarely said a word, and I certainly wasn't going to say anything, yet the experience was one of fullness. Once, after we'd walked for two hours and were just getting back to the ashram, he said, "I shit on all architects." In New York there's beautiful old architecture and then there are all these new ugly buildings, which is what he was referring to. In two hours, those were the only five words spoken, and it didn't dissipate the fullness at all.

Understand how much energy we expend through mindless chatter and in defense of the ego. When people function from that state, they don't know whether anyone else heard a word they said, and mostly they don't care. They're too busy talking. You must know when talking is an act of unconsciousness. It could be mindless chatter or the unconscious act of demanding or defending. In having the discipline of speaking from stillness and centeredness, it becomes very clear when talking is the correct thing to do, when it's an extension and a flow. When you find yourself talking from reaction, contraction, and tension, just stop and get quiet. And if all else fails, use duct tape.

THE UPĀYAS, FURTHER THOUGHTS

While *anupāya* is considered the highest means—the flash of insight, one glance from the guru, one touch from Śiva, and that illuminating light becomes clear—the other *upāyas* are about discovering that we didn't have to do all that work at all. All we had to do was simply recognize the highest part of ourselves. In some ways the discussion of the *upāyas* is not different than that of *prakāśa* and *vimarśa*, the unfolding of Śiva's light and the self-referential capacity to see that light. The *upāyas* are the means of achieving that light: the path of individual effort; the path of energy (surrendering into the flow of life); and the path of awareness, of simply letting go, all function at the same time.

If you're trying to engage your life from the very highest Consciousness and find yourself not doing so, what do you do? Take a breath, feel the flow, open your heart, surrender. Opening and feeling your heart could certainly be described as *āṇavopāya*, the path of effort. When new students come in to my meditation practice, for example, the first instructions they receive are: "Open your heart, feel the flow, and surrender." This is *āṇavopāya*, *śāktopāya*, and *śāmbhavopāya*.

We surrender our limited experience by surrendering the limited consciousness causing us to have a limited experience. This is critical. If we want to live in a higher experience, we must transform our own consciousness, and we do that through the process of freeing ourselves from it. When Abhinavagupta says there is no other Divine fire able to consume duality than *kuṇḍalinī*, this is what he's talking about. Duality is our experience of the world, not Śiva's. This is why whatever struggle we find ourselves in is of the ego, the part of us that demands to hold on to its limited consciousness, thinks it's separate, and is going to fight to the death to prove it.

Focusing on Freedom

It is the transformation of our awareness in the moment—whatever that moment presents us with, whatever level of difficulty—that is the demonstration of our spiritual mastery. Even the silliest, stupidest little argument can have the same binding effect as some major difficulty in our life, i.e., the experience of contracting instead of opening. Isn't that amazing? The second through fifth chapters of the Tantrāloka are a discussion of the *upāyas*. What it all boils down to is the focusing of our own individual consciousness into a higher consciousness, and doing so from a place of joy and celebration. Then there's no more struggle in life, only the focusing of our awareness to penetrate through our misunderstanding of the situations and conditions we perceive as difficult.

Each of those means or strategies—*upāyas* are sometimes called strategies—is simply our conscious choice to be aware of our own state, to recognize when it limits us, and to choose a state that's not limiting. As soon as we understand this, our life, and our engagement with every dynamic in it, will be transformed. Since Śiva's will is the perpetual expansion of freedom, through all the *upāyas*, through our functioning within all the *upāyas*, we learn to say, "May my will be Your will." We begin to let go and free ourselves from the incessant demand that life be the way we think it should be and that we get what we think we should have. From the first moment of our spiritual *sādhana*, our life becomes one of service, of serving Śiva's intention for freedom to express itself. That service is first expressed in ourselves, and offered to the people around us. We serve our own freedom by not needing people to change, and we serve and free the people around us by not needing them to change.

Our individual effort of taking a breath, wishing to grow, and opening our heart is *āṇavopāya*. *Śāktopāya* is living in flow and allowing it to free us of all impurities. At the same time, recognizing that Śiva wishes us to be free is *śāmbhavopāya*, simply living in Divine Presence, in the state of surrender, in the heart-space. None of these are in conflict. In our engagement with the world, we don't function from the highest and not be able, as we meet a difficult situation, to take our awareness inside, which is *āṇavopāya*, and not engage from contraction or tension. Once we're centered, we can listen and engage with what's going on. We can create a flow and understand there is a dynamic interchange of energy happening. If we can stay in that flow long enough, we'll have an insight. We'll be in *śāmbhavopāya*, the path of awareness.

No matter what *tattva* we're operating from or what *upāya* we're using to ascend from one *tattva* to the next, it is only our capacity to surrender that gives access to the transformation of our own limited consciousness. Surrender is the foundation of every *upāya*, every level of practice. If Infinite Consciousness exists within us and we don't have access to it, it is the uncovering of that Consciousness that our *sādhana* is all about, the dissolution of our misunderstanding and our dualistic experience. The *upāyas* are the means by which we uncover ourselves and recognize our Divine nature.

There is actually even a double-secret *upāya*, called "you-*upāya*," meaning that you and your life are your means to liberation. Everything that happens in your life is part of your process of unfolding your higher nature. Every aspect of your life is your means to liberation. Every moment and every challenge in your life is an opportunity for freedom. Your life is perfectly and Divinely offered to you as your means to liberation. This is why every moment of your life, every experience in your life, should be experienced as joy.

The Four Gates: Inner Practice, Grace, Devotion, Selfless Service

9

The Four Gates: Inner Practice, Grace, Devotion, Selfless Service

At its highest, Trika tradition asserts that we are already free, and there is nothing to be done in terms of practice. Yet for most of us, that recognition unfolds gradually through a combination of God's Grace, our personal wish to grow, and some form of spiritual *sādhana*. In looking at the Śiva's Trident *maṇḍala* we'll see there are four gates, which in my teaching I describe as inner practice, Grace, devotion, and selfless service. These are the portals back into the field of Consciousness from which we arose.

We have to reenter our own life. We have to enter the spiritual dimension through these gates. In my view, this image describes the heart of God and our own heart. These are the four gates into our own heart. While there is no outside of the heart, we perceive ourselves to be outside of it, and we either function from within that centeredness and openness, or we don't. These are the four gates into the heart through the involution process, which is how we get back home.

These four gates are all interchangeable and intermixed; so a person can't be the greatest meditator on the face of the earth and be self-centered. The result of meditating every moment of life if we're not willing to serve is nothing. It's an act of self-centeredness. We can't enter through the gate of service and then not practice. All four gates are the entry points for our penetration back into that field of Consciousness. None of them is more important than the others, although, like the *upāyas*, one may have a predominant expression of action at certain times in our life.

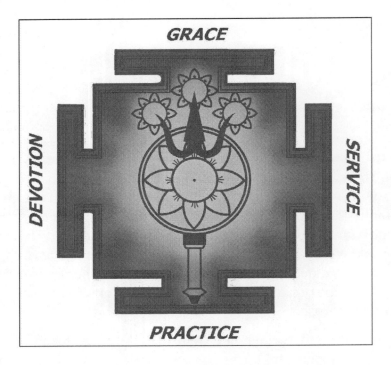

The most important aspect to recognize about the trident *maṇḍala* is that the field of Consciousness it represents is ever present. The consciousness of freedom is the choice to enter that space, through one or all of the gates simultaneously. Inherent within the discussion of the consciousness of freedom and becoming one with Śiva, the source and holder of the powers of the universe, is the recognition that we get to choose. At every level it's a conscious choice. At every level it's an effort. The efforts we make as we move from *āṇavopāya* to *śāmbhavopāya*, and from one gate to another, may have a different *rasa*, or flavor, but they are all simply ways of focusing and directing our awareness back into that field of Consciousness. Let's discuss the four gates in turn.

THE GATE OF INNER PRACTICE

Sādhana, or practice, is fundamental to discovering the highest within ourselves. We can't buy spiritual liberation at the 7-11. We must do the work of transforming our own consciousness. Contemplating one's identity with Consciousness again and again in the state of meditation and in daily life is *sādhana*. The first thing to understand about disciplined inner practice is that it should be our response to the Grace in our life. When Grace begins to reveal our highest Self, the only true response is gratitude and devotion—expressed through our disciplined inner practice.

Part of disciplined inner practice is the engagement with a teacher, which we will discuss further below. That relationship is Grace for it allows us, at any point in the day, to tune in and identify with the field of energy and Consciousness that is the power and Grace of a lineage. Part of that *sādhana* is conscious choice. The highest conscious choice we can make at any moment in our life is to recognize our freedom instead of identifying with our bondage.

The Tantric practices of my lineage are based on the psychic body, particularly the awakening of *kuṇḍalinī*, the vital energy of life and the individuated expression of Divine energy, and the remerging of it back to the heart-space, back into Śiva. As stated in the opening quote, Tantric tradition asserts that there is no other Divine fire able to consume the whole of duality than *kuṇḍalinī*. The Tantric masters are making an emphatic statement that this is the only way liberation happens: It is the penetration of our individuated life force back to its Source that brings freedom, and this happens in the *suṣumṇa* through the opening and piercing of each *cakra* and the dissolving of the *granthi*. All levels of misunderstanding are burned up by the rise of the *kuṇḍalinī* back through the *suṣumṇa* to its own Source, Śiva. This is the freedom to experience unity with God, the purpose of all spiritual life and practice.

The *suṣumṇa* is an infinitesimally fine filament, a Divine thread, and it reaches to God. When I discuss breath, *cakra*, flow, and Presence, I mean to encourage you every day of your life to become established in flow, internally and with the world. Establishing that flow internally is what refines and burns the impurities within the *suṣumṇa*.

The essence of our inner work involves the technical capacity to awaken the *kuṇḍalinī*, and then allowing it rise through the *cakras*, burn impurities, and create openness and flow within the *suṣumṇa*. As that happens, we become aware of the internal breath and gain access to that filament, that internal light. The internal breath allows us to feel into and experience that Divine thread that comes from our deepest core and rises up through to God. This is why the Tantrics say it is the rising of the *kuṇḍalinī* through the *suṣumṇa*—dissolving all *tattvas* and merging back into Śiva—that brings liberation. This is the practice of Kuṇḍalinī Yoga.

The flow, the awakening of the *kuṇḍalinī* and allowing It to rise through the *suṣumṇa*, is the continual reintegrating and opening that allows the energy to dissolve the *granthi* from the inside out. The dissolving of the *granthi* is the effect of the rising *kuṇḍalinī*. The *granthi* in the base of the spine is dissolved as we turn our life force back inside ourselves. We free ourselves from lifetimes of externalizing our life force and the karma we created. The psychic mechanism is our own personal refinery, and it refines our consciousness. Rudi called our work "psychic Drano," because if we think of the *suṣumṇa* as a pipe, the flow is what cleans it out, so that ultimately there is enough openness for the center of the *suṣumṇa* to become perceptible.

Our meditation practices are what we engage in to create the structure within ourselves to hold higher consciousness. It's like a large room in which the weight of the ceiling is supported by pillars. The structure is what holds the openness, which suggests to us that the effortlessness of our experience comes only after we've had the discipline and courage to live our *sādhana* and do our inner practice. We are developing higher levels of inner capacity through our meditation, and if we don't spend the time we will not develop the capacity.

The Double-Breath

As I've touched on earlier, of the many extraordinary gifts of Rudi, one of the greatest is the double-breath exercise, which brings the energetic flow down to the base of the spine and allows it to rise through and purify the *suṣumṇa*. This is a profound practice because it allows us to understand that as we process the energies of life, we can draw into ourselves this emission, this *visarga*, this energy that expresses itself as manifestation. We can recycle and internalize that energy and use it to refine our own psychic mechanism.

The double-breath is about attaching our awareness to the breath and drawing in energy to nourish the *cakra* system. The double-breath brings energy into each *cakra*, opening and exercising it. We bring the energy down the front, where it opens in the heart, expands in the navel, moves to the base of the spine, and back to the top of the head. As we develop this vertical flow of energy and feel it moving through the *cakra* system, through the *suṣumṇa*, out the top of the head and back in through the base of the spine, we are internalizing our life force. This is what cleans out any debris in the *suṣumṇa* and dissolves the *granthi*.

As we create openness in the psychic body, we allow the energy to fill and hold that openness. We attach our awareness to the gross breath to bring our focus inside. We're trying to expand the *cakras* to increase their capacity to hold and channel energy through the psychic body. We're bringing the energy down, ultimately trying to get to that goddess's door in the base of the *suṣumṇa* because that's where the treasure is: the latent energy we want to awaken and rise up through the *suṣumṇa*. We're delivering croissants and café-au-lait to the energy that's dormant within us, and saying, "Wake up and rise." When that happens we feel it as flow extending beyond the boundary of any particular *cakra*.

It's not different in our meditation than in our engagement with people. It isn't just an internal flow; it is between us and our life, between us and other people. We must internalize our energy with our eyes open and dealing the pressures and tensions of life. We're not spiritual ostriches sticking our heads in the sand. There is no separation between the world and us. We use the world and its energy to discover ourselves, and that's its purpose. The purpose of our life in the world is Self-discovery, to experience Śiva's bliss and the will that created us out of that bliss. Day-to-day life is how the Divine chose to experience Itself, so it is also our moment-by-moment opportunity to understand Unity.

We must seek and practice that experience in meditation, and we must seek and practice that during our day. When some misunderstanding happens in you, for example, just take a breath. When you get into a tight situation with somebody, if you stop slinging your sledgehammer long enough to just start to feel, all of a sudden it changes, and there's a dialogue of energy, a flow. How amazing. There is no separation between us and the world; there is no separation between Unity and duality. We penetrate the appearance of duality by consuming the misunderstanding that it is such.

This is the gift Rudi gave us. We consume the life we project from our limited understanding back inside, refine it, and project it into a higher state of clarity. By being established in this flow throughout the day as we engage our life, we are penetrating through and absorbing that emission and refining that energy back into ourselves. All that manifestation of our own will, knowledge, and action is consumed. It's a continual process of refining. The energy moves out the top of the head then back to the base of the spine in a perpetual internalization of our own life force so that it can be refined through the subtlest of the subtlest. Only in its subtle state can the energy rise into higher states of consciousness, through the *suṣumṇa*, through the psychic body, through God's body. This is not different than what Abhinavagupta teaches, which is that life is energy, and we must consume it.

All of life arises and unfolds from that single *bindu* point of Infinite Consciousness in the middle of the Śiva's Trident *maṇḍala*, which is God's Presence. That unfolding is God's expression of the consciousness of freedom. Spiritual practice is the involution, the returning to that point, which is what any authentic practice is about. As we return to that point, we penetrate through and understand each dimension of consciousness and energy we connect to as not separate from its source. Penetrating through and consuming that emission allows us to make contact with the Creator of that emission.

The Internal Breath

The practice of the double-breath internalizes our energy and opens the psychic system. It is the doorway that opens us to the internal breath, that subtlest breath, which is the rising of the Divine energy and Consciousness that created us back to its Source. The maturation of the double-breath, of establishing ourselves in flow, leads to the experience of the internal breath, which ultimately leads to *dvādaśānta*, back to Parā. The source of that flow is the internal breath, which is really the potency and vitality within the *suṣumṇa*. At its subtlest it is simply the pulsation of Consciousness, and it takes a great deal of time and stillness to find it. The internal breath, the center of the *suṣumṇa*, is the only place we can move from the center of the head to the top of the head. It's that filament, the *bindu* point of the hourglass, that incredibly subtle thread, which is our connection to God. It takes a very refined mechanism and capacity to be able to tune in to that and move through it. You may want to download and practice the meditation now (see Appendix), before proceeding with the rest of the discussion.

As we practice tuning in to the internal breath, the internal filament within the *suṣumṇa*, the first thing we experience is flow, that is, energy moving palpably through our system. The next thing we realize is that our gross breath is an effect of the internal breath. As we begin to disconnect from the gross breath, we understand that it has a source. Breathing gives rise to the sensations of the body and thoughts. This is where the body and thoughts emerge from, the physical breath giving life to the body. We're not alive because we breathe or have a body. We have a body and we breathe because we're alive. The breath is irrelevant, ultimately. As we penetrate deeper we understand that there's a source to our breath, the internal breath. The importance of tuning in to the internal breath is that now we are free from our body; it's not the body that experiences this.

Discovering the internal breath is never about holding the breath or stopping breathing. It is a powerful, subtle practice that converts the body's need for breath into light and energy. It's not that the body stops breathing but that we become free from the misperception that we are alive because we breathe. While the experience will be one of not breathing, we don't need to stop breathing in order to have that experience. As we penetrate through that, we recognize that the body is draped over the psychic body, and that the psychic body is sustained by energy. You begin to feel yourself as flow, as a nonlocal vitality that contains its own source.

Rudi described it as "being breathed," and as you practice you'll feel it. As you tune in deeper and deeper, at a certain point you realize that you are not breathing. You are being breathed by the power and energy of Consciousness. That's why I say in the guided meditation, "When you feel like you need to take a breath, don't. Take a breath from inside." The sensation of being breathed is the recognition that you are in existence because Śiva is breathing. You are not the doer. The *Aham* mantra means "I am," and it is the sound of Śiva's breath, the pulsation of Consciousness or *spanda*, the quivering forth of Consciousness into energy. This is the internal breath, and it is how we create the space inside us to install Śiva's Trident.

There's a wonderful line that says the *sādhaka* who focuses on the internal breath first recognizes their breath as a moment, then as a minute, then as a day, then as a month, and then as a lifetime. This is how we transcend time, because there is no time in the internal breath. Nityananda says those who do not breathe through the mouth or nostrils have no desire. How amazing. He is describing how the practice of the internal breath, the experience of being freed by Śiva, frees us from desire. The state of desirelessness is recognizing that you are complete in yourself.

If we wish to penetrate into that higher realm in our meditation we must discover the internal breath and allow it to become the energetic highway on which our consciousness travels—not just up to the center of the head to the crown but through to *dvādaśānta*, the emission of Śiva's own powers. We need to look for that stillness, that internal breath, as we reach up to knock on the door of Parā, the supreme goddess.

That Divine thread goes from the base of the spine all the way to God. Ultimately, we become aware of ourselves being God being aware of that Divine thread. As we become adept at it, we no longer see this meditation as separate or different from the double-breath. It is simply the maturation of our own conscious capacity. Rudi said it very simply: "You can now do in five minutes what it took you five years to do." At a certain point, it's already functioning when we get up in the morning, and our job is simply to participate in it.

Our ability to feel our own heart, to feel energy moving through us, is fundamental and imperative. What matures and emerges from that is the experience of the internal breath. These are powerful, subtle, advanced practices. If we don't have the discipline to sit down in the morning and feel our heart, use the double-breath, and begin to establish ourselves in a sustained flow throughout the day, we will never develop the capacity to access the experience that these advanced practices offer.

This exercise requires subtlety of awareness to move through the center of the head and the crown, allowing our awareness to be able to extend up into *dvādaśānta*. We can think of the Divine thread as the center of the *suṣumṇa*. It is a thin filament, rising from the base of the spine, all the way through the psychic system, and out. It takes such subtle discriminating capacity to tune in to it that we don't want our breath to get in the way.

Bringing Practice Into Daily Life

Our experience of the *suṣumṇa* is not different than our experience of life. There is no distinction between that inner experience and our engagement in the world. We cannot achieve freedom in one without achieving it in the other. If we find it in ourselves, we'll see it in the world. If we look the other way around, we're taking the long loop and probably won't get there because we're trying to find Unity in manifestation when we haven't yet developed the sensitivity to see it. This is why it's important to understand both, why the Tantrics refused to reject the world. If the world is a reflection of myself, how can I ignore it? How can I claim to be pure if I can't hold on to that purity and clarity as I engage the very reality projected from within me?

The reason we can't look to experience Unity only in our meditation but we have to experience it in the world, is because that very process transforms our limited individual will, knowledge, and action into Divine will, knowledge, and action. So often, we meditate and we find Śiva in our heart, then we open our eyes and it's like, "Which way did He go?" It is through that penetration, in dissolving the experience of duality, that we move into those states of higher consciousness. We move into and become established in the experience of Unity, and we see the world completely differently—as an extension of our own awareness and the playground of our own experience. We begin to comprehend that it is the merging of those two experiences into one experience that we seek.

It is in our meditation, the diligence of our capacity to refine our own awareness, that we discover that highway, that Divine filament that we just climb up. It is the internalizing of our life force, allowing it to refine itself through the *suṣumṇa*, that begins to offer us those moments of insight. Our capacity to be established in that flow ultimately means we're established in *śakti* and living in the flow of life.

You are connecting yourself to that highest experience; you've connected the deepest place in you to the deepest place in God's heart. Merge your heart with God's heart. That's the heart-space, the individuated heart within you that is not separate or different from its own source: God's heart.

Open Your Heart, Feel the Flow, Surrender Everything

In my first book, *Depth Over Time*, I gave this as the secret teaching, because it's really all you ever need to do. As I've said, the first thing I always tell new students is to feel and open their heart, because this begins to dissolve the *granthi* in the heart. Bring your awareness into your center, Śiva's center, the *bindu* point in the middle of the *maṇḍala*. If you focus on your heart *cakra*, every higher experience will come from that, because the natural expansion and contraction of that process will open and ultimately dissolve the *granthi* in your heart, allowing that awareness to rise to the center of the head.

"Open your heart, feel the flow, and surrender everything," describes how you dissolve the *granthi*. Opening your heart is freeing yourself from the mind and becoming centered in yourself. It is functioning from the mind, and the struggles and karma we create from that, that causes the *granthi* in the heart to keep getting bigger and bigger.

When I say to open your heart, I don't mean just be open and nice to people. I'm talking about feeling the God within your own heart, which has an infinite capacity to open and experience itself. You are alive and have the capacity for consciousness because you have been given your own heart. It's not your small heart; it is the biggest heart in the universe. If you don't come to the place in your day where you feel profound gratitude, you haven't opened your heart. The experience of deeply living in your heart will melt you. The gratitude and devotion that ooze out of it is the experience you will have every day if you open your heart every day.

Focus on that. Keep your energy focused inside enough every day to find that experience, and then allow what opens and blossoms from that to show you the next level of expansion. You can even have that experience when your mind is going crazy, because one is not connected to the other. Your heart will change the experience of your mind, not the other way around. The mind cannot perceive the heart. It isn't big enough, and it is too attached. The mind is a prisoner of itself.

After opening your heart, I always suggest feeling the flow. What I mean is that your psychic system generates that energy within yourself, and as the energy gets bigger and bigger, it sustains itself, moves up, and penetrates the *granthi*, removing misunderstanding. It is the build-up of energy that creates that discriminating capacity. Flow is the energetic highway on which your consciousness expands, and that discerning capacity is held within that flow. The stronger and bigger the energy, the more impurity it has freed within the *suṣumṇa*, and the more capacity it has to continue to do so.

The discernment comes from the expansion of energy, which allows for the expansion of consciousness. Having a powerful flow within you is meaningless if it doesn't expand your consciousness. When you see people seduced by power, they have enormous energy in them, but their consciousness hasn't expanded with it, and they didn't surrender to the source of that power. Be conscious as the energy expands, so when you're fully established in it, you are not saying, "Look how much *śakti* I have!" but "Thank you, God, for this *śakti*."

After we open our heart and feel the flow, we must surrender everything. This is such an important aspect of our inner practice that the next chapter is devoted to it entirely. Consciousness is *vimarśa*, the capacity to be aware. You must bring that awareness to your moment-by-moment experience in order to recognize what level of consciousness you are identifying with within yourself. When you identify from your ego, you see the world as duality, which you mistakenly think can affect your state. Recognizing this misunderstanding is an important revelation because it's the moment of choice. We've seen in the layout of the *tattvas* that *buddhi* is above ego and mind. That discriminating choice is like a ray of light that gets through that says there is something other than darkness, and something other than "me, me, me." The place you look for this awareness is in your meditation. You make contact with that clarity. You let go deeply enough that the eternal Grace that's always functioning can start to get out, or get in, or both, so the deepest part of you begins to emerge and the flower of your heart blossoms.

What so often happens is: We get up in the morning, we meditate, we open our hearts, and we expand. Then we engage our day, and we feel some contraction because something didn't go according to our plan. Suddenly that state of openness we thought was expressing God's will wasn't really God's will because it didn't go our way. Maybe some jerk coming up to you and spitting in your face is God's plan. Are you willing to open? Understand that from within ourselves we create the very dynamics in the world that will really test our willingness to not be attached to the dynamics of the world. What a trick that is! Our life is painted on the canvas of our own consciousness. When Rudi talked about being tested this is exactly what he meant. The very wish to grow, and the vibration of that wish, attracts to us—in the manifest world in the power of action—some form (i.e., a person or situation) that will test whether or not we were serious.

Through our inner practice, what we are asking for is to have our limitations and barriers to Pure Consciousness exposed. The first thing that usually happens is that we see those limitations with clarity. We see ourselves more clearly than ever, with all our faults and misunderstandings. Because we have those pure powers of will, knowledge, and action and the capacity to recognize our own state, we must then make the conscious choice to surrender ourselves, to surrender our tension, to surrender all that keeps us from Śiva.

We start to realize that we are the common denominator in our experience of suffering. We may change our partners and our careers, but we are the common denominator in our own tension. We are the common denominator in trying to change the people around us so that we can love them. This is an enormous clue. This is the very thing we are asking for when we go inside and say, "I wish to grow. I wish to know God. I wish to be free of my suffering." Whatever the request, when we internalize the wish to grow, we are asking the highest Consciousness that is always present and available within us to expose our misunderstanding so that we can change. As I so often remind students, "If you want to change your life, change your consciousness."

Whatever limitation, thought-construct, pattern, or karma that gets exposed in the process of the energy rising and penetrating back through itself, we must understand it as form created out of the energy and density of our own consciousness. So where else would this form show up in our lives except as people, situations, and conditions that challenge our capacity to live in stillness? As we learn to look at such density as nourishment for our own growth, we simply say, "Ah, lunch," and we consume it. As we consume enough of that density and externalization, all of a sudden there's an opening, and we're light enough to move through it.

What we're talking about is the surrender required to break through the *granthi* in the center of the head, which represents duality. Our life force is no longer projected into the world, and we are centered in our hearts. We have freed ourselves from thought-construct and are ready to free ourselves completely from duality. All the energy we previously used to create and sustain duality is now internalized. We now have all of our life force to focus on truly transcending, penetrating, and freeing ourselves from duality.

We can reach for God all we want, but if we're not deeply surrendered in the process, and if our wish to grow isn't coming from the purest place in ourselves, we never rise high enough to penetrate our own ego, the black hole of consciousness. So I suggest we rev up the engine and get a running start. When rockets are blasting off, they rev until there's enough internal force to penetrate through the inertia of gravity and achieve lift-off. Sometimes they may get off the ground, but if they haven't generated enough internal force to penetrate through the density of gravity, they fall back to earth. Our own limited consciousness is not different than that. So we need to do everything we can to generate as much of that force to lift ourselves up. It is only our intention to generate that force that allows God to reach down and say, "Here, let me give you a hand."

Inner Practice and the Upāyas

The *upāyas* are ways of focusing our consciousness. What they beautifully describe is the moment of choice that we always function in. Sometimes we aren't still enough to function from our highest awareness, but at least we can have the discipline to not act on our tension. We must go inside and begin to exercise more control over our energy and awareness because when we're just blowing out our energy and scattering our awareness, we don't have any control over where it's going, nor do we care. Discipline is holding our awareness inside long enough that any emotional energy and binding thought-construct, and the tensions that arise from that, can begin to be absorbed back into us until we understand them as just energy. We can internalize that energy, put it into the flow, and refine it. As that energy is refined, it takes us deeper inside ourselves, where we discover the source of that energy that takes shape as form but is ultimately Consciousness. The reason it's called spiritual "practice" is because we don't always get it right.

If we apply the progression of our practice to the *upāyas*, the first step in *āṇavopāya* is to make an effort. We learn to take a breath and open our heart. With *śāktopāya*, we learn to create a flow and to dissolve some of our tension, misunderstanding, and patterns. That matures into *śāmbhavopāya*, pure awareness of that filament, where there's nothing to obscure the rising. At a certain point, you experience all of them at the same time. There is just pure flow and awareness and joy, even when you may be dealing with the most difficult things you've ever dealt with.

Ritual is *āṇavopāya*, the path of the individual, and so people learn ritual as a daily practice and meditation. The reason daily ritual is given is so people can do it every day if they want. The ritual is simply our internal breath repeating itself. This is the highest ritual, the highest experience, and the purpose of ritual is to take us to that moment, to that place.

To arrive at a place of openness, stillness, desirelessness, and knowing this is God's will, requires enough practice that we have freed ourselves from our limited thought-construct. This is *śāktopāya*. It is transforming the limited awareness that functions in our mind and putting it into flow. It is the understanding that our thought-constructs bind us so that the thought-free state, sometimes called *nirvikalpa samādhi*, is not just an idea but the conscious choice to free ourselves from the bindings of our own thought-construct. At that very moment we can know there's a deeper place we can function from, and we choose to let go. We surrender even our thoughts.

Even living through our karma, which manifests as the difficult things we go through, is an opportunity to live with consciousness, recognizing that it is because we were self-centered and willfully tried to control a situation that we created the karma, and now here it is again. We can say to ourselves: "This time I can recognize the pattern of self-serving that created the karma in the first place, and I can free myself of it." It is God's will that you free yourself. Even in the most challenging moments we can recognize God's Grace in our lives. Because of the self-reflective capacity to know ourselves, even as we engage in some powerful, difficult, karmic situation, we can recognize it as an opportunity to be free. This is *śāmbhavopāya*, the path of awareness.

Through our spiritual practices, we develop our capacity to internalize our awareness, to simply feel our heart and open it, to live in flow and allow it to free us enough that we can live in a state of surrender. This is the progression of our *sādhana*. This is moving from living in duality to living in Unity. In the state of *śāmbhavopāya*, *anupāya* is so close that they're not separate.

Liberation is a Ph.D.

Our capacity to integrate the teachings and practices rests upon our capacity to do the inner work. The foundation of spiritual work is sitting down every day and meditating, finding the deepest place inside ourselves, and then getting up and engaging life from that place. We cannot expect to find the deepest truth in ourselves without that level of discipline.

Spiritual practice is discovering and recognizing that the part of us that knows home is trying to go there. It is surrendering to God's process, to Śiva's will, the perpetual expansion of freedom. Liberation is a Ph.D. It is mastery over our topic. It is having such a profound, astute capacity to decipher and function within the higher levels of consciousness that we dissolve our limitations and allow the highest capacities to function as us. Doesn't that sound pretty good?

Mastery comes from practice. It takes twelve years to learn to surrender, twelve years of surrendering daily. Rudi called it depth over time. This is how we become masters. To quote the Dalai Lama, "There are thousands of paths to God. Choose one, and become a master in it." Become a master in the one that has shown up in your life.

THE GATE OF GRACE

The field of Consciousness that the Śiva's Trident *maṇḍala* represents happens by God's Grace, yet Grace is also one of the ways we reenter that field of Consciousness. The reason Grace is depicted on top is that it is by God's Grace that we are able to make the choice of freedom. While every tradition speaks of Grace, the Tantric tradition speaks of it specifically as the descent of Grace through *śaktipāta*, which is the descent of the highest form of Consciousness and energy through the *tattvas* to free the individual.

Kashmir Shaivism describes several levels of *śaktipāta*. The highest level, and the most rare form of Grace, is receiving our spiritual freedom directly from Śiva. A person like Nityananda would be understood to have received this level of *śaktipāta*, or direct transmission from God. The next level of *śaktipāta* is receiving that Grace a bit more indirectly, through a teacher, through a relationship with the energy field of a teacher. The third level is the Grace that awakens in you the wish to know your highest Self.

Throughout my teens, I was a declared atheist. All of a sudden, at the age of nineteen, walking around the corrals of Odessa, Texas, all I could think about was God, even though I had never thought about God before in my life. Shortly thereafter I heard about Rudi, and took a circuitous route directly to his door. That's Grace descending and saying, "Okay, he's not ready for direct enlightenment. He's not really ready to stand in front of his teacher, so I'll create some wish in him that will bring him to that point."

What I realized later was that I *had* actually been thinking about God all along—because I was saying there is no God. That just shows you the power of Śiva's Grace, that He thought, "Here's this jackass denying Me My existence. I will show him that it is impossible to do so." That's why, in one sense, it's only our response to Grace that's important. I don't spend much time wondering why I received so much Grace in my life, but I do spend a lot of time trying to respond to It.

Grace Flows Through a Teacher

Grace Itself is God's will, emerging from His Consciousness and bliss and His will to express that. We exist because of God's will to perpetually expand freedom, joy, and Consciousness. Ultimately, our freedom is dependent on our direct connection to God. Because it is rare that individuals recognize that they have received Grace directly from God, in the Tantric tradition Grace manifests as a teacher. A teacher is simply a messenger, and a lineage is a series of messengers. The purpose of that relationship is Grace. There is only one God and thus one source of Grace, but because we're a little dense we don't always recognize that Grace is all around us. We can't feel it because we're a little self-absorbed and not quite as sensitive to the Grace that is our life at every moment. A teacher is a beacon for us to connect to and from which to receive Grace. Our relationship with a teacher is the opportunity to respond to Grace. Grace manifests through a teacher as *śaktipāta*, which is transmitted by a teacher in four ways: through look, touch, word, or thought.

The Bhagavad Gītā says this about Grace and the role of the teacher: "Fixing your mind on Me, you will by My Grace cross over all difficulty, but if through the ego you do not listen, you will perish." It further goes on to say, "Absorption is difficult to attain without the firm Grace of God and without the Grace of the teacher, who has become pleased by the devoted service of the disciple."

Grace is the freedom-bestowing power of the Divine and represents the highest relationship with the Divine. The following anecdote represents a powerful descent of Grace — in the form of word — that I experienced in relationship to my teacher.

Not long after I met him, Rudi initiated me as a teacher and I started my own ashram in Lafayette, Indiana. A few months later, I invited Rudi to come and teach there for the first time. There were about fifteen people who lived there, and we had spent a lot of time fixing the place up and preparing for Rudi's visit. As I was only twenty-one at the time, and having been made a teacher within about five months of meeting Rudi and now with my own ashram, my peacock feathers were getting bigger and brighter and more full of color.

After picking him up at the airport, I drove Rudi to the ashram and started giving him a tour of the first floor, showing him the meditation room we had created. Next we headed up the stairs. About halfway up the stairs I noticed him looking around, so I said, "Rudi, what are you looking for?" He said, "Where's the corpse?" and then he just kept walking. He didn't have to say another word because, believe me, the corpse, i.e., my dead ego, was there immediately. I had gotten so full of myself. I had this big ashram and had spent all this time getting ready. What Rudi was looking for, however, was the surrender, not this twenty-one-year-old punk thinking, "Look at me, look what I did, I'm a big teacher now." What he saw was the energy of arrogance, and he just cut right through it before he took twenty steps into the house. He wanted the death of that level of ego.

That was a pivotal moment in my relationship with Rudi. It was the first time I felt that samurai sword—the steely sharpness and cold precision of his *śakti*, as words—cut right through me. Instead of one slice, it was like in the cartoons when we see a number of layers cut through all in a split second. A multitude of experiences arose within me in that moment. One was the pain and agony of being sliced and diced. Yet, in the same instant, there was the elation of recognizing what part of me I had been focusing on and growing: my plumes! It was an amazing experience that shifted my understanding of the purpose of my relationship with Rudi. Every time I saw him after that I handed him a bag of bones and dust. All he had to say were those three simple words, "Where's the corpse?" This is the power of Grace: the fact that I, being a relatively dense, young, not-so-capable person, somehow had the capacity to hear and respond to that correction. I've never regretted any of it, in terms of the amount of burning that I put myself through, and continue to, in response to the Grace in my life.

Abhinavagupta gives the most eloquent description of the Grace that is the teacher-student relationship:

> *Ultimately, entering into a relationship with a teacher is the conscious choice on the part of the student to place his finite awareness in direct confrontation with the expanded consciousness of the teacher, which is the unbounded consciousness the student wishes to attain. This meeting of finite and infinite consciousness represents the very condition of vimarśa, Consciousness doubling back on itself, the method of realization that abides perpetually in and as the Divine heart. As the student comes into the gaze of the guru, his finite consciousness encounters its own source in the person of the teacher. It releases the inner meditative current, the liberating Grace, the Self-referential nature of the unbounded Consciousness of Śiva. In the process, the teacher binds the student to*

> *service and growth and the inner practices required. The single purpose of the binding is the attainment of freedom. The teacher acts as God's agent to free the student from himself. This all happens through śaktipāta, the will of Śiva that has taken the disciple into the gaze of the guru.*

The purpose of a teacher and lineage is to facilitate, nourish, and guide us toward making permanent, direct contact with the God within our own heart. There is no other purpose. How could there be? There is no other purpose for life.

Grace and the Fivefold Acts of the Divine

The fifth act of in the Fivefold Acts of the Divine is revelation. This is Grace, the freedom-bestowing power of the Divine. It is because concealment exists that Grace must also exist. Remember, Śiva concealed Himself by manifesting the universe. Because He was smart, before He did that, He said, "In this process, even in the unfolding, there will be revelation, because I may forget Myself so much that I won't remember that I forgot Myself." This is the very mystery of Unity, that the experience of duality is held within the experience of Unity, and vice versa.

The concealing starts at *māyā*, the limiting and covering up of the true nature of Consciousness. Grace is the anti-concealing salve. The solution to concealment is Grace. Grace comes along for one reason, not to make life easier or more fun, but to reveal our misunderstanding and free us from the veils of duality. Living in Śiva's Grace is the transcendence of duality. Grace doesn't care whether our life changes. It cares whether our *experience* of life changes.

The processes of unfolding and expressing God's powers is the emission of the universe. That emission is the creation, the maintenance, and the dissolution of life itself, and that process is either concealing itself or revealing itself. It's Grace that it's happening at all. It's also Grace that we can say, "Wait a minute, maybe this moment is a revealing and not a concealing," and we can then make a choice.

It is always a conscious choice. So often, we don't make that choice, and then we wonder, "Why am I not experiencing joy and bliss and freedom?" The essence of Grace, and the highest expression of our own Consciousness, is the capacity to recognize and choose our own state. The purpose of life is the recognition and the freedom of the God who dwells within our heart. All the experiences we go through are trying to take us there. The reason there is reincarnation is because God is benevolent. We don't get only one chance. God is so benevolent He says, "It's your choice; take a thousand lifetimes or take one." The capacity to recognize and transform our own state is the Grace of Consciousness implanted within us. Our capacity to recognize the state of our connection to our highest Self—and to do something about that connection—is the essence of spiritual practice, and of conscious choice.

We don't have to sit around waiting for Grace to appear in our lives. We have this nice fantasy of how perfect everything will be when Grace finally happens to us, which is nothing more than a projection of the mind. As we free ourselves from our mind, as we open our heart and get quiet and still, we will recognize and experience the unbounded Grace that is creating us at every moment. At the same time, at each and every moment of our lives, an experience of joy or freedom or love or gratitude or devotion is always available to us, unless we choose to connect to something else.

Grace is the descent of Consciousness through the *tattvas*, the descent of that pure highest awareness as it seeps down through these levels of consciousness that have condensed into tighter and tighter form. Our experience in life is our experience of consciousness. Whatever level of consciousness we experience creates our experience of life. Because every one of those dimensions of awareness that are expressed in the *tattvas* is available to us at any moment, we get to choose which one we function from. As we're walking along through life with our tension and drama and feeling sorry for ourselves, what would change that experience? Grace, a higher state of consciousness descending into us and revealing to us that we have a choice.

One of the reasons it takes us so long to truly experience Grace is that we're always trying to define what Grace should be giving us. So often, we try to define Grace, which is God's will, as what we have, don't have, or should have had. None of that is the intent of Grace, which is that we live in the joy and effulgence of our own existence. We have all already had the experience of not living in the effulgence of our own existence, which is called suffering.

Grace is ever present. Yet it is our choice to lay down our confusion and be aware of It that truly allows Grace to come through. When Grace shows Itself like a beam of light, and we have a "wow" moment, it is our response to that moment that determines the rest of our life. The challenge for us as *sādhakas* is to remember that moment in the next moment. Unless we can internalize and consciously hold on to and express that experience—not the particular experience but the awareness that it opens in us—we lose it.

We're like a dog with a big bone. We go out and bury it for a rainy day, and then, particularly us old dogs, we forget where in the hell we buried it. In the face of all of our struggles and difficulty, we forget that Grace exists. And then what happens? Our energy and awareness get absorbed into our mind and our ego, and they cannot perceive God, even though they are the expression of God. We forget that effulgent moment and start looking outside ourselves for some sense of fulfillment. Inherent within us, the deepest part of our consciousness wants one thing: fulfillment, completeness, and yet we spend our lives searching for that fulfillment in places that cannot fulfill.

That completeness is found in the simple, profound experience of feeling the fullness of our own heart. Then our difficulties have no grip on us anymore. This is Grace repeating Itself, saying, "Okay, you didn't get it last time; let Me show it to you again." When we have the experience of fullness and completeness, we recognize that no condition in our life, nobody in our life, no dynamic in our life, can take that away from us, although we can choose to give it away.

In many Tantric scriptures it is stated emphatically that only Grace frees. So then we think we don't have to do anything; all we have to do is sit here and Grace will come along and free us. Not exactly. What really frees us is our response to Grace. It's like the old line, you can lead a horse to water, but you can't make it drink. When Grace shows up in our lives, we must drink It. We must be aware of It. Because for so much of our lives we function from a limited consciousness that can't perceive Grace, we somehow miss It. We chalk up those "wow" moments to some fleeting experience.

It is not in everyone's life that Grace shows up as the longing to know God, to know our highest Self. I suggest that the deepest gratitude and devotion—reflected in the choices we make to free ourselves from our limited experience—is the only response to the Grace that has shown up in our life. So focus on Grace. Grace is always present in our life. It is God's will that It is present. We are alive because of Grace, and we experience Grace because of Grace. Do not use your free will to reject the Grace of your own life. How is it that we receive and respond to Grace? By opening our heart, feeling the flow, and surrendering everything.

THE GATE OF DEVOTION

This is such a powerful line in the Bhagavad Gītā that it bears repeating: "Of thousands of men, only a few strive to attain perfection. And of those who strive, only a few know Me in truth." It's such a beautiful statement, and it makes clear one thing: the importance and power of our wish to grow. What distinguishes one person from the other thousands who strive? What distinguishes the person who knows God in truth? It is the strength of their wish. Rudi built his entire freedom on that premise, on discovering that wish within himself when it wasn't there, holding on to the wish when something tried to get in the way of it, and surrendering himself to that wish no matter what the cost. As he told us regularly, "the wish is the most powerful force within a human being."

The fundamental energy and awareness behind the wish to grow is devotion. Only our devotion to God sees us through. Only our devotion to God allows us to surrender in the face of all adversity and be willing to sacrifice any level of limited consciousness we find ourselves functioning from. The energy of Śiva's Grace is not different than Parā, His will, and the stillpoint of truly living in His Grace is devotion. Devotion is the conscious opening to God's Grace, and the offering back of our lives in gratitude. It is this self-reflective response to God's Grace: "I offer my life in service, without thought of price, to do with as He chooses."

What we are trying to do through our practice is to awaken those five Divine forces—Consciousnesss, bliss, will, knowledge, and action—within ourselves, allow them to dissolve our limited understanding of our true Self, and begin to live from them. It isn't just interior or exterior practice that does the work but our devotion. By practicing the internal meditations, we are awakening those highest energies specifically within our psychic body and allowing them to rise through, creating a place for those goddesses to rest. Not any less important than those practices is the inner discipline required to actually live by those powers and states of consciousness. That discipline is the devotion.

As we discussed above, Grace is the freedom-bestowing power of the Divine. Amazingly, Grace is not only Śiva's freedom trying to show itself in us. It is also our capacity and willingness to respond to Grace that is Grace Itself, and the response to Grace is devotion. Devotion is the fire of Consciousness in which we sacrifice our own limitation. To be clear, sacrificing our individuality and our lives is meaningless if we don't also sacrifice our tensions, our holding on to our limited perspective, and our limited willingness to serve. As Rudi said to us, the only thing you must give up is your tension. Why would he say such a simple thing? He's really saying that the ultimate tension is holding on to our limited self, because that's the thing we're always willing to fight about, rather than fighting for our freedom.

During our *sādhana*, as we make the individual effort to cultivate a wish to grow, to let go, and to understand, we begin to say to ourselves, "I may not fully understand God's will, but I do understand that mine hasn't gotten me very far. In fact, what mine has brought me is pain and agony." Even as we begin our practice, we can find enough devotion in ourselves to say, "Okay, I'll let go for a while. I've had enough fun doing this lifetime after lifetime."

Nityananda says, "As is your devotion, so is your liberation." The Bhagavad Gītā states, "I am the ritual action, I am the sacrifice, I am the offering. I am the myrrh, I am the mantra, I am the clarified butter, I am the fire, and I am the oblation." It further elaborates, "Renounce the fruit of action to understand devotion. It is the giving up of the fruit of any action that is prompted by desire that is the true understanding of desirelessness." Desirelessness and devotion are not separate or different.

Sacrificing Our Limitations Is Devotion

The central theme of the Bhagavad Gītā is the internal battle within Arjuna, the warrior-prince and hero of the story, about doing his duty, which is to the will of God. His dilemma was whether to fight in a great battle in which he would inevitably kill many of his own kinsmen. But slaughtering his family was just details. It was the soap opera. Only devotion to the will of God is real, and Kṛṣṇa taught Arjuna that his highest duty was to serve God's will. We could say that devotion is our duty to our own freedom. Devotion is not doing what we want to do; it is to the will of God. There's only one thing to remember about the will of God, which is that it is the perpetual expansion of freedom and joy. Devotion is the *homa* of fire, the ritual sacrifice we perform each day by saying, "I want to be free of this misunderstanding, and I am willing to sacrifice myself."

Devotion is expressed through our conscious choices and disciplined actions. We make choices that serve God and not ourselves, no matter what the personal costs. Devotion isn't real if it's not expressed in response to the Grace in our life. What other response could we have to Grace but the devotion of our own lives to that freedom?

How does the test of our devotion come to us most often? As a request. Our life requests something of us, which may be in the form of our partner, our children, our teacher, our boss, etc. This is Grace requesting something of us. This is, to use Rudi's language, God testing us. Are we really devoted? Or are we devoted only when it's convenient? Are we devoted when it's easy? Are we devoted when it doesn't cost us anything? I'm sure we can all say yes to that. The issue is, are we devoted when it's *not* easy? Are we devoted when it costs us something? Are we devoted when it requires us to change? Only then is it really a conscious choice. Either we choose to change or we choose not to change. We talk, dream, and fantasize a lot about how much we're willing to give, but when our life requests that we express freedom by giving and serving unconditionally, this is the test of our devotion to that freedom. This testing happens in every dimension of ourselves.

Devotion must be expressed, and it must be expressed at the time it's asked for. Devotion is the only appropriate response to Grace. If we're not prepared to respond by sacrificing our limited capacity at the time it's called for—whenever life asks it of us—then it's not true devotion. This is about entering into the gate of devotion. Once we've entered into the bullring and truly committed ourselves to growth and freedom, there is no escape. We close the door, nail it shut, and proclaim, "This is where I will make my choices, from within the field of Consciousness." This surrendering of our will and living in God's will is the expression of our devotion. Do not let the form of your life create the experience of your life. Where is the form in devotion? There is none. Its essence is no form.

Devotion and Surrender Are the Same

Nityananda says, "The ocean is vast. The amount we take from it is dependent on the size of the container we bring to it." In your endeavor to find your liberation, it is the size of the container that you bring to it that determines the discovery. You are trying to fit the infinite within your own heart. The energy of Grace, of a lineage and a teacher, is there to help expand the size of the container. Your response to that Grace determines the depth you receive. All the surrender, the service, the sacrifice, the slicing and dicing of the ego, is simply our response to Grace in our lives, which can only be devotion. Devotion is the fire of Consciousness in which we surrender and sacrifice our own limitation, and service is the expression of devotion. When you find yourself with some lesser response to the Grace in your life, stop and ask, "What is it that I really want? How am I responding to God?" The third act in the thirty-six-act play of Śiva is Divine will. The very same act of the thirty-six-act play that is the drama of your own life is your own will. The leverage in this play is in will, which is your wish to grow.

Vimarśa, the self-reflective capacity to know ourselves, is God's love for us. Devotion is our love for God, and our willingness to sacrifice in that love. When we feel devotion, what emerge are surrender, gratitude, joy, and simplicity. Abhinavagupta tells us of that experience, "The entire universe shines forth within the Self, consciously articulating the universe as an expression of the nectar of sweetness of its own Self-awareness." He ends with, "I offer my homage to the wondrous delight of that Consciousness which is supreme and unsurpassable, and which is effulgent by Its own light." This is a description of *prakāśa* and *vimarśa*, the awareness and the experience of life that is our Divine right, and the depth of understanding that is available to each of us.

Devotion is simply the surrendering into God's perspective. Our devotion to God is the letting go of our limited awareness so that we can see life from His perspective. I'd say it's a pretty good trade-up. It is through our internal practice that we awaken our contact with Śiva's Divine energies and activate them so that they begin to function in our lives at their highest levels. Through these energies, we find their Source, which is Śiva, God's Consciousness. If devotion is living in God's Consciousness, how and when do we realize that? When we surrender our limited perspective and begin to truly experience our life from those higher levels of consciousness, as Śiva.

What we come to understand over time is that devotion is not devotion to anything. It is the recognition of our own Self, *vimarśa*, self-reflective awareness. There is extraordinary power in the path of devotion, the path of recognizing ourselves as God. What greater devotion to God could we have than that recognition? That's all He really wants from us.

Devotion, Sādhana, and the Upāyas

When we first come to our spiritual practice, we experience our *sādhana* as something we are doing. In the *upāyas*, it is *āṇavopāya*, the path of effort, that describes this. We are sitting down to meditate. We are breathing. We are doing *pūjā*. We are doing service. This is the path of *āṇavopāya*, and we have the sense that we are doing it. When we do that long enough, we begin to have the sense that something deeper within us is the cause of our effort. This shift starts to move us into the path of energy, the path of *śakti*, called *śāktopāya*. We feel the flow, the *śakti* of life, and it is expressing itself through us. While there's an effort, it's a different effort. We're living in the flow. That flow of a higher awareness takes us to *śāmbhavopāya*, the path of awareness. Here, we are aware that we are doing nothing. Even what appear to be dualistic experiences of us doing *sādhana*, such as bowing in devotion, are ultimately perceived as Śiva expressing Himself as us.

In the path of *anupāya*, the no-path path, all experience of duality has been dispersed, and Śiva's Grace and bliss simply express themselves. Remember, Śiva's bliss isn't dependent on any condition—it emerges out of the awareness of His own existence. It is simply the joy of expressing its own self-awareness, *vimarśa*. This is why it is the transcendence of conditionality that frees us to live in bliss.

It is from bliss that God's will emerges to express that joy. Therefore, shouldn't what emerges out of us be the will to express our own joy? If we're not experiencing that, then perhaps we're not living in God's will. Perhaps we're pushing from our own willfulness, trying to create something, and missing the simplicity of that joy, the essential bliss of being. Remember, Parā is Śiva's expression of His own will, and her abode is *dvādaśānta*, the place from which manifestation emerges, the place from which we came, as if dropped out of a cosmic eyedropper. This happens because of Śiva's will. When we talk about surrender, it's not about surrendering this thing or that thing. The highest surrender is the surrendering of our will to God, and this is the highest devotion.

In some ways we can't perceive that it's that simple. This is part of the whole mystery of *sādhana* in the sense that we have to make an effort, we have to reach inside, we have to use our own consciousness, our wish, and our own will to penetrate into some deeper part of ourselves. When you do that, and you make contact with that deeper part of yourself, then let it open. Keep your awareness there. You could say that devotion is keeping your awareness on that experience of openness and not allowing anything to close it down. That requires tremendous devotion. Then it's not this big discipline or drudgery but a natural expression of gratitude. Understand that the part of you that can't sustain that openness, your ego, is powerful. It will create dynamics and conditions to see if it can steal the energy of that experience of openness.

Eventually, what we discover—and this is amazing—is that we exist because of Śiva's devotion. We are the expression of Śiva's devotion—to Himself. Then any experience of dualistic devotion starts to be transformed. So be devoted, even be dualistically devoted to Śiva, because if you're truly devoted and willing to surrender your perspective to hold on to that devotion, you will find a still deeper awareness of devotion. You will understand that Śiva's devotion is to the expression of His own freedom and bliss.

What qualities does devotion require? Commitment, service, surrender, humility, gratitude, courage, sacrifice. In order to lift ourselves out of our limited perspective and function from a higher awareness that already exists within us, our *sādhana* is to live by these qualities, and to recognize when we resist and are no longer living from them. We are gaining access to the highest Consciousness, and that happens by penetrating through and freeing ourselves from dualistic awareness. That happens first in our meditation, and then later because we can hold on to the awareness that we found in our meditation as we open our eyes and face life.

Every one of us has had the incredible experience of sitting down and finding God in our heart. What's even more incredible is how often we open our eyes and immediately lose sight of Him. From the dualistic point of view, our devotion is to finding God with our eyes open. The point of meditation is to discover something that's already within us, that's powerful enough that we bow down to it. That's why meditation and *sādhana* are so often described as "discipline." It is doing our practice day after day, year after year, decade after decade until we make that discovery that reveals to us the depth of our own devotion. Our discipline is a reflection of our devotion.

Most importantly, we must consciously express our devotion through ever-deeper effort and ever-deeper surrendering. When we open our heart, even in the expression of devotion we are absorbed still deeper into the source that's given us the capacity for devotion in the first place. Ultimately, what we seek to experience is not our devotion to God but God's devotion to us. Open and receive that, because this is a place of simplicity that you can live from.

In a certain way, all other means are meaningless without that depth of devotion. You must find a place in yourself that is devoted to living God's will, which is that you live in joy. When you find that joy, when you recognize the seed of it, then plant it, water it, nurture it, make sure it gets some sunlight, and let it grow within you. When the weeds start to come into the garden, pull them out. From that place you can begin to penetrate and discover the source of that simplicity and joy, which is God's heart, and which is also your heart.

So start with devotion. You might think, "I'm not that devoted yet." Start with it anyway, because that is how you'll find it. Devotion is Śiva's expression of joy and freedom, with no form, content, story, or drama attached. It is just pure devotion. If you simply offered yourself into that joy, the first thing that would happen is you would discover it. The second thing would be that you'd never let go of it. Devotion is the fire of Consciousness in which you sacrifice your unwillingness to be free. If you're lucky you'll have a teacher who's throwing kerosene on that fire on a regular basis.

THE GATE OF SELFLESS SERVICE

The Bhagavad Gītā says, "If you are unable to seek Me through the practice of yoga, then devote yourself entirely to My works. By performing actions for My sake, you will attain perfection." In other words, if you can't do yoga, if you can't take a breath, if you can't feel your heart, then serve. The reason for this is that service begins to transform our energy. It retunes our resonance from one of incessant demand to the simplicity of wishing to give and to receive. Service is an expression of the highest Consciousness, and, in my view, it completes the gates. You cannot separate any of those four gates, as they are what complete the container.

In my own teaching and practice, the reason service is emphasized so much is because it is the active expression of devotion; it is devotion in action. When you serve from gratitude, from truly living within the Grace of your life, you always want to serve, because it is the simple response and expression of gratitude for the experience of the unbounded joy of your own existence. We serve at whatever level we can in order to expose a deeper capacity to serve. In the process, we will come up against all our limitations, resistance, and hidden agendas. True serving is doing whatever you have been called on to do. Serving God starts with serving the people in front of you. Even serving at the highest doesn't negate your duty to serve in simple ways, such as sweeping the stairs when they need sweeping.

Selflessly Serving, Selflessly Receiving

True service has two aspects: selflessly serving, which is giving what is wanted without being asked; and selflessly receiving, which is receiving what is given without asking for that which was not. This is true service and surrender, the very center of the lotus called bliss, because it arises from the profound abundance of simply being alive. It arises from the experience of completeness and effulgence—of being so full we give without worrying about how we might be diminished in the process. It is being so full we can simply receive and experience what manifests in our life as what we need. In fact, need isn't even part of the equation. It is being so full that need doesn't arise.

This state of consciousness emerges from understanding that God's will truly functions within us. The profound sweetness of that experience—of living in the subtle balance point between giving what is wanted and receiving what is given—marks the end of struggling with life, the end of needing to reach for anything. We simply recognize that our life is projecting itself from the highest Consciousness within us, creating the perfection of that experience.

Service is the willingness to truly serve God's will, but in order to accomplish that, we will come up against the moment-by-moment challenges to doing so—of letting go or thinking we shouldn't have to serve. As discussed earlier, traditional training in spiritual practice required prospective students to dig ditches for twelve years before receiving teachings. This was a test for gurus to determine if potential *sādhakas* were serious about serving and about receiving what they were asking for. Were they prepared to pay the price? Were they willing to give up their life? Were they prepared to dig the ditch and throw the corpse of their misunderstanding into it? Twelve years is a long time to prove one's worthiness.

Rudi recounted that at an early age, he heard the voice of God say to him, "Never forget, you're not here to serve the world. You're here to serve Me." What an incredible experience to have had as a child. Without negating the world, he understood that serving people and situations is how we serve God's will. So we serve in the world; we serve people and situations. If we're lucky enough we have a child to serve. If we're really lucky we have a guru to serve.

The people right in front of us, the people we love, are where we start. If we demand they give us something in return, we're not serving them; we're serving ourselves. Service isn't even just giving another person what they want; it's not giving them what they don't want, which is our garbage, our need to have life be the way we think it ought to be, or our need for people to change in order for us to love them. How great a service would it be to the people around us if we could just simply be in the flow and give of ourselves?

In our relationships with the people we love, if we function from a place of demanding anything from them other than the possibility of loving them, then we're expressing our conditions and our will. Yeah, you say, but what if I love them and they still don't change? Whether they change or not is irrelevant. What's relevant is whether we change, and whether we did our best to love and serve them. If we can do that, we get something groovy out of it, which is freedom. We get to function, experience, and express from the unconditional joy of needing nothing outside ourselves in order to have the highest experience within ourselves. So while it looks like we're giving up this or giving in to that person, all we're really doing is offering ourselves in service.

In serving people and situations in the world, we begin to understand the underlying energetic dynamic of our existence, which ultimately leads to the awareness of serving Śiva. While we may still perceive them as outside ourselves, and therefore different and separate from us, we begin to recognize the people and situations in our lives as energy. We experience and understand that serving the people in our lives, engaging in challenging and difficult situations, and doing so from a place of openness and joy, is how we serve Śiva. It's in that way that we truly serve the highest.

SERVICE IS JOY

From the very beginning of our *sādhana*, our service must come from its own source, which is joy. Gratitude is the emergent quality of joy and freedom and service. Gratitude is *vimarśa*, because it arises from the recognition of our own experience. We all know how wonderful it feels to just give something to someone else without condition. When we can give and serve without all the attachment and demand and negotiation, it means we've really let go; we're just breathing and serving and allowing the flow of energy between us and another person to express itself in our actions.

If we can serve from joy, we function from an entirely new place in ourselves. Instead of bringing tension and contraction to our effort to serve, we bring openness, awareness, and the self-reflective capacity to see that while it may be difficult, we'll do it anyhow. We understand that when it's difficult it is because we're still trying to serve through our own need.

Service is not negotiation, and if it comes from some hidden agenda it's not really service but an attempt to manipulate life into giving us what we think we should have. We all know the resonance of agenda, and we often try to fake service. When you feel that agenda, serve so that you are using the action of service to understand instead of mindlessly doing the action. Then there's no distinction between what is and isn't service; there is simply the joyous offering of ourselves.

True service has the power to uncover our layers of confusion and unwillingness to truly discover what life is about. Serving isn't about you. It isn't about what you want. It is about what God wants. Don't wait for someone to convince you that you should serve. Your life is trying to suggest this to you at every moment. I can say from personal experience that it costs nothing, because all the things we think we have to give up in order to truly give are ultimately recognized as meaningless. Service will expose everything in you that you think you shouldn't have to give up, yet these are the very things you should give up.

The single purpose of action is the acquisition of the highest knowledge, the involution of our own consciousness back from the experience of the duality of the world to the understanding of where the world comes from. The Bhagavad Gītā says of the yoga of action, "In order to truly understand action, you must be free from the fruit of action, detached from the expectation of any result of the action."

When we are quiet and still, we experience wholeness, the feeling that we don't need to do anything. Yet we must, because true action, true service, is the expression of wholeness, and it is through such action that we transcend duality. We understand we aren't acting for the sake of getting anything in return but simply because we are expressing the joy and will of God. This is selflessly serving and selflessly receiving, and when we do it, we feel how incredible, simple, and unencumbered it is.

True action is the expression of consciousness, and never separate from it. If we are individuated expressions of Divine Consciousness, then we are Śiva in action. It is only when we misunderstand this that we think we're doing something instead of being done. To be a servant of God is to recognize that we are just pawns in the game of life, and we are happy to be the pawn. It is glorious to be the pawn, because all our actions are designed for one thing: to allow the will of God, which is the perpetual expansion of freedom and joy, to express itself.

There is never a moment we shouldn't serve. Service is foundational to any possibility of freeing ourselves from ourselves. We can't free ourselves from the limitations of ego if we can't express and extend into the world the understanding that it is really about allowing a higher purpose to express itself through us. That's what we are serving. All the details and the different things we do to serve are really only different acts of the play. How powerful, this voice of God telling Rudi, "You are here to serve Me and not the world." Service is how we come to understand that statement. Duality is misperception. Liberation is the understanding that there is no "us" and "them," yet we serve God by serving the world.

There is only one service, which is to God's will. That highest will expresses itself on every level; helping someone up the stairs is service, for example. The point is, we must serve at every level, because there is no higher or lower service within this understanding. If we sit down and offer our life in service, from that point on there is no question, confusion, or doubt about what is and isn't service. Our whole life is service. Ultimately, it is only Self, only God, that we serve.

In the context of our larger discussion, service is the willingness to take that fifth Divine energy, the power of action, and perform the actions of God, the actions of giving. These are the actions that arise from the Divine knowledge of what we're here to do, and from the will that emerges from the bliss of being a conscious entity.

SERVICE AND THE UPĀYAS

Āṇavopāya, the path of individual effort, is the effort to begin to function beyond our own need, to be willing to let go of our need and place someone else's need above our own. *Āṇavopāya*, the fundamental basis of spiritual *sādhana*, is the first crack in the walls of the prison of our own limited consciousness. It is the first crack that shows us that we can live in a bigger place than we have been. Then the struggle isn't to control; it's a struggle to let go.

Service in *āṇavopāya* is the wish to serve God. Well, guess what? Imagine that all those jackasses out there in the world have the word "God" written across their foreheads. We all know the story of Jesus coming to the door as a beggar and people dismissing him. We can serve for the rest of our life, but if we're grumpy about it we're just going to get constipation. That's not service. The willingness to just give, whether or not others give back, takes a lot of courage and surrender, but if we can do it long enough, we begin to function from *śāktopāya*. Our understanding shifts from "I'm doing" to the recognition that "God is doing through me." We experience Unity in diversity. We are still our individuated self, and we see life happening through us. God is doing through us, expressing His Divine will of perpetual freedom through us.

Whatever dynamic we find ourselves in, as we function from the willingness to give in simple ways and do what's needed when it's asked, or even before it's asked, we begin to let go of our own limitations and offer the energy of our own life into serving God. We live in the flow of life. This is what's meant by sacrifice: the burning of our limited consciousness, the offering of our own life force back to its source. This is *śāktopāya*, transforming our experience of living in the grip of our own mind and our misunderstanding, which is caused by the thought-construct of our sense of separateness. This is how we free ourselves from the one fundamental thought-construct that we function from, which is: I am separate. This is the basic foundation of our individual experience, which translates into the mantra of stupidity: "What's gonna happen to me?"

As we learn to function from this flow of energy, we see how that mantra continually repeats itself in our resonance, and we surrender it. We offer the density of our awareness back into the flow, refine it within our psychic body, and extend from that place. We begin to truly offer our own life in service. There have been great saints in every tradition. What they have in common is the resonance that functions within them. Their life is their offering to God in service, and they make that offering in the world. They don't sit in a cave. They're engaged in the world and allow their own energy to be part of that flow. They serve from that place of offering to God, and whatever limitations they confront in the process, they surrender and burn in the fire of Consciousness, the fire of *kuṇḍalinī*, of flow.

The shift in capacity to simply receive what is given, without reaching for that which is not, is really the test of whether we will live in God's will. When we surrender our incessant demand that life be the way we think it should be, we simply receive what is being given and recognize the perfection of that. Our misunderstanding, our experience of not being complete, is burned in the fire of God's will. We begin to truly live in service of God, understanding that God is doing through us. If we do that long enough, experiencing the joy of our own individuated existence, we begin to understand that God is not doing through us, God is just doing. This is *śāmbhavopāya*, the path of awareness. God isn't doing *through* me; God is doing *as* me.

Surrender Is the Key

10

Surrender Is the Key

If the four gates discussed in the last chapter—inner practice, Grace, devotion, and selfless service—are the entryways into our own heart, into the field of Consciousness from which we arose, we can think of the practice of surrender as the key that unlocks each of those gates. Recall that the central lotus in the Śiva's Trident *maṇḍala* is a depiction of bliss, a representation of surrender and unconditionality. This is because bliss is the state of surrender and unconditionality, meaning there is no condition that can ever affect our permanent state of joy.

In any authentic practice, surrender, ultimately, is the foundation, the structure, the wiring, and the final building in terms of our spiritual freedom. As I've said, the first and most important instruction I give students is "open your heart." The practice of surrender starts there, because we must first surrender everything that keeps us from opening our heart. Next, we must surrender everything that blocks the flow in us from showing itself. Then we must surrender everything we don't want to surrender.

We must consciously decide if liberation is what we want, because it is not possible without surrender. *Svātantrya*—the absolute, autonomous freedom that is the underlying field of awareness in the *maṇḍala*—is not separate or different than the state of surrender. This is the consciousness of freedom, the experience we seek, the purpose of spiritual practice, the purpose of our life. In deciding that liberation is what we want, we must understand we are also deciding to live a life of surrender, which is the conscious choice to let go and joyously offer our limited self back to God. This is how we come to recognize our true Self. The point of *sādhana*, and the point of our life, is to experience the joy of our own existence. If we're serious, then we surrender everything that gets in the way of that experience. As Nityananda says, "Surrender everything that keeps you from Śiva."

There is never a moment or situation in life in which surrender isn't the key to our freedom. Surrender is the highest form of the consciousness of freedom, the highest expression of our own choice and our own will. What could be more powerful than surrendering ourselves and our will? Every dynamic we find ourselves in offers the same fundamental choice: to open our heart or to close it. We must make a conscious choice to be free of our limited understanding. This too is surrender. There is no level of interaction in which surrender isn't valid. It is *śakti*; it is bliss, yet from our side of duality, we must practice surrender until it becomes the state we live in. In order to arrive at that state we must make choices that express our willingness to surrender.

The highest prayer in the Sufi tradition is *Fana fi Allah*, which means: May I be annihilated in God. How beautiful. The same Divine will that creates and sustains the universe is our will, given to us to do with as we choose. This is the freedom of the gift of Grace. Divine will is the perpetual expansion of freedom and joy. We were created for that purpose, in that purpose, and to serve that purpose. Let's choose to live a life of joy—right here, right now—and surrender everything that gets in the way of that choice. Now that I've described how easy it is, let's discuss how hard it is.

SURRENDERING OUR PERSPECTIVE

There are a number of dimensions of surrender we need to function from because there are a number of traps outside the door of Unity. One of them is our perspective. Since it is outside the door of Unity, our perspective is of duality. Duality can only experience duality. All our perspectives of who we think we are, what we think we need, where we think we have to go, what we are or aren't willing to sacrifice, are all limited if we function from outside our center, if we function from our mind, which, as we know from the *tattvas*, is several levels down from the highest Consciousness.

Our *sādhana* is about transforming our perspective, and to transform our perspective we must let go of it. We must understand that we function from a limited perspective. It is only our surrender and devotion that enable us to live from God's perspective and see the big picture, and, believe me, it's a really big picture. It's only when we somehow think we're the center of the universe that we get confused.

We are so attached to our thoughts and perspectives because we think we are actually doing something, which is the very perspective that needs to be surrendered. Surrender is also trusting that we can let go of our perspective, our need to control, and finding that place inside that trusts that life is expressing itself perfectly as it is. The reason we don't surrender is that we don't trust God. It is the surrendering of our perspective that leads to the possibility of seeing God's perspective. The practice is to not act from our own perspective. This is a twofold practice: non-acting and surrendering. We can't act on our perspective and surrender it at the same time. That's just more duality.

There's always a dynamic interchange between our own inner experience—the one we seek to create through our meditation practices, *sādhana*, service, and devotion—and the expression of that experience as our world. The world we see when we open our eyes in many ways is not the same world the next person sees when they open their eyes. It ought to be, but it's not. There's part of the rub, we don't all see things from the same perspective.

Stop trying to fit life into your perspective and filter it through your understanding. Instead, let the highest understanding open and show itself to you. It will not fit into the duffle bag of your understanding. It just won't fit. Let go of your limited perspective. You won't arrive at the highest truth from that place. It's impossible to understand Unity from duality. Seek to know God's perspective; cease to be so attached to your own. Even when you find yourself in the middle of an argument, understand that the possibility of surrendering your perspective may lead you to see God's perspective.

Surrendering the Mind and Thoughts

The Spandakārikā says, "The rise in the bound soul of all sorts of thought marks the disappearance of the bliss of supreme immortality. On account of this he loses his independence." Abhinavagupta says, "For those whose minds are not purified, even continuous practice will not bring freedom. Even those initiated into the Saiva mysteries and [who] possess a means of attaining enlightenment fail in their efforts as a result of mind. The mind must be purified." The mind is the device the ego uses to sustain itself. As long as our identity is wrapped around our mind, we are bound. When our identity is wrapped around God's heart, we are free. There are no thoughts in God's heart.

As a thought arises, we give it form because we put energy into it, thus declaring its validity. The Spanda school of Kashmir Shaivism suggests that as a thought arises, before it takes form and leads to action, we should surrender it. What happens most of the time is that a thought arises, it does its song and dance, and if we don't engage it, it subsides. It is just energy arising and subsiding. When we surrender our thoughts we are surrendering ourselves. Rudi says, surrender yourself and then you can change. Surrender yourself and you will be changed. Your consciousness will be transformed.

The ego and its grip on us are real. I'm not suggesting that our pain doesn't hurt or our confusion isn't real. I am suggesting we can be free of it by surrendering, which is the highest practice for freeing ourselves from the grip of the ego. As we consciously choose not to engage in any mental, emotional, or psychological dramas, we're recognizing the limited dimension that's functioning within us, and we're surrendering by not allowing it to dictate our action and reaction. We take the energy out of it, pull it back inside, and consume it, creating nourishment for our psychic body. This is *śāktopāya*. This is sacrifice. This is *śakti*, the burning of lesser things, the transmuting of dense energy into Consciousness and flow.

It is at the very moment of contraction that the possibility of openness exists. This is where our self-reflective awareness comes in and we recognize: I am contracted; my attachment, my misunderstanding, my thought-construct, my willingness to serve only myself, is the energy and resonance I'm functioning from in this moment. Because we're self-aware we can see our contraction and choose not to function from that place. This is how discipline and devotion can lead us to surrender.

You're either aware you're stuck in your mind or you're not. When you realize there's a boundary to the internalization and refinement of your own awareness, just sit there with it and let go. All of a sudden your thoughts fall away. Thoughts are just the perspective of a limited thing called the mind. Until you are free from attachment to your mind, you will be bound by your mind. The problem isn't the mind itself but your attachment to the identity it creates. Stop listening to and fighting with your mind. Surrender your mind and your struggle with it. Find a deeper place. Feel the wish to grow. Open your heart and let go.

Arriving at a place of openness, stillness, desirelessness, and knowing God's will requires enough practice that we have freed ourselves from our limited thought-construct. Tantric exposition categorically states that thoughts are the source of bondage because limited knowing in the form of thought-construct is what binds and limits our awareness. *Śāktopāya* is transforming the limited awareness that functions at the level of mind and putting it into flow. It is the understanding that our thought-constructs bind us, and that *nirvikalpa samādhi*, the thought-free state, is not just an idea but the conscious choice to free ourselves from the bonds of our own mind. At that very moment, we know there's a deeper place we can function from, and we let go. We surrender even our thoughts.

It is only in the surrendering of the mind and the attachment to thought that we are freed from the constraints of thought-construct. Abhinavagupta says, "Freedom from thought-construct is the miracle of the dissolution of human consciousness into Divine Consciousness." In other words, human existence is for the discovery of Divine existence. That's its purpose. Why fight with our thoughts when we can connect to Divine Consciousness?

SURRENDERING THE NEED TO CONTROL

We must start by surrendering control over things, people, ideas, thoughts, and the dynamics in our life until we reach the point where we recognize we are not surrendering anything but our misunderstanding. Surrender in *āṇavopāya* is letting go of our need to control how somebody else looks, acts, and feels; it is letting go of our need to control every moment of every day of our life. Tension arises from our need to control life and our inability to accept life as it is. In other words, it arises from our perspective, especially when someone else doesn't agree with it. This is how we create the *granthi* inside ourselves; it is the continual wrapping of tension around Spirit. We can either blame ourselves for having a thought or perspective, we can fight to defend it, or we can surrender it. Any particular thought or perspective we have may be right, but it's our attachment to it and our willingness to get tense about it that's the issue.

We must surrender our idea of control because it is the reinforcing factor of the veil of duality that we are the doer, that we are doing anything. The opposite of surrendering to God's will is willfulness, the need and attempt to control life. It is our complete misunderstanding that we need to change life in order to be happy, and our perpetual attempts to do so are what make us so unhappy. Isn't that interesting?

Every dynamic we find ourselves in is the Grace of God giving us the opportunity to discover our own bliss. Until we can find it in all of them, we won't discover true joy, because it only takes one thing to hook us. As Rumi says, "When I surrender, I always find myself holding on to one thing." It doesn't matter what one thing we hold on to as a condition or circumstance that determines our experience. If it still hooks us, we're still hooked.

The devotion deep inside us that knows there's a deeper awareness we can live from is what allows us to surrender, even when we don't understand and we're petrified to let go of our need to control. Ultimately, we understand we only really have the illusion of control. We come to the point where we ask, "Why would I want to control anything? Why would I suggest I'm smarter than God? Why wouldn't I let God show me my life, and the perfection of my own existence?"

The consciousness of surrender happens in the very moment surrender is needed. You must make the conscious choice to surrender in the same moment the patterns, tensions, insecurities, and fears arise. As Rudi said, "Tension is the expression of limitation. Surrender is the expression of ability." There is no story in surrender; it isn't surrendering this or that. It is simply letting go. It is you letting go of you letting go. Surrender is the highest trust. It is the complete letting go of everything in your life and trusting that it will show itself in its own perfection.

Surrendering Attachments

After the challenge of surrendering control comes the challenge of surrendering attachments. The equation around attachment is this: The thing we're attached to isn't the issue; the *attachment* to the thing is the issue. Whether it is a thing, a person, a perspective, a belief, a non-belief, or a doubt, we cannot be free if we are attached. It's not what we've surrendered that matters. It's what we haven't surrendered that matters. It's not what we've surrendered that binds us. It's what we haven't surrendered that binds us. As Rudi put it, "To surrender is to surrender completely, not just what you wish to surrender or think needs to be surrendered, but a total letting go." Rudi's mantra to himself at the end of his life was: "I surrender all things, thought, form, matter, and sound. Everything." That was his way of penetrating through the powers of emission.

Nityananda says to us, "True desirelessness is freedom." In other words, taste the pleasures of life, but never lose yourself in the process. Love your life. Celebrate it. Consume it. Devour it. Just don't be attached to it. This is one of the fundamental tenets of Tantric practices. There is nothing to be rejected. There is nothing that is not part of the whole, therefore having is never a problem, except for the unhappiness that surfaces in our attachment to whether we have or don't have. You can want anything in this life; you just can't be attached to it.

It isn't even relevant what we are attached to because attachment is only about one thing: our attachment to our identity, that is, who we think we are. Anytime you find yourself reaching for something you think you need, let go. Everything you need in your life is there at every moment of your life. If it's not there, you don't need it. Sometimes we need something in our life for some period of time and then it's gone. It means we don't need it anymore.

We're so afraid to surrender and sacrifice our attachments, but we sacrifice our own freedom in order to hold on to them. Our unwillingness to surrender is, in fact, the surrendering of our own freedom! At some point we stop wanting all of this other stuff more than we want to live with God because we understand that wanting all the other stuff is keeping us from living with God. So then, with our own will, of our own choice, we let go.

Whenever we are surrendering anything, the first thing we are doing is letting go of our limited understanding of it, recognizing that in letting go of our limited understanding, we now have access to the energy previously bound in that misunderstanding. We can then draw that energy inside and refine it, which will gives us still more energy to refine our own understanding.

If we don't have the courage to be honest with ourselves about the life experience we are creating, we will never come to the place of surrender. As we turn inward and offer our misunderstanding back to Śiva, our experience of life begins to change. The moments that are uncomfortable and difficult and that require us to change are the very moments of freedom. Even really challenging situations, like your teacher flying into the side of a mountain, become opportunities to understand freedom. To do that, we have to surrender our perspective and see from God's perspective. You can't hold on to yourself and change at the same time. That's why I often say, "Surrender, and allow yourself to be changed."

Surrendering Our Patterns

Our patterns are simply our resistance to change, and they are the result of our not changing. Patterns are how we use our will to say, "No, I don't want a different experience in life. I just want to keep doing what I'm doing." Patterns and tensions coalesce together and create the blocks, the *granthi*, in our psychic body. Dissolving patterns is a twofold process. It's always Śiva and Śakti working. First, there is the conscious awareness of the pattern and the part of us that is doing it, and the surrendering of the perpetual repetition of that. Then, there is the drawing of the energy out of the pattern and back into flow that allows us to actually transmute the density of the energy trapped within a pattern.

Our patterns are our incessant need and demand to control life. This is the most powerful pattern. Instead of living in the effulgence of Śiva's will, we're constantly pounding on life, usually in the form of our partner, our children, or other loved ones, to change. Every time you want to react or complain, just stop. Open your heart, feel the flow, and surrender. Not some of the time, but every time. This is an incredibly important discipline. If you do this, you will come to that moment of liberation. This is all you need to do, but it only works if you use your God-given right to choose your state and experience.

We try to complicate it and think we have to do more than just this, but it's that simple. There's no guilt involved or penance you have to do. There's simply letting go and saying, "I won't do this again." It's about moving into a deeper internal place than the place that created the pattern, and recognizing, "I created that because I misunderstood. I don't want to keep living in this place. I'll go deeper." Then whatever action or service is required to undo it, you do out of gratitude and joy. Only the mind wants to complicate it and make a drama out of it. A pattern is simply bound energy. It has nothing to do with details or form.

Surrendering Our Individuality

Ultimately, there is only one thing we must surrender. We may surrender a thousand other things just getting to it, but that one thing is our ego, our sense of separation. That is where the pain is. It is interesting to compare how Rudi and Nityananda describe the experience of surrender in two different-same ways. Rudi says, "Surrender yourself, and then you can change." He didn't say, change and then you can surrender. Nityananda says, "Merge into the heart-space and your individual identity is dissolved." They are both describing the same experience: the surrendering of our separation from our own Divine Source, which is liberation.

When you get to that point when you've freed yourself from any attachment to your individuality, your work is about to begin. Think, "Hallelujah. Let's get rid of this whole thing called 'me' as fast as I can so I can get on with it." Rudi described stopping short of that as going to a big feast and then just standing at the door and eating peanuts. Getting rid of all your stuff—your patterns and attachments—is just eating peanuts. Enter the feast, and remember that you're trying to penetrate through any sense of separation, because if there's no separation there can be no duality, only Unity. When you start to glimpse that you are Śiva, surrender is like flushing the toilet. So you have to do all that work surrendering your thoughts, control, attachments, and patterns to come to the point of recognizing that you didn't have to do all that stuff.

Once you get serious and stop fighting with all the nonsense you fight to be free of, you start to get down to the reality that what you're really trying to be free of is your separate identity. You want to be afraid of something? Be afraid of losing your separate identity. I'm down with that, because at least you're getting real and dealing with a profound reality of what's keeping you separate from God.

The point of Trident Man and the practice it reveals is to surrender our individual, limited understanding and to allow the highest Consciousness that's already given life to us to finally remove enough of the filter that Śiva's light shows through. Then life is so clear. We're living to serve God's will, and whatever comes out of that is clear. We always say, "Yeah, but then I won't be there to experience it." Well, hallelujah, because God will always be there to experience it. What do we really want, our own experience or God's experience? Until we're willing to surrender our notion of freedom through our own filter, we won't begin to perceive or understand it.

Only a rare few have the capacity to completely surrender, so we surrender one part of us at a time, one mental projection, one thought-construct, one holding-on, and that becomes an exponential process. Surrendering some little mundane thing becomes the capacity to surrender lots of mundane things, until suddenly it isn't mundane things we're surrendering anymore—it's our own sense of identity and separation.

Surrendering Our Will to God's Will

At some moment in our life, if true, unconditional freedom and joy is what we really want, we must be willing to surrender our will. We must be willing to surrender the idea that we are doing anything other than living in the unfathomable joy of the recognition that God is doing it all, and He's doing it through us. If His intention is the perpetual expansion of freedom, what happened in the translation? Our will got in the way. We forgot who we were, and we began to have the experience of being separate from that will, of being separate from God. And if we're separate and different, we get to do anything we want, which is true. We *can* do anything we want, but if we are seeking the highest truth in ourselves, our actions should be held in that context, and should reflect what we want most in life.

So when you find yourself in that moment where you know you need to make that offering of your will, and you begin to feel afraid, reach inside and ask for help. Simply ask, "May my will be Your will. May I live in unconditional bliss." This is the power of your will, the power of your wish to grow. This wish turns into commitment to growing, and ultimately the surrender to growing no matter what the condition, whatever we get or don't get. This is the importance of Divine will as it manifests within us.

When we surrender the misunderstanding of thinking we are the doer, God just expresses himself through us, with no particular plan. His plan, his will, is the expression of freedom. The problem is that we want to make even surrender a material thing. Don't think because you surrender totally into the will of God that you're just going to sit there for the rest of your life. Out of God's will emerges the knowledge of what to do and the capacity to do it, the state of illuminated clarity. You don't need to question whether it's God's will or yours. It's crystal clear.

Here's a clue. If we're struggling about whether something is or isn't our will, that's the ego. The reason we don't understand this is because we want to attach a result to everything we do, even to our surrender. The only result of surrender is surrender. It doesn't have to look like anything. It is a state of awareness and freedom.

Often, when we surrender our will, we're still trying to get something. There's still this subtle negotiation. As Rumi would say, that's why everything we do has some weird sense of failure in it. So what's a *sādhaka* to do? Keep going, but use the power of your own self-reflective capacity to see where you function from, to see that even in asking for freedom, you're really asking for freedom from suffering instead of the freedom of joy. The objective of freedom from suffering still has some subtle form attached to it.

When any substance is purified, impurities get released. In us, our own impurities are our misunderstandings, which present a barrier to Śiva's illuminating radiance and clarity. This purification requires a conscious choice: as your attachment to yourself and your will surfaces, you must surrender your will in that moment and say, "Thy will be done."

In traditional *homa* ceremonies, the word *svāhā* is the sound of offering. It is a letting go of something, and throwing it into the fire. In our inner work it is the same. We consciously choose to not engage in dynamics that create tension. *Homa* is sacrifice. *Pūjā* is worship. Sacrifice, worship, and surrender are not different. All are offerings. In making the conscious choice to surrender, at some point we must sacrifice the level of life we're engaged in. This is done out of the subtle discrimination of seeing that the level we're on is binding us and keeping us from opening to a higher state of awareness within. Seen from that point of view, sacrifice is a joyful offering of whatever limitation is binding us and saying, "God, please take this from me."

The most difficult situations, the ones that test our limited understanding, are the most powerful opportunities for freedom. To offer our life in service to the Divine is the sacrifice of our own will and the surrender to God's will. If we're aware that it is our conscious choice to live in freedom, then whether we're giving up or receiving, it is all part of the same dynamic. All of the challenging moments are the gifts of Grace. These are the moments that we can change. When everything is groovy, what pressure is there on us to change? The fact that we need some pressure on us to change is because we're pretty dense. We either just drown in the ocean of *saṃsāra* or we live on that raft of devotion so that we can float across it. If we choose devotion, when those really difficult things come along that we don't understand, we can deeply ask to understand, and we can really let go.

In trying to find the state of freedom, we must at some point surrender our will. This is the highest service, and the highest state of freedom. First we practice doing this in our meditation, and then we have to learn how to do it in our day. Since the energies of action and knowledge and will are the same capacity for us as they are for the Divine, we must begin to align those powers with those of the Divine, and to express freedom and service in all our actions.

Attempting to do so will require incredible surrender, beyond what you ever thought you would have to surrender. If you aren't willing and able to function from that place as you engage your life and the people in your life, then you aren't expressing freedom, that highest will. Instead, you're trying to use higher energies for your personal benefit, saying, "I want to be blissed out and full of power and will, and I want to be able to do whatever I want with it." You can't sit there in meditation and find some profound deep state of surrender, and then when you open your eyes use the power of that surrender to express your own will. We have access to extraordinary power. What *are* you going to do with it?

Resistance and Testing

It is the moment that we surrender ourselves and offer our lives in service that we begin to function from a place of devotion that says we are ready and willing to surrender our will. But isn't it interesting that when we talk about service and surrendering our will, suddenly there's this tension that arises within us? If we say, "I am willing to live in the joy and freedom of myself," then we feel open about it. Yet there is really no distinction or conflict between those two things. Even as we make a commitment to serve and surrender, and we feel some hesitation come up, we can be self-aware and understand that part of us is resisting and still holding on. Part of us is saying, "Maybe I'm right. Maybe it *is* all about me. Maybe my will *will* be done."

Often, when we express our will, instead of bringing us everything we thought we should have and some kind of permanent joy, willfulness brings us suffering. Yet we continue to express our will over and over again, thinking next time it will be different and turn out the way we want it to.

When we offer our lives in service to God, we'd better mean it because we will be tested. Anyone can make a commitment. It is the test of the commitment that makes it real. It doesn't work to say, "I'll surrender myself in this situation, but not in that situation."

In recalling Rudi's beautiful analogy of the designer and the weaver, he made it clear that we are not the designer; we are only the weaver:

> *Those who pick apart the threads weaken the fabric of creation by applying their own mind to the design, because to them, God's will is not acceptable as their own. We must first surrender to the miracle of creation, then the pattern will emerge. Life is composed of an endless variety of threads of many colors. The need to reduce them to a*

> *certain type of design constricts the creative output. All the tensions we put into the weaving are man's limitation of God's purpose.*

All the tension we feel in our life is our limited understanding of God's will functioning through and as us, perpetuating freedom.

Somehow we think that we can design it a little bit better, that perfection would show up if we designed it. Your life is already perfect because it is trying to free you. What could be more perfect? You will never have that experience of perfection until you ask for it and are willing to truly let go of the idea that you are the designer, and that your life needs to be redesigned. Start with, "Thy will be done." There is no more struggle, no need to change anything, no need for things to be different, only the recognition of the perfection of your own life, as it is in this moment. Don't try to redesign your life; allow your consciousness to be transformed. Then it doesn't make a difference whether the thread is blue or black or yellow. We simply recognize it, and we don't need to change it.

If we could for one moment truly let go of everything we think we need and perpetually reach for, we would be free. Our will is how we do that. Are you brave enough? Are you big enough? Don't worry if you're not, because you will be. Make the offering. And then Śiva will come along with a chest spreader like the ones used in open-heart surgery, put it into your heart, and start cranking.

Sometimes when we're in pain and can't surrender, our openness isn't enough. We haven't gotten big enough. This is God taking that heart crank and cranking it and saying, "Open up. Understand this from a perspective beyond yourself." When this happens and you start to struggle, fight, and contract, that's the moment to let go and recognize that God is trying to make you bigger. That profoundly subtle fear you come up against that says, "Yeah, but if I do it...," has to be surrendered. The end of the sentence is not relevant. If you let go in those moments you discover the power of bliss, the power of unconditional surrender. They're not separate. Bliss is the joy of experiencing your own existence as it is at this moment.

All the different levels of surrender—surrendering tension, mundaneness, things, and needs—are simply practice for the ultimate unconditional surrender of saying, "May my will be Your will." The moment we allow that mantra to become the resonance we function from, we have accessed the Divine powers of Śiva's Trident; we recognize, I *am* Śiva. I *am* Parā. I can do anything I want, and because of that, I don't need to do anything. All I want is to be Myself. All I want is to sit in this infinite joy, and whatever arises from that is just so perfect that there's no thought that starts to dissect the fabric or question the design.

You must recognize the resistance of your own will, because how are you going to give it up otherwise? If you're not meeting your resistance, you're not growing, and that applies to the surrendering of your own will. The highest expression of your individual will is to surrender it, to offer it back to that Divine will, because that's the point of having that individual will. The point of Divine will is the perpetual expansion of freedom. If we use our own will for that purpose, we no longer have any thoughts about how our life manifests. We no longer question whether it is our will or God's will. It's just freedom expressing itself, and it's perfect. It's only when we start to say, "Wait a minute, this isn't so perfect," that we contract again into our own individual will. That is the moment of surrender. We get bigger, and then we start to get a little smaller. That's natural. What's the next thing to do? Open and expand again.

In Tantric spiritual practices there are really three things a practitioner surrenders to: God's Grace, the energy, and the teacher. At some point we discover that they are not separate or different. At some point we stop surrendering things and simply surrender to and receive God's Grace, which is available to us at every moment. We must surrender to that Grace. Why wouldn't we?

There is really only one moment of surrender, and then there is the work we must do to live up to that. There is the joyous offering of ourselves, and then the surrendering of everything that keeps us from living up to that offering. The practice of surrendering all the details is just practice for surrendering the one thing you have to surrender: yourself. Try it for one second; turn it into an hour, a day, a month, and allow it to turn into your lifetime.

The State of Autonomous Joy

We spend our life force trying to change the conditions around us. If you truly surrender and discover the joy of your own existence, you will not need to change anything or anyone in order to live in that joy. That is the pathway to freedom. You can take all the sledgehammers you want to life, and all you will do is beat it into some other form. You can do that forever, and it will still just be form. It will still just be a set of conditions. There are no conditions in unconditionality. There, your life is about the consciousness of freedom, the discovery of truth, rather than the defense of non-truth. Instead of defending yourself and what you think you know, surrender and let God reveal the truth.

The state of surrender is the expression of unconditional joy, of not being bound by any condition, as ugly and intense as it may get. The conditions of life are mirrors, projections of our own misunderstanding, perfectly created for us to penetrate through that emission, perfectly created from within ourselves to provide us with the very dynamic we need to test our understanding, to see if we can penetrate duality. Because life looks, feels, acts, sounds, and behaves like it's outside of us, we get confused and think we have to change it or run away from it, instead of changing in ourselves. This is why life is so perfect—because it sets up so many conditions!

I talk regularly about surrender being something we do, but it is really a state of awareness, a state of consciousness. In the state of surrender we have surrendered the veils of duality, and it is God's will, God's knowledge, and God's action that take place; we are just along for the ride. Remember, Śiva surrendered Himself in order for all this to exist, for the pure joy of it, and for the expansion of that joy. In that surrendering He forgot Himself, for the joy of remembering. If Śiva can do it, we ought to be able to do it, since we are not different than Śiva. Surrender is the state of living as the God within. It is living beyond all condition, ours and everyone else's. It is the highest practice, and it can happen in every moment.

If you don't understand liberation, focus on joy. Understand that all of of life emerges from the joy of God's liberated state of Consciousness. So whenever you are grumpy, angry, self-rejected, rejecting somebody else, you can spend eternity trying to fix it, but you don't have to if you just go inside and find that unconditional joy. How else could you describe surrender more beautifully than unconditional joy? Ultimately you're not surrendering your stuff. You're just surrendering into joy and unconditionality.

Love and Surrender

There isn't a tremendous amount of discussion of the term "love" in Kashmir Shaivite scripture, yet in trying to understand that literature, the term always comes up. Rudi taught that we have to love life and love God if we want our freedom. The problem is that we always misinterpret love as wanting to be loved by someone else. When we're filled by someone loving us, if they stop loving us we feel a loss; we feel empty. This isn't to deny the beauty of that sharing, but it should help us understand that only God's love for us is permanent and unconditional.

When I was in India with the scholar and translator of Abhinavagupta's Tantrāloka, Mark Dyczkowski, he gave an incredibly beautiful lecture on *vimarśa*, our self-reflective awareness. He described *vimarśa* as love. What he meant was that since our capacity for *vimarśa* allows us to see, know, and recognize ourselves, it also enables us to consciously choose to see, know, and recognize somebody else. The eloquence of that insight is reflected in our description of surrender as the state of bliss and unconditionality. The reason *vimarśa* is love is because it's not separate or different from *ānanda śakti*, the unconditional state. To really love someone is to love them unconditionally.

The highest expression of surrender is to be able to transcend all duality and to love unconditionally. This is the highest fulfillment in life. All the things that we have to surrender are what we have to surrender to be able to come to that place where we can love unconditionally, so that we can experience God's unconditional love. If you want to be happy for the rest of your life, love your life without condition, and learn to love the people around you without condition.

In order to achieve that state of surrender and clarity, we practice reaching for it in the moments we haven't achieved it. Ultimately, it must, it will, it cannot do anything else but bring us to that moment of clarity in which we understand that love and surrender are the same. All this is God's will, which leads to the luminous light of knowing: All this is My will. I am the light. I am the way. How extraordinary that each of us has the opportunity to experience that.

SURRENDER IS THE KEY

Surrender is the key to living as an expression of God's will. Ultimately we are trying to recognize that we are alive and experiencing our life because God willed it. Anything else is an act of limited consciousness. In trying to get back home to Divine Consciousness, all *tattvas* must be purified in Śiva. All manifest and unmanifest expressions of Consciousness are reabsorbed back into their source, purifying the misunderstanding that they are separate from or outside of Divine Consciousness. This is what we are asking for in our wish to know God in truth: for all the divergent, condensed levels of consciousness to be purified and absorbed back into that infinite state.

The notion of surrender and sacrifice in spiritual practice is the surrendering of the limited self into the higher Self. Sacrifice is always shown as fire. Your life is your own crucible, so make an offering. Offer your pain, suffering, mind, and emotions—everything that keeps you from your Divine Source. In the process you'll recognize you were given those things for the very purpose of surrendering and offering them. *Svāhā*. . . .

Here's the thing about surrender. You get to choose *whether* you surrender. You don't get to choose *what* you surrender. Surrender is a state of unconditionality. It is the response to the Sufi prayer, "May I be annihilated in God." We can talk forever about the details, but there is only the question: Did you or didn't you? Will you or won't you? At some point you recognize that surrendering is the most joyous act, because it's no longer a giving up; it's only a receiving.

At the age of twenty-one I recognized surrender as the key to spiritual freedom. That recognition was made very clear to me in 1973, when Rudi died. Rudi did two great things for me: allowing me to meet him, and dying. His dying sixteen months after I met him was one of the pivotal moments of my life. For the first thirty seconds, it was the most intensely painful experience I ever went through. The work that was required of me in order to understand that what was real about Rudi hadn't died is what freed me from the notion that there is such a thing as death. His energy is as alive in me at this moment as it ever was. I would have preferred to learn that lesson some other way. As a twenty-one-year-old, I didn't have much higher consciousness, but in that moment, life was saying to me, "You had better get conscious—and fast."

Without surrender I could not have survived Rudi's death. I am eternally grateful for that experience because in the process I recognized that surrender was the only way for me to express my gratitude for the gift he'd given me while he was alive, and to not allow anything to diminish that gift. Continuing to surrender allowed that gift to grow and dissolved everything in the way of its unfolding.

Many of Rudi's students had their practice derailed by his death, because of the pain of the misunderstanding that there was a loss, instead of doing what was required, which was tuning in to a more refined expression of that same energy. We create our own experience every moment, determined by the level of consciousness in which we function. Only by Grace was I able to transmute the pain of my own sense of loss to the recognition, thirty seconds later, that Rudi was free. Within the span of thirty seconds, that same experience was interpreted through a different understanding, one we might call "forced surrender." It was surrender because there was no other choice, but it enabled me to understand the same experience from a completely different perspective. This was Grace.

Whatever your experience of pain has been, it is either nourishment for your change, or justification for not changing. You can, in this moment, surrender everything. Will you or won't you? These are the moments in which you decide whether you are willing to surrender yourself completely, to become Śiva, to not need to do anything but simply be God.

The highest practice, the highest meditation, the highest way of living your life, is living in surrender. You come to understand that no matter how much it hurts and what it costs, you must let go of your limited experience of life if you want that higher experience in this life.

When you're not sure, when you're in pain, ask for help. Ask for Grace. God, free me from myself. Not, God fix this or God, make it go away. Free me from myself. These moments truly help us understand we are not our bodies, our thoughts, our egos, or our limited experience of ourselves. When your consciousness contracts, when you feel pain and think, "I'd better inflict some pain on someone else," know that you're not functioning from, or moving toward, the highest in yourself, and let go. Use the power of your own self-reflective awareness to say, "This is not the experience I want," and surrender it. This is the power of the consciousness of freedom, to say, "I choose freedom. I choose to not live in pain. I choose to let go of my attachment to the limitations and misunderstandings that make me unhappy."

In any difficult situation, when you are being crucified, burned alive, and everything in you wants to run away, this is the moment of Grace, the possibility of true transformation. When Rudi died it was one of those moments. There have been very few moments in my life that have compared. It is in those moments that we truly surrender. We surrender our will and recognize God's will. We make the choice to live in freedom.

Ultimately, there is no practice, no set of techniques, and no teacher that can serve you unless you can surrender. I will end this chapter with a quote from Rudi:

> *The last year of my life has prepared me for the understanding that Divine Consciousness can only come through unconditional surrender into our own nothingness. That state is reached by surrendering*

ourselves and the tensions that bind and restrict us, keeping us from expressing the power of creation that is our true essence. It is God flowing through us and showing us that we are nothing but Him. I want to live as an expression of that higher creative will and from a deeper sense of surrender....

Those were Rudi's last words before his plane crashed into a mountain. How amazing that even with his very last breath he was expressing that surrender is how we go to God.

Śiva's Grace:
The Heart of it All

Conclusion

Śiva's Grace: The Heart of it All

The more *sādhana* we do, the more we come to understand that our freedom, and the point of all our efforts, is to arrive at the place in ourselves where we are truly able to live in God's Grace. So much of the challenge for us as spiritual students is to discover the awareness that Grace is the reason we're alive, and that Grace is the reason we have the opportunity to live from that awareness. God's Grace is ever present in our lives. Spiritual *sādhana* is the awakening of the Consciousness within ourselves to be able to see it, hear it, feel it, and most importantly, to live by it.

The *maṇḍala* of Śiva's Trident represents the field of Consciousness from which everything arises. It's a profoundly simple and elegant representation of the Trika understanding of how, through the Grace of Śiva's power—therefore our power and experience—we can recognize ourselves as the source and holder of the powers of the universe. The *maṇḍala* simultaneously expresses both universal awareness and the individual's capacity to perceive and experience that.

The point of life is to experience unconditional freedom and joy. All the hubbub Śiva goes through in manifesting the universe is all part of His infinite joy and bliss. This is true even of the process of forgetting Himself, because it's just so much fun and just so beautiful. Self-discovery is the highest experience, and if those highest levels of awareness were not concealed we couldn't experience the Grace of the revealing. The distinction between Śiva and us is that no form or condition ever changes His own essence, or His experience of His essence.

Out of the dynamic interplay between the Self-illuminating light of Consciousness and Its own capacity to bathe in that light, emission—*visarga*—happens. As we ascend back up the *tattvas* through our internal practice, we penetrate through that emission. Just as in the simple adage "You end up back where you began," the source from which all of life emerges is the same point to which it returns: unconditional joy. In terms of our experience, this means that our *sādhana* is to live in bliss. The difference between the state of bliss and our incessant search to find something outside of ourselves to make us happy is the difference between freedom and non-freedom.

The meaning of Śiva's Trident is that freedom, even Śiva's freedom, is the product of His own union with that which emerges from Him. How powerful for us to understand this in our own lives. The *maṇḍala* is emphatically showing us that our own existence is the effect of Śiva's powers, yet it is neither different nor separate from them, reminding us once again: Our life is the expression of God's freedom. So, we ask ourselves, "If that's true, then why do I suffer? Why don't I experience infinite bliss?" There is only one thing that stands in the way of that experience: our limited understanding, and because of that, our failure to reach for the highest. Yet that failure is not something to blame ourselves for; it is simply something to recognize.

Our capacity to free ourselves begins with our willingness to free ourselves and truly surrender the world we create out of our thought-construct, which causes us to experience binding and suffering instead of joy and freedom. Our willingness to free ourselves begins with our willingness to say, "Maybe I ought to let somebody else do this for a while. Maybe I ought to let Śiva do this. Maybe I ought to listen to what my teacher is telling me about my patterns and how I keep repeating them, creating the same experience over and over again. Maybe I ought to not trust my limited understanding and surrender to a higher understanding." That all starts with willingness, which is actually Śiva's Grace, His Divine will functioning within us, saying, "I will create My freedom."

We must find the place in us that not only believes in but also feels the pure potentiality of life. We must really start to feel it and live it, and we mustn't stop until we see the white of God's eyes. The whole exchange between Kṛṣṇa and Arjuna in the Bhagavad Gītā is not simply a discussion of the impending battle. It's about living God's will—whatever the cost. The last line in the entire epic is, "Thy will be done." This epic went on for eons, yet it's all finally over as soon as the last line is stated: "Thy will be done."

It's important to understand that all of Śiva's powers are our powers, and they're all wrapped up in one power, which is the power of the choice we have to decide where we live in ourselves. All of the levels of consciousness exist within us like a thirty-six-floor high-rise called The *Tattva* Towers, and we can decide which floor we live on. The fact that the rent is higher in the penthouse means you get what you pay for. Decide what it is that you're looking for in this life: the highest truth or some facsimile thereof. When you think you're too busy, that you have too much pressure, or that your stuff is special, stop and ask yourself where those thoughts are coming from. Use your God-given will to choose the highest in yourself. Isn't it amazing that there's so much fear and resistance to living in the deepest, stillest, most joyful place in ourselves?

"Yeah," you say, "but then I have to work and sacrifice and serve." Remember that those efforts are the natural expression of the simple choice to discover your own source. Then all of life is part of that. Whatever you have to do or not do is all part of the process of discovering the highest within yourself, so don't get caught in any of the details along the way. Live in the world and infuse it with your own awareness and meaning. If you do this, the attempt to find meaning in the world becomes nonexistent because its meaning will simply be your own expression of the joy of freedom. The very act of engaging in the world, of being in the world yet free of its conditions, will allow you to discover the truth, and that's the purpose of the world. Ain't it grand?

Living Beyond Condition

The discussion we had about devotion is the recognition that Śiva's Grace is His devotion to our freedom. More specifically, Śiva's Grace is His devotion to His own freedom, expressed as all of us. It could be said that we are the object of Śiva's Grace, and that Śiva is the subject of our devotion. It is the merging of those two things that brings us the experience of Oneness, where there is no separation between subject and object, between the Supreme Subject and all the objects that are expressed from It.

The subtle negotiation that we think we need to engage in with God arises from the subtle misunderstanding that we're separate. The highest *upāya*, *anupāya*, translates into the end of all negotiation. We all know that in negotiating with ourselves we never win, so why negotiate with God? This is the power of *ānanda śakti*, the bliss from which life emerged. God didn't create out of suffering and lack. He created out of His own effulgence. Try that in your own life. And know that anytime and every time you aren't functioning from that place it is your choice not to do so. Even if you cannot find that most expanded, unconditional place, you still have the discriminating awareness and self-reflective capacity to offer whatever level of unconsciousness you're functioning from into the fire and say, "*Svāhā.*" This is the joy and consciousness of *sādhana*: I will not be bound. Ultimately, you're even demanding of God, "Stop screwing around and beam me up." And just like that your life will change. Grace can penetrate through any level of density to reveal Itself.

If every time you feel difficulty or resistance, when you feel lost or confused, just close your eyes and feel God's love for you, and in less than five minutes of feeling God's love, everything will change. You will have made contact with the fullness that exists within you. In functioning from that place, you will have a different perspective. We could say you have God's perspective. Ultimately, all our individual effort, our deep wish to grow, the sacrifices we make, and the willingness to simply allow the flow of life to show us our life, all lead to the state of *śāmbhavopāya*, the recognition that all along, our life was Śiva's will. All along, it was Śiva perpetuating His own freedom and joy, and no condition we find ourselves in can ever limit that, unless we choose for it to do so.

We begin to recognize that all of this activity is the effect of Śiva doing. The whole discussion of the *tattvas* and the goddesses of will, knowledge, and action is about Śiva's power and energy to execute His own freedom, to express the incredible perfection of life. He didn't even have to predesign it all because what He's expressing is perfection. Herein lies another clue for us: There is nothing that is not part of that perfection. Śiva doesn't care whether you have money or not, whether you are a boy with a boyfriend or a girl with a girlfriend. These details are just how Śiva's will takes form.

Because Śiva's will is the perpetuation of freedom, how could any effect or form that shines forth from that freedom be separate or different than that freedom? How could it ever be anything but perfect?

What's wonderful to understand about the five highest energies of Śiva is that not only are they levels of consciousness, they are power and energy. Divine Consciousness is not inert awareness. It has a vibrant, radiant reality, which is the reality that gave birth to you out of Its own Self-experience of that radiance. Infinite Consciousness and the bliss of that awareness are never separate. What this says is that if we're conscious, we can experience joy. We are never separate from our consciousness. The issue is which level of consciousness we function and understand from.

The Grace of *vimarśa* is that we have the capacity to know our own state. We can be aware when we're functioning from a limited place and choose not to. We can be aware of when we need to open and be bigger, and when we need to become even more open and even bigger. When Rudi talked about everything in life being a test, that's what he meant. The wonderful thing about growing is that if you don't get it right this moment, the next moment comes around to give you another chance to get it right. Because God's Grace is ever flowing, those moments come back over and over again, moment by moment. There is never a moment in your life that freedom is not available.

If we are fully conscious of our true Self, the only experience can be joy. Our devotion is our perpetual search inside ourselves to have that experience and to firmly establish ourselves within it. This is a beautiful description of devotion. We are devoted to knowing and loving God so much that we are willing to surrender and sacrifice all of the other levels of awareness that take us out of that. Open your heart, feel the flow, and surrender. It's that simple. The eloquent expositions around the *tattvas* and Trident Man reveal the reality and the potential of our individual experience. It is the descent of Consciousness and Its ascent back into Itself that is the fire of *kuṇḍalinī*.

Mokṣa and Bhoga

The term *mokṣa* means liberation. *Bhoga* means enjoyment, celebration. What good is liberation if we don't enjoy it? This is the Tantric canon: There is no duality or conflict between liberation and enjoyment in life. Shaivism understands Śiva and Śakti as *mokṣa* and *bhoga*: freedom and the expression of that freedom. The union of Śiva and Śakti is the celebration of freedom. That's where all of life comes from, out of that perfection. It just emotes. Go forth and be passionate about that emission. Be passionate about celebrating your life. If there's a conscious choice we make, it's the celebration of life instead of the suffering of life, and however we express that in the world, it's no problem. The problem is we get caught in limited joy, and then when conditions in our life change, we lose that joy. In merging with God we make contact with permanent joy, which no condition can ever take away or even enhance.

Rudi was profoundly passionate about living, about the extraordinary Grace, beauty, simplicity, dynamism, and chaos of life. He devoured it. He ate it for lunch, dinner, breakfast, and for a 3 a.m. snack. We should be passionate about living our lives from the joy that all of creation emerged from. Whatever you do in life, be passionate about it. Just remember that passion is the expression of perfection, joy, and freedom — not the search for those experiences. The key is that all of it, even the difficult times that we face, should be understood as a celebration. What would our experience of life be if every day we got up and said, "It's time to celebrate!"? Probably a little bit better. If we could only see the perfection of it all, we would be free. Instead, we try to beat life into our version of what we think is perfect. Having our own particular version of a "perfect" life doesn't translate into understanding the perfection of life. My idea of a perfect life included Rudi staying alive, and yet he didn't; how perfect.

If we wake up every day and the first thing we do is find our heart, so much of the drama and tension just fall away. We simply live in the devotion of God's will. When is it that we find ourselves struggling? When we want to take a different route than the one set out before us. Always remember, the source of Divine will is unconditional joy, bliss. The purpose of surrendering to God's will is to discover that place of unconditionality, to live in that profound joy, which is the purpose of our life. We can then recognize that when we express our individual will in ways that resist God's will, we're going in the opposite direction from God's bliss.

Grace is always descending. Use your own freedom to allow it to touch your life and raise your awareness. Understand the extraordinary opportunity for absolute freedom and unconditional joy that is available to you. It has always been available to you, but you now have the vehicle. You can get in it, turn on the engine, step on the gas, and go exactly where you want to go. Plug this in on your GPS: *dvādaśānta*. Go left, take a breath, and let go. You have specific directions. As you drive there more often, you'll understand the direction inside the direction: You are being lifted into that space.

The world is manifest out of Śiva's joy, extended outward from and yet still held within Himself. Let your life be an extension that flows outward from you, instead of the other way around. Your experience will be radically different. Recognize that your life is expressing itself from your own state of consciousness. The state of consciousness that you are tuned in to within yourself is what determines your life, and your experience of your life.

Building a Foundation

People always say to me, "It's so easy for you." That's because I've spent the last forty years developing mastery over the foundation by opening my heart and feeling the flow. Don't forget the foundation on which you are building your life. The foundational technique is your wish to grow. If you don't feel that wish, then sit down and find it or you will never be able to say, "I wish to surrender myself completely." You are building a structure for higher consciousness within you. Don't build it on quicksand. Build it so it can withstand the elements and the storms. Your practice, and the release of potency within you, expands exponentially. So decide what you really want, because the power and energy will be there to support you.

This will take a lifetime to master, so why not start today? This is the highest experience: union with the Divine, the recognition that there is only one thing in life and that is the joy of our own existence. If you have to surrender and sacrifice and struggle, it's worth the price. If you don't achieve it, understand that you made the choice not to. There is no limitation on any of us except the ones we choose. Our *sādhana* is the expression of our choice. At the end of our life, the result of our *sādhana* will be the effect of our choices. If freedom is available to us in this lifetime, then not having it ultimately becomes our choice. How amazing it is that this is our responsibility. If God dwells within us and infinite freedom is always available to us, then not having it means we valued something else more.

The whole world—every level of it and everything that happens within each level—is perfection. It is not separate from God; it is God's creation. Because we have the discriminating power of consciousness, we get to choose our own state of awareness from among all the dimensions of resonance within us. Whatever level of density you find yourself in, freedom always exists there, because it exists everywhere. Instead of focusing on freedom from suffering, focus on the freedom and joy inherent within you. It is a matter of perspective. If you look at life from tension and fear, you manifest tension and fear. If you look from freedom and joy, that is what you manifest. So move into the state of unconditional joy, and live your life from there. You will have transformed your consciousness, and your experience of life will be completely different.

It is truly only by God's Grace that we can know Him. It is by God's Grace that we have the consciousness to know Consciousness Itself. The power within the choice to use that consciousness is the power that can free us. This is the power of your choice, and nobody else can make that choice for you, not even God. If you truly want to know God, you must give your life back to Him, which is simply the burning up of the idea that it's your life in the first place. You may delay that moment as long as you choose, but if you truly want freedom and unbounded joy, you will come to that moment. When you do, you simply understand that Divine Consciousness gave you life in order to celebrate Itself. If that's true, how could your life, even the ugly parts, not be perfect? This is bliss, the unbounded joy of experiencing your own existence, *samāveśa*, immersion in God.

At some point you recognize that you are not even freeing yourself. Śiva is the doer, and He is freeing you. That is the most excellent sunrise, and it is Grace at Its highest. There is no separation between that highest Grace, which is God's will to express freedom, and the simple Grace of choosing to sit down on your cushion, take a breath, and open your heart. So open your heart, and know that freedom is available when you choose it.

Appendix: Guided Meditations

The Double-Breath Exercise

The double-breath exercise developed by Swami Rudrananda is a very important tool for meditation. It will help you to experience and deepen the flow of vital force. The double-breath integrates the wish to grow with awareness of the breath, the *cakras*, and the flow of energy within, all into one smooth process. With the double-breath, you are working to establish a flow of energy down the front and up the back. Use the double-breath every ten minutes during meditation to sharpen your inner focus. Use it throughout the day.

1. Take a deep breath, let it go, and relax.

2. Be aware that the breath is filled with spiritual energy and nourishment.

3. Draw the next breath into the heart *cakra*. As the breath moves through the throat *cakra*, swallow. Without forcing the breath, allow it to fill and open your chest. Relax in the heart *cakra* and feel an expansion taking place. Feel a deep wish to grow. Ask deeply to open your heart; ask deeply to surrender your worries, problems, and boundaries. Hold the breath in the heart for about ten seconds or until it naturally releases.

4. Release about one-fifth of the breath and deeply let go. Keep your attention and energy in your heart.

5. Breathe in again, through the heart, bringing the breath and your attention into the navel *cakra*. Hold gently and relax deeply. Feel your belly open and soften with the expansion of energy. Hold

the breath and your attention there for about ten seconds. As you release the breath, feel the energy naturally expand across the sex *cakra* and into the base of the spine.

6. Relax the base of the spine and allow the energy to rise up the spinal column to the top of the head. Feel the energy there.

At other times during meditation, when not doing the double-breath, remain very aware of your breath, and focus your breath and attention on the heart *cakra*. Be aware of the flow of energy moving down through the *cakras* and up the spinal column to the top of the head. At the end of each outbreath, let go, and then let go again. Feel the expansion in yourself. Surrender inside, allowing something deeper and finer to fill you. It is this ever-deepening practice that mobilizes your inner energy to facilitate a very profound and lasting change in your consciousness and in your experience of life.

The Internal Breath Meditation

1. Sit up straight, with your back erect but relaxed. With thumbs and forefingers together, place your hands, palms facing up, on your thighs. Relax your body.

2. Bring your awareness to the arising and subsiding of your breath. As you follow the arising and subsiding of the breath, notice that your awareness becomes more focused on it. If your attention wanders or thoughts arise, bring your attention back to the breath. Deeply feel the arising and subsiding of the breath.

3. Feel the breath as it arises and subsides in your heart. With each arising and subsiding, feel your heart open more and more. Be aware of the pulsation in your heart as it gives rise to the breath. Feel the arising and expansion of that pulsation. As it reaches its apex of expansion, relax and let go. At the natural release at the end of the outbreath, let go again.

4. Feel the openness as it expands, opening and giving rise to the breath, which gives rise to the expansion. Feel the boundary that it reaches, and at the outermost edge of that boundary, let go. With the natural release of the breath, follow that openness as it reaches the other edge of the boundary of release, and let go again.

5. Allow your awareness to become deeply centered in the center of your heart. Remain aware of the subtle pulsation that gives rise to the breath. Let go.

6. Without holding your breath, feel the breath as it comes to a stillpoint. When you feel the need to take a breath, don't. Instead, breathe from within your heart. Feel the breath arise from the base of the spine, opening and filling the heart. When you feel the need to release, instead of allowing the breath to externalize, allow the energy to rise from the heart to the center of the head. Let go.

7. Keep your awareness in your heart. Don't hold your breath, but as you feel the need to breathe, feel the energy and awareness rise from the base of the spine, fill the heart, and softly expand it. If you feel pressure, release without externalizing the breath, allow your awareness and the energy to rise to the center of the head. Let go. Feel the breathing inside. Feel the breath as the arising and expansion of the energy within you. Release, and allow the energy to rise to the center of your head. Let go.

8. Each time you feel you need to take a breath, simply draw the energy from the base of the spine into the heart, filling the heart, and opening into the center of the head. When you feel the pressure that wants to release, without externalizing the breath, allow it to rise from the center of the head to the top of the head. Let go.

9. Feel the potency and vitality of the flow of energy pulsating within the *suṣumṇa*, opening from the base of the spine, opening and filling the heart, expanding into the center of the head, and releasing through the crown. You are centered in the *suṣumṇa*, being breathed from that place. Let go.

10. Without losing contact with that openness from the base of the spine, into the heart, center of the head, and top of the head, feel into the space about 12 inches above the crown of your head. Allow the energy and awareness from the base of your spine to open, expand in the heart, and rise to the center of the head and to the crown. Allow it to rise to that space above your head. Let go.

11. Feel the openness above your head, and keep your awareness there. Feel the pulsation of that openness as it lifts the energy from the base of your spine through your heart, expands in the center of your head, moves through the crown, and rises into the space above your head. This place is called *dvādaśānta*, the abode of Śiva.

12. So simply focus your awareness in the center of that space above your head. Let go into that center. Keep your awareness there for 5 to 10 minutes, and continue to let go.

13. Don't lose contact with the energy as it moves from the base of your spine to *dvādaśānta*, the space above your head. Without losing that contact, take a deep breath into you heart *cakra*. Feel it open, expanding into the navel, and release.

14. Allow the awareness and the energy and the breath to rise up through the *suṣumṇa*, back to the heart, back to the center of the head, through the crown, and back to *dvādaśānta*. Be aware of the flow from that space as you draw the energy into yourself, down the front, and as you release in the base of the spine and allow it to rise back to its source. This is Śiva's Trident.

15. Bring you hands together in front of you in Namaste. Feel the deep gratitude in yourself, and allow that gratitude to rise back to *dvādaśānta*.

Dvādaśānta Meditation

Due to the intricate nature of this meditation, written instuctions are not provided. Please download the guided meditation (see below).

Links to Online Downloads

To hear guided meditations leading you through the double-breath, internal breath, and *dvādaśānta* exercises, go to *TrikaShala.com* and click on the Writings & Photos page. Under the Guided Meditations heading, click the link for *Shiva's Trident* readers and enter the code TRIDENT (all caps). Note that the meditation entitled "Opening the Heart and Creating Flow" includes instruction in the double-breath.

Glossary and Pronunciation Guide

Trika tradition reflects the understanding that Sanskrit is a sacred, revealed language, its phenomes imbued with Śakti's power of manifestation. In honor of that view, the Glossary of Terms is presented in both transliterated Sanskrit with diacritical marks and Anglicized form where needed to aid in pronunciation. Sanskrit words are generally pronounced as in English, with some exceptions. Readers can use the key given here as a guide to proper pronunciation.

Vowels

Sanskrit vowels are long or short. In English transliteration, long vowels are marked with a horizontal bar over the letter. The vowels "e" and "o" are always pronounced as long vowels.

ā	the long a, as in palm
e	as in wave
ī	the long i, as in deed
o	as in home
ū	the long u, as in pool

Consonants

c	ch, as in chat
ñ	as in canyon
ṣ, ś	sh
th	as in anthill

Aham
Śiva's eternal mantra, "I am," the sound of Śiva's breath.
Ahamkāra
Tattva 15, the level consciousness known as the ego.
Ānanda śakti [Ananda shakti]
The energy of Divine bliss, the infinite bliss of existence.
Āṇavopāya
One of the *upāyas*, the path or means of individual effort.
Anupāya
The highest *upāya*, the path of Divine Grace, or no means.
Anuttara Trika
The highest practice, the penetration of Śiva's three energies of emission.
Aparā
The goddess of Śiva's power of pure, infinite action.
Avadhūta
An enlightened being, Pure Consciousness in human form.
Bandha
An energetic or physical lock or contraction that directs and intentionalizes awareness.
Bhakti
The path of devotion to God.
Bindu
A single point.
Bhoga
Celebration, enjoyment.
Brahmā granthi
The lowest knot in the psychic body, in the base of the spine.
Buddhi
Tattva 14, the higher mind or intellect, the capacity for subtle discrimination.

Cakra(s) [Chakra(s)]
(lit., wheel) An energy center in the psychic body.

Cit śakti [Chit shakti]
The power of pure, supreme awareness, Consciousness Itself.

Darśana [Darshan]
The viewing of a saint; to be in the presence of a holy being.

Dvādaśānta
The space 12 inches above the crown of the head, the abode of Parā, Parāparā, and Aparā, the goddesses of Śiva's Divine powers of will, knowledge, and action.

Granthi
Energetic knots or blockages in the psychic system made up of lifetimes of karma, tension, and patterns.

Guru
(lit., dispeller of darkness) A Self-realized spiritual teacher.

Icchā śakti [Iccha shakti]
Śiva's Divine power of pure will, His intent to express infinite freedom and joy, synonymous with the goddess Parā.

Īśvara [Ishvara]
Tattva 4, another name for *jñāna śakti*, perfect knowing, Śiva's Divine knowledge of all things.

Jīva
See *puruṣa*, an individuated expression of the Divine whole.

Jīvanmukti
The state of spiritual liberation attained while alive and embodied.

Jñāna śakti [Jnana shakti]
Śiva's Divine power of perfect knowing, synonymous with the goddess Parāparā.

Jñānendriyas
Tattvas 17 to 21, the senses of perception: hearing, touch, seeing, tasting, and smelling.

Kāla
Tattva 10, time, the limitation of eternal Presence.

Kalā
Tattva 7, the limitation of omnipotence.

Kañcukas [Kanchukas]
Tattvas 7 to 11, the limitations of the five powers of the Divine.

Kaṇḍa
The bulb four fingers below the navel in the *suṣumṇa* containing the lowest five *tattvas*, the union of the energies of the three lower *cakras*.

Karma
Energy trapped in a pattern as a result of lifetimes of limited actions; the energetic principle of cause and effect.

Karmendriyas
Tattvas 22 to 26, the limited powers of action: speaking, grasping, locomotion, excretion, and procreation.

Khecara
The state of spiritual freedom that comes from the liberation of the mind from thought-construct.

Kriyā śakti [Kriya shakti]
Śiva's Divine power of pure action or doership, synonymous with the goddess Aparā.

Kuṇḍalinī
(lit., coiled one) Divine energy expressed as the individual.

Līlā
Manifest reality as the play of Divine Consciousness.

Mahābhūtas
Tattvas 32 to 36, the gross elements: ether, air, fire, water, and earth, of which all matter is comprised.

Manas
Tattva 16, the level of Consciousness discussed as the thinking mind and thought-construct.

Maṇḍala
A sacred, diagrammatic image used in spiritual practice for contemplation and ritual worship.

Māyā
Tattva 6, Śiva's power to limit and obscure Divine Unity.

Mokṣa (Moksha)
See *Jīvanmukti*; spiritual liberation.

Nirvikalpa samādhi
The thought-free state.

Niyati
Tattva 11, localization and specificity (space and causation), the limitation of omnipresence.

Parā
The supreme goddess who sits atop Śiva's Trident, the energy of Śiva's Divine will and Grace.

Paramaśiva [Paramashiva]
The field of Absolute Consciousness from and within which all of life and manifestation arises.

Parāparā
The goddess of Śiva's power of infinite knowledge.

Prakāśa [Prakasha]
The eternal light of Divine Consciousness that illuminates all of life.

Prakṛti [Prakriti]
Tattva 13, *puruṣa's* outer, objective realty of the world and manifestation.

Pratyabhijñā
Spontaneous recognition of the Self.

Pūjā
Ritual worship, part of the path of *āṇavopāya*.

Puruṣa [Purusha]
Tattva 12, individuated consciousness, Śiva limited by the powers of *māyā*.

Rāga
Tattva 9, limited desire, the limitation of completeness.

Rasa
Flavor; the subtle energy of sweetness.

Rudra granthi
The energetic knot in the center of the head; the arbiter between duality and Unity.

Sadāśiva [Sadashiva]
Tattva 3, another name for *icchā śakti*, Śiva's pure will.

Sādhaka
A spiritual student or aspirant.

Sādhana
Spiritual practice engaged in for the process of transformation.

Śakti [Shakti]
Tattva 2, pure Divine energy, not separate from Śiva or Divine Consciousness, the dynamic aspect of Śiva.

Śaktipāta [Shaktipat]
(lit., descent of Grace) A spiritual initiation awakening the *kuṇḍalinī*.

Śāktopāya [Shaktopaya]
The path of energy, the means of transforming the energy of the mind.

Samāveśa [Samavesha]
The state of complete immersion in God Consciousness.

Śāmbhavopāya [Shambhavopaya]
The path of awareness.

Saṃnyāsa [Sannyas]
Formal vows of renunciation.

Saṃskāras
Impressions or memories from past lives embedded in the psychic body.

Śiva [Shiva]
Tattva 1, the supreme reality and supreme awareness, Pure Consciousness, God.

Spanda
The subtle vibrating pulsation of Consciousness whereby all matter and experience pulse into and out of being.

Śuddha-vidyā [Shuddha-vidya]
Tattva 5, another name for *kriyā śakti*, Śiva's Divine power of action.

Suṣumṇa [Sushumna] The central and most important energetic channel of the psychic body.

Svātantrya
Pure, autonomous, infinite freedom.

Tanmātras
Tattvas 27 to 31, the subtle elements: sound, touch, form, taste, and smell.

Tattva(s)
(lit., that-ness) The 36 levels of consciousness, or categories of existence.

Upāyas
Methods, means, or pathways to spiritual liberation.

Vidyā
Tattva 8, limited or categorical knowledge, the limitation of omniscience.

Vimarśa [Vimarsha]
The Self-reflective capacity of Divine Consciousness to know Itself.

Visarga
The creative emission of the universe as an expression of Divine sovereignty.

Viṣṇu granthi [Vishnu granthi]
The energetic knot or block in the center of the heart *cakra*.

About the Author

Swami Khecaranatha has practiced and taught Kuṇḍalinī MahāYoga since 1972. With a mastery derived from more than four decades of dedicated inner practice and selfless service, he is an authentic adept of nondual Tantric Shaivism and an initiated lineage carrier in the *śaktipāta* tradition of Bhagavan Nityananda and Swami Rudrananda (Rudi). Based on the profound spiritual transformation he experienced in his own life through the practice of Kuṇḍalinī Yoga and the Grace of his teachers, he offers inspirational and practical guidance that can change a reader's life as well.

Khecaranatha was born in 1951 in Illinois to an American family in circumstances comparable to those of most of his students and readers. His own life has demonstrated that it is possible to live fully in the world while developing and maintaining one's conscious connection to the Divinity within. After meeting his teacher Rudi in 1971, he moved into Rudi's ashram in Indiana, and Rudi recognized him as a teacher within this lineage in 1972. After Rudi took *mahāsamadhi* in 1973, Khecaranatha continued to work with Swami Chetanananda, the spiritual leader of the ashram, and lived as a member of that community as it subsequently moved to Cambridge, Massachusetts, and finally to Portland, Oregon.

Serving as the head teacher under Chetanananda, he was, through the years, instrumental in helping to develop the ashrams that Rudi started. While living in an ashram for thirty years he also held several "real-world" jobs, including that of CEO of a multimillion-dollar consulting business. This personal experience strengthened his conviction that there is no separation between spiritual life and life in the world. In 2001 Khecaranatha moved to Berkeley, California, to start Sacred Space Yoga Sanctuary, a spiritual center. Sacred Space offers in-depth instruction in Kuṇḍalinī Yoga through its TrikaShala program. In addition to teaching, Swami Khecaranatha currently serves as director of Rudramandir: A Center for Spirituality and Healing, which is operated by Sacred Space.

In July of 2002, Khecaranatha took formal vows of *saṁnyāsa* and was initiated into the Sarasvatī order by Ma Yoga Shakti, a swami based in New York. He was given the name Swami Khecaranatha, which means "Moving in the fullness of the Divine Heart." A swami, or *saṁnyāsin*, is unconditionally committed to serve, love, and support other people in their spiritual growth. To fulfill that undertaking, Khecaranatha continues to teach and to serve as the spiritual leader of a community of practitioners at TrikaShala.

Swami Khecaranatha's other books include *Depth Over Time: Kundalini MahaYoga, A Path of Transformation and Liberation* (2010), *Merging With the Divine: One Day at a Time* (2011), and *The Heart of Recognition: The Wisdom and Practices of the Pratyabhijna Hṛdayam* (2013). More information about his practice, books, and guided-meditation CDs is available at *SwamiKhecaranatha.com*.

About TrikaShala and Rudramandir

Swami Khecaranatha is the spiritual leader of TrikaShala, the meditation program at Sacred Space Yoga Sanctuary, a nonprofit organization in Berkeley, California. TrikaShala teaches Kundalini Meditation through classes, retreats, immersions, and engagement with a spiritual community. Weekly classes, which include *śaktipāta* transmission, are free of charge. For more information about attending your first Kundalini class or retreat, please call (510) 486-8700 or visit *TrikaShala.com*.

TrikaShala is located at Rudramandir: A Center for Spirituality and Healing. Its mission is to serve the community by offering a breadth of programs to aid in the exploration of each individual's full potential. The experience of celebration and expansion at Rudramandir is enhanced through the adornment of the space with sacred art in the form of sculpture, painting, and architectural elements, evoking the magnificence of Spirit. Additional information is available at *Rudramandir.com*.

Made in the USA
Lexington, KY
07 January 2014